PERGAMON INTERNATIONAL LIBRARY
of Science, Technology, Engineering and Social Studies
The 1000-volume original paperback library in aid of education,
industrial training and the enjoyment of leisure
Publisher: Robert Maxwell, M.C.

CRITICAL READINGS
IN PLANNING THEORY

To John,

I wish we
could have done it
together... But in a
way we did.
Fraternally,
Chris.

THE PERGAMON TEXTBOOK
INSPECTION COPY SERVICE

An inspection copy of any book published in the Pergamon International Library will
gladly be sent to academic staff without obligation for their consideration for course adoption
or recommendation. Copies may be retained for a period of 60 days from receipt and returned
if not suitable. When a particular title is adopted or recommended for adoption for class use
and the recommendation results in a sale of 12 or more copies, the inspection copy may be
retained with our compliments. The Publishers will be pleased to receiv̶e̶
revised editions and new titles to be published in this important Internation̶

CRITICAL READINGS IN PLANNING THEORY

Edited by

CHRIS PARIS
Research Fellow of the Urban Research Unit
Australian National University

PERGAMON PRESS

OXFORD · NEW YORK · TORONTO · SYDNEY · PARIS · FRANKFURT

U.K.	Pergamon Press Ltd., Headington Hill Hall, Oxford OX3 0BW, England
U.S.A.	Pergamon Press Inc., Maxwell House, Fairview Park, Elmsford, New York 10523, U.S.A.
CANADA	Pergamon Press Canada Ltd., Suite 104, 150 Consumers Rd., Willowdale, Ontario M2J 1P9, Canada
AUSTRALIA	Pergamon Press (Aust.) Pty. Ltd., P.O. Box 544, Potts Point, N.S.W. 2011, Australia
FRANCE	Pergamon Press SARL, 24 rue des Ecoles, 75240 Paris, Cedex 05, France
FEDERAL REPUBLIC OF GERMANY	Pergamon Press GmbH, 6242 Kronberg-Taunus, Hammerweg 6, Federal Republic of Germany

First edition 1982

Library of Congress Cataloging in Publication Data
Main entry under title:
Critical readings in planning theory.
(Pergamon international library of science,
technology, engineering, and social studies)
Bibliography: p.
Includes index.
1. City planning--Addresses, essays,
lectures. I. Paris, Chris. II. Series.
HT165.5.C73 1982   307.7′6   81-21027

British Library Cataloguing in Publication Data
Critical readings in planning theory.—(Urban
and regional planning series; v.27).—
(Pergamon international library)
1. Social policy
I. Paris, Chris II. Series
361.6′1   HN18

ISBN 0-08-024681-8 (Hardcover)
ISBN 0-08-024680-X (Flexicover)

Printed in Great Britain by A. Wheaton & Co. Ltd., Exeter

Preface

Becoming aware of planning: a personal view

I first became aware of town planning as a child, though it was through the eyes and with the mind of a child and thus a particular and personal view. I grew up in a bungalow in the Lea Valley, on the Hertfordshire side of the river, in an 'unplanned' struggle of dwellings more or less focused on a pub and general store at Dobbs Weir. Most of the bungalows had been hand built by working men and women from the East End of London on virtually worthless sites purchased before the Second World War. There was no gas or public water supply and the height of luxury was a good chemical lavatory. The place was not served by public transport and most children had to travel at least a mile by foot or bicycle to get to school.

In the increasingly planned post-war world such places have become anachronisms, more and more destroyed or taken over as weekend communities of city workers. I did not realize this at the time as it was an exciting place to be a child, neither quite 'town' nor 'country', with open fields and the river but with a main commuter railway to Liverpool Street Station only a mile away.

Our relatives, many of whom were East Enders, often called on summer Sundays, usually unannounced but still expecting tea. Theirs was a busier, dirtier, world, though some had moved to new council flats in Walthamstow or Dagenham. Only later did I come to understand the economic and historical circumstances of such population movements. As a child it was merely a fact to note and forget, between the much more interestering stories of old East End life.

My first experiences of a 'planned' town was Harlow, which I often visited on Saturday mornings. The eight-mile cycle ride through lovely Essex countryside ended in the broad streets and central square of Harlow New Town. I went mainly for the outdoor market, where, I remember, I used to trade old Adventure comics at a secondhand book stall.

The contrasts between the three places - the three worlds - of which I had differing experiences was enormous. The 'folk history' of the East End which invariably filled those summer Sunday visits was of a communal warmth in a physically decaying inner-city nighbourhood. My immediate existence in our little world by the river was very happy; what we lacked in material possessions was more than compensated for in a close and devoted family. I took for granted the need for the lavatory to be emptied in the back garden and luxuriated in the new electric water pump which did away with the old hand pump. Most summer holidays were spent in or by the river and seem to go on forever. But Harlow was something of a puzzle; I knew that it was a 'New' town but nobody ever explained why it had been built or what it was for. Even so, with many other things to do and think about, such minor problems of understanding never took up much of my time.

My first real lesson in town planning came when I was in the sixth form at a local grammar school. Having been refused access to council housing for over ten years, suddenly, out of the blue, came an offer of a council house and a bid (from a local councillor) to buy our bungalow. Only later did we find out that the land had been re-zoned for industrial purposes. The bungalow was demolished and no doubt the councillor made a tidy profit. Such trivial examples of minor abuse of public office, are, of course, commonplace and do not require further elaboration. But something *changed,* both in the real world that I inhabited and knew, and in my understanding of the forces and processes that had shaped that world.

It was about that time, too, that I thought I was a communist. We held a mock general election at school to coincide with the real election then taking place. Nobody else was prepared to stand as the communist candidate so I volunteered, at first 'for a laugh'. I had always been interested in politics though uncritically supporting Labour. During this mock election I settled down to read the manifestos of the various parties and only one made any sense to me at all. I was fired by the urgency of the critique and the passionate sense of social justice in the Communist Party's manifesto. I despised Conservatives then, much as I still do today; Labour's dream of technocratic advance sounded hollow and I assumed then that the Liberals were more or less the same as the Conservatives anyway and so could be ignored. I came second to the school 'Conservative candidate' who is now a sociologist at Bradford University.

During the later 1960s I was painfully aware of the gulf between the world outside my University - Vietnam, Paris '68, the Hippie Movement, the British economic crisis - and the sterile imperatives of my teachers. 'Objectivity in all things, Paris' one tutor used to insist, but I never could become objective about napalm in Vietnam and riot troops used against strikers. As an undergraduate I failed to reconcile my growing commitment to communism and my tentative first attempts to read Marx with the 'objective' world of a geography degree. I was not aware of a body of radical literature that could help me criticise my teachers, and they did nothing to introduce me to one. I felt totally alienated from their complacent world but had no intellectual response. A final-year course in urban geography was the last straw, as we ploughed through archaic 'theories' of urban structure and form and finally came to discussions of planning.

It amazed me then, as it amuses me now, that so many geographers assume that 'planning is really applied geography'. It is, of course, nothing of the sort, but it is a nice comfortable illusion for academic geographers to hang on to when the intellectual basis of their discipline is collapsing around them. Time and again my teachers' attempts to bring urban geography up to date resulted in descriptions of planning schemes, at greater and lesser spatial scales. *Planning* became the focus of study and appeared to be the major force shaping changes in the spatial structure of modern Britain. In part this was convincing, as there were clearly vast numbers of plans and a huge apparatus of planning, so there was clearly *something* going on. But I was sceptical of the extent to which planning in itself was important. Had planners somehow got things 'wrong' which 'better' planning would have got 'right' or was there more to it than that? My political perspective said there was, but nothing in geography could give me any clues.

I did my intellectual growing up at Glasgow University, in the Department of Town and Regional Planning. Although one of the Department's aims was to produce planners to work for the state, there was a fundamental commitment to free and critical thought. I had open access to scholars both within the Department and outside and spent more time reading political philosophy and social theory than town planning texts. An inspiring course in urban sociology taught by Peter Norman (now running a housing association in Salford) enabled me to develop a new perspective on planning - as a bureaucratic activity, predominantly carried out in large, complex (state) organizations, set up by law and with varying relations to and with many other complex facets of modern British society. Most town planners would respond, 'Of course, what else could anyone think planning is?' Planning literature, however, and much that passes as planning theory, systematically ignores and obscures this central reality and reifies planning and planners as autonomous agents of change. Perhaps I should have used the past tense, as the self-doubts which possess all but the most brutal technocrats and cynics in planning are today based on the understanding that planning is indeed *not* more than a bureaucratic state activity or private enterprise employed by or against the state.

The hope remains for many that planning *could* be otherwise and that, under different economic and social circumstances, planning would necessarily be part of the quest for a fairer and more humane way of life. That, for me, remains the central contradiction of planning, and it is a theme underlying many of the contributions to this book. A better society will not just happen, it will have to be worked for, communally planned, and can only come about through making mistakes and learning from them. But institutional planning in a capitalist society is not about such progressive change and so the practice of planning is a different thing altogether.

Courses in town planning will continue to attract young people for good reasons - concern for creating a better physical environment, concern for social justice and commitment to others. Unfortunately, despite attempts made by many teachers in planning schools to take a critical stance, the only saleable product of such schools is 'planners' who work within planning *as it is,* not as they would have it be. I have put this book together to help students of planning who want to understand planning as it is, and to provide them with a set of readings which can assist them in their intellectual development towards a critical perspective on planning.

Chris Paris

Acknowledgements

I am, first of all, grateful to all the authors of the papers in this collection, both for agreeing to republication or for preparing essays specially for this book. I am also pleased to acknowledge permissions given by copyright holders: The University of Newcastle-upon-Tyne, publishers of *Planning Outlook,* for the articles by Thomas and Faludi; Penguin Books for permission to reprint the chapter from Pahl's *Whose City?*; The *National Westminster Bank Quarterly Review* for permission to reprint Pickvance's essay; Tavistock Press for permission to reprint the chapter from Davies' *The Evangelistic Bureaucrat*; Richard Peet on behalf of *Antipode* for permission to reprint the Preteceille article; Pluto Press for permission to reprint the chapter from *The Local State*; *The Journal of the American Institute of Planners* for permission to reprint the Mazziotti paper; the Benwell Community Project and the Home Office for permission to reprint part of *Gilding the Ghetto*.

It has not been possible, however, to make contact with the author of one paper, Donald F. Mazziotti, who was formerly at the University of Iowa and subsequently at Portland State University; inclusion of his paper is therefore on the basis of copyright clearance alone.

Many other people have helped me in the preparation of this book. Some years ago, at the suggestion of Andreas Faludi, I started work on a similar project with Mike Gibson, then a colleague at Birmingham Polytechnic UK, and John Palmer, then at Central London Polytechnic and now with the UK Housing Corporation; ideas and work collectively developed at that time have been incorporated freely in this book. The project was revived at the initiative of Derek Diamond, Reader in Regional Planning at the London School of Economics and Political Science. I have been given invaluable help and assistance by Peggy Ducker of Pergamon Press: she patiently put up with many delays caused by my travels backwards and forwards between the UK and Australia and also gave sympathetic assistance during my long period of unemployment following the closure of the Centre for Environmental Studies.

Finally, I am grateful to friends and colleagues at the Urban Research Unit of the Australian National University for providing a stimulating and supportive milieu within which I have been able to finish what has proved to be a much bigger job than I originally expected.

Chris Paris

Contents

xii   *Contents*

Part Four: Alternatives and Contradictions

Part Five: The Future

Contributors

MARTIN BODDY: Lecturer at the School for advanced Urban Studies, University of Bristol, England.

CYNTHIA COCKBURN: Formerly at the Centre for Environmental Studies, London, England.

COMMUNITY DEVELOPMENT PROJECT: this is a collective of workers from various Community Development Projects, publications available from The Benwell Community Project, 85/87 Adelaide Terrace, Benwell, Newcastle-upon-Tyne, NE4, 8BB, England.

JON GOWER DAVIES: Senior Lecturer in Social Studies, University of Newcastle-upon-Tyne, England.

NORMAN FAINSTEIN: Professor of Urban Planning, Rutgers University, New Jersey, USA.

SUSAN FAINSTEIN: Professor of Urban Planning, Rutgers University, New Jersey, USA.

ANDREAS FALUDI: Professor of Planning, University of Amsterdam, The Netherlands.

NATHAN GARDELS: Special Consultant to Governor Brown of California and Executive Director of the Governor's Public Investment Task Force, USA.

CLIFF HAGUE: Senior Lecturer, Department of Town and Country Planning, Heriot-Walt University, Edinburgh, Scotland.

ROBERT KRAUSHAAR: Associate Professor, School of Architecture and Environmental Design, State University of New York at Buffalo, New York, USA.

JOHN LAMBERT: Lecturer in Social Administration, University College Cardiff, Wales.

DONALD MAZZIOTTI: was Assistant Professor in Urban and Regional Planning at the Univesity of Iowa and Associate Professor in Urban Studies at Portland State University, USA.

xiii

RAY PAHL: Professor of Sociology, University of Kent, Canterbury, England.

CHRIS PARIS: Research Fellow, Urban Research Unit, Australian National University, Canberra, Australia.

CHRIS PICKVANCE: Senior Lecturer in Interdisciplinary Studies, University of Kent, Canterbury, England.

EDMOND PRETECEILLE: Professor, Centre de Sociologie Urbaine, Paris, France.

MICHAEL THOMAS: Senior Lecturer in Planning, Oxford Polytechnic, Oxford, England.

PART ONE

A Critique of Pure Planning

Introduction by the Editor

Is it possible to understand planning in the abstract, and to develop theories about planning as an activity *in itself*? It was suggested, at least as long ago as the mid-1950s, that there could be two quite different kinds of planning theory, though in practice these should be thought of as overlapping. The difference was put forward as a conceptual thing, rarely to be expected in real examples, but as a useful way of organizing our understanding of different theoretical perspectives on planning.

Used as a simplifying device this distinction is unexceptionable. It has, however, come to be more than that, and to form the basis of a particular style of 'planning theory', most frequently now associated with the work of Andreas Faludi (1973b, 1978). Faludi's scholarship and readiness to enter into debate enlivened discussion of planning during the 1970s and he has undoubtedly made a major contribution to the development of a critical understanding of modern planning. But his critics believe that Faludi has taken an *analytic* distinction and treated this as a real division in the nature of planning as a human activity. In other words, he takes the simplifying device too far and by so doing obscures the reality of the interaction between the social context of planning, the theories that planners hold (consciously and unconsciously) and the internal procedures of planning practice. It is thus argued that he wrests the practice of planning from its social, political and economic context and consequently operates on a mythical patient of his own creating.

An excellent critique of Faludi's theoretical provision is Mike Thomas' article reproduced below, in which it is argued that, despite his disclaimers to the contrary, Faludi systematically obscures the political context and content of planning.

Faludi's response is also included below mainly to give readers the opportunity to judge the merits of the alternative positions for

3

themselves. It would be both too easy and unfair for me to leave it at that; I must make my own position clear, for the rest of this book is a function of where I stand on the Thomas-Faludi debate.

I believe that Thomas is substantially right and Faludi correspondingly wrong. However in order to leave readers free to judge the merits of the two papers I shall put my position in general terms rather than focus on the particulars of their debate. Indeed, the perspective that I outline below is far broader and, in my view, provides for a more comprehensive critique of procedural approaches to planning than that provided by Mike Thomas. It is a position that can be termed historical materialist as it is based on a materialist conception of society elaborated through a concern for real historical social development.

Whilst I do not consider it a particularly useful term, I must accept that others will think that my theoretical and political position is Marxist. I consider the term inappropriate for three reasons. First, it is frequently used as a mark of bravura by militants who have no knowledge of Marxist theory and practice and, hence, devalue the category of Marxist. Second, many right-wingers, equally mindlessly, denounce as 'Marxists' all and any of more radical complexion than themselves, thus transforming the category into a generalized form of abuse. Third, and of more consequence, Marxism is a living, developing and changing *perspective* on capitalism and hence should be thought of as a dynamic body of knowledge and action, whereas the term 'Marxist' used loosely can imply adherence to a set of ancient texts which few contemporary marxists would dream of using biblically.* Clearly, some of the contributions in this book use marxist analysis, but I have avoided doing so wherever possible: not because marxist categories of analysis are wrong but in order to develop arguments that are easily followed by those unfamiliar with marxist terminology.

Where marxist analysis is used, and may cause problems for the uninitiated, then I am careful in my introductory comments to each section to explain the terms and concepts being used by the different authors.

*For example, few contemporary Marxists would agree with Marx's claim that 'The country that is more developed industrially only shows, to the less developed, the image of its own future'. (Preface to the German edition of *Capital*.)

In this introductory section I have deliberately avoided extensive annotation and references in order to keep discussion general and to smooth the flow of argument. Extensive references are included elsewhere, in the contributions themselves, in the introductions to other sections, and notes on further reading. I have chosen here mainly to refer to a few major or seminal texts.

My own perspective on planning theory proceeds through three stages. First of all, I address the concept of a 'theory of planning' in the sense of theories about planning as an activity and how to 'do' planning. Second, I turn to the nature of town planning in capitalist societies. Problems raised and conclusions drawn from those two considerations lead on to a new perspective on planning ideology.

The Theory of Planning

The theory of planning rests on a distinction between (a) theories used to comprehend the milieu within which planning operates and (b) theories of how planning itself works. The theory of planning is concerned with the latter as opposed to, for example, 'economic theory' and 'social theory' which planners and others use to structure their understanding of economy and society. The proponents of the theory of planning thus argue that 'procedural knowledge' is distinct from 'substantive knowledge' and that this distinction holds for all types of planning:

> Planning theory deals with those features of organizations and procedures of planning which are similar in all its field, including their systematic variations. (Faludi, 1978, pp. 163-4.).

Central to this approach is a belief that such organizations and procedures are, can be, or *should be* based on 'rationality'. Thus Faludi argues that different types of planning - using the examples of economic planning, social planning and physical planning - have their own procedures for comparing and evaluating alternative courses of action against desired ends and selecting 'the best course of action' (p. 164). He goes on to define rationality:

> Rationality is therefore a feature of decision processes aiming to identify what best to do in given situations (pp. 164-4.)

'Planning' is thus represented as a set of activities, albeit affected by external 'constraints', which rationally provide for the solution of 'problems'. It is a neat and persuasive way of closing off discussion of the very logic on which the argument rests. But that logic requires further analysis, critically because it depends on the separation between *doing* planning and the social, economic and political milieu within which planning as a specific form of institutional activity takes place. If that separation is false then there can be no separate and distinctive theory of planning.

In order to explore the separation we have to ask what is 'planning'? At one level it is no more and no less than all conscious attempts to organize action in order to affect future outcomes. As such it is a generic and universal human activity for which no special training and qualifications are required: it is what most people normally do with greater or lesser degrees of calculation. It is, however, an activity which is intrinsically bound up in the interplay of choice and constraint that defines particular social worlds and thus takes different *forms* under different circumstances. To talk of planning in this way is both to define it as an axiomatic human characteristic and also to reduce the significance of 'rationality' as a guiding principle of 'planning' to so general an element of social interaction that its analytic value is virtually nil. Planning is rationality is planning, and so on *ad infinitum.*

The use of rationality as a guiding principle of planning is thus tautological: *of course* planning should be rational, what else could we have it be? That, however, tells us nothing specific about 'planning' as it exists as particular institutional or 'professional' activities. Indeed, it obscures what is specific about planning as an occupation, i.e. the very institutional contexts in which it operates, which vary considerably over time and between societies. Thus 'urban planning' in contemporary USA, 'town and country planning' under the Town and Country Planning Act, 1947 in Britain, and early post-war Soviet economic planning have been quite different things. To presume otherwise is to operate a principle of universality to 'planning' which utterly disregards what actually happens; it is a static, technocratic and ahistorical view of social relations which cannot explain why particular *forms* of 'rational' planning exist under different conditions of social and economic organization. Faludi takes a general observation which is irrefutable and uncritically applies this to the analysis of quite specific institutional forms: 'economic planning', 'social planning' and 'physical planning'.

To view planning theory as a separate, internally coherent set of procedural logics, operating in 'given situations' is thus to ignore what is crucial for any real understanding of particular forms of planning, i.e. the inter-relationships over time between the *development* of such forms, the practice of 'planning' as a job or profession, and the significance of those forms and practices within particular societies. At best it is a cookbook of instructions for doing planning-as-a-job but at worst it could be a deliberate attempt to focus on the uncontroversial and the mundane at the expense of a critical understanding of the nature and significance of specific institutional forms.

Town Planning under Capitalism

Town planning has existed in many different societies at different periods, and has been catalogued by 'planning historians'. Typically, such historians infer continuity and progression through learning, implying a continuous thread of development. With a few notable exceptions, however, most planning historians fail to relate town planning activities to the social and economic contexts within which they occurred. Town planning is seen as a real and distinctive phenomenon that may be analysed in its own right. Major social change has been viewed as some kind of backcloth to be hurriedly referred to and then forgotten before focusing in on plans and planners.

The objective of this book is quite the reverse: it is to provide a set of readings which concentrate on the practice of planning under specific and distinctive social and economic circumstances - twentieth-century capitalism. Axiomatic to this approach is the view that particular social forms can only be comprehended through an analysis of their development through time and their relations with society as a whole. Thus the significance of town planning is not merely that is is a form of 'rational' behaviour applied to urban development, but that it has developed in a particular socio-legal context, during a period of social and economic change, and has been part of a process of social transformation and class struggle. It has not been separate from other changes, rather it has been part of, reflected, and contributed to such change.

Crucially, urbanization under capitalism has reflected new logics of social and economic organizations arising out of the fundamental exploitation of labour by capital. Town planning is a state activity, regulated by law, carried out by state bureaucrats and private entrepreneurs in a relationship with elected politicians, in the context of continuing private accumulation of capital. Ironically, one of the few books which has sought to focus on planning from a materialist perspective, Gwyneth Kirk's *Urban Planning in a Capitalist Society* (1980), fails to draw out the necessary connections between the development of British capitalism, capitalist urbanization and town planning. She convincingly demolishes the myth that Britain is 'no longer capitalist', and rightly argues that 'it is the contradictions of British capitalism which account for the contradictions of land-use planning' (p. 92). Unfortunately she does not go on fully to explore the specific contradictions of *British* capitalism and at times falls into the trap of using analyses of planning in the USA or continental Europe and applying these uncritically to Britain. Even so, her book is a very good corrective to many conventional wisdoms of British planning.

As will be apparent from the range of contributions in this book, I am not narrowly concerned with Britain, but is is essential to bear in mind the differences between state stuctures, forms of institutional planning, histories of class struggle and capital accumulation in different capitalist societies. The fundamental thing to acknowledge is that town planning under capitalism necessarily reflects, in the British case, a history of institutionalized class struggle mediated by Parliamentary institutions, most fully developed in the specific post-war Welfare State compromise between capital and labour. The apparatuses of town and country planning that were established, as well as the consolidation and extension of 'regional policy', were part of a major reconstruction of the state and its modes of intervention. But the world did not stand still to be planned, and the practices of planning were only part of the dynamics reshaping the British space-economy: central was the drive for continued private accumulation of capital both through productive investment and speculation in money, land and the built environment.

The detailed operation of the post-war planning system up to 1970 has been adequately described by Peter Hall and his colleagues (1973). Although they never set out to develop a materialist critique they admirably demonstrated the very limited autonomy of planning as a regulatory or developmental activity, though they do show that planning was *one element* in the 'containment' of British towns and cities. Urban growth, however, clearly continued, usually in ways that were planned less by planners than by developers and industrialists.

A whole new scenario has now emerged. British capitalism is critically affected by world recession and going through a process of major restructuring. The political emergence and current dominance of a monetarist Conservative Government - the 'New Right' - has led to a rapid acceleration of unemployment, growing bankruptcies of small capitalists, and a concentrated attack on both the assumptions and institutions of the Welfare State. Whatever town planning has been (as it is analysed by many contributors in this book), it is likely to have changed dramatically by 1990. Such changes will be a direct result of changes in the relations between the state and capitalism during this period and are surely of infinitely greater significance than forms of logic which might or might not be used within 'given situations'.

Planning Ideology

The logic of the last two sections leads me to take a distinctive view of planning ideology. Many critics of planning, particularly sociologists, have discussed ideologies in planning. Typically they refer to both general and particular beliefs held by planners which consciously and unconsciously affect their work. One of the best essays of this genre, Foley's study of diverse 'threads of influence' on British town planning (reproduced in Faludi, 1973a, pp. 69-93), examined three potentially conflicting elements:

1. Town planning's main task is to reconcile conflicting claims for the use of limited land so as to provide a consistent, balanced and orderly arrangement of land uses. . .
2. Town planning's central function is to provide a good (or better) physical environment: a physical environment of which good quality is essential for the promotion of a healthy and civilised life....
3. Town planning, as part of a broader social programme, is responsible for providing the physical basis for better urban community life: the main ideals toward which town planning is to strive are (a) the provision of low-density residential areas, (b) the fostering of community life and (c) the control of conurban growth. . . (*Op cit.*, pp. 76-8.)

Foley considered that one of the major achievements of British town planning was the bringing together of such elements, but that this task was inevitably accompanied by ideological inconsistency: there was an underlying tension which posed the threat of disintegration. He noted as have others, the ideology of professionalism in planning (see also Dennis, 1972; Davies, 1972) and the inherent problems of attempting to be 'comprehensive' when much was uninfluenced by planners' actions.

His observations were, and remain, valid. But they only tell part of the story. Their weakness does not lie so much in what they study and conclude: rather it is in what they *exclude* from consideration. Their explanations are not so much wrong, as one-dimensional and consequently fail to highlight the *central* ideology of planning.

My version of planning ideology follows from my conclusions concerning the 'theory of planning' and the nature of town planning under capitalism. The theory of planning obscures, by definitional exclusion, the relationship between the practice of planning and its social, economic and political context. That context, in contemporary capitalist societies, is the continuing dynamic of capital accumulation. The form of institutional town planning, its practices and its effects, vary in response to different processes of actual historic development, but under capitalism the underlying rationale is constant: state institutions, operating apparently independently of class relations, appear to modify processes of urban development in the general interest and such 'intervention' is supposedly both desirable and possible.

Now, clearly, much 'planning' happens; armies of trained planners daily earn their living from doing planning. What do they *do* and to what effect? They produce plans, and to varying degrees they implement plans by advising on investment decisions and regulating development according to bureaucratically determined rules. Most urban development, however, is but marginally affected by all this activity. Such minimal effect, despite the paraphenalia and trappings of professionalism and the rhetoric of a welfare state based on intervention in the public interest, leads to the conclusion that it is the objective existence of planning which is in question. To put it another way, the activities of planners and the apparatuses of planning present the appearance of a (potentially) rational system of decision-making and resource allocation which helps to obscure the real workings of the space economy. Thus conceived it is planning itself which is an ideological phenomenon and the belief in the possibility of planned urban development is the ideology of planning. By concentrating on the internal mechanics of doing planning and the beliefs held by planners, this fundamental insight into the ideology of planning has remained obscured.

It is only when we question the very *possibility* of rational town planning and critically assess the meaning and significance of town planning in capitalist societies that we can develop meaningful theories about planning. It is the aim of this book to provide a set of readings which contributes towards that critical understanding. Finally, it should be emphasized that it is only once we can demystify what *appears to be* a system of planning urban development, and understand the real limits on equitable urban imposed by the process of capitalist accumulation, that we can move forward to a genuinely humane and equitable system of urban and regional planning.

References

Davies, J. G. (1972) *The Evangelistic Bureaucrat,* London, Tavistock.

Dennis, N. (1972) *Public Participation and Planners Blight,* London, Faber

Faludi, A. (1973a) *A Reader in Planning Theory,* Oxford, Pergamon

Faludi, A. (1973b) *Planning Theory* Oxford, Pergamon

Faludi, A. (1978) *Essays on Planning Theory and Education,* Oxford, Pergamon

Foley, D. C. (1969) 'British town planning: one ideology of three?', *British Journal of Sociology,* Vol. 11. (Reproduced in Faludi, 1973a)

Hall, P. *et al.* (1973) *The Containment of Urban England,* Vols. I and II, London, George Allen Unwin.

Kirk, G. (1978) *Urban Planning in a Capitalist Society,* London, Croom Helm.

The Procedural Planning Theory of A. Faludi

MICHAEL J. THOMAS*

Introduction

Procedural planning theory deals with the making and implementing of plans. It is concerned with the processes and techniques which are employed by planners in theory work as well as the operating modes of planning agencies. Consequently, it is overwhelmingly focused on the means of planning and not the ends. Andreas Faludi is one of the leading exponents of this type of planning theory. His work has attracted a great deal of attention in this country and the USA. Faludi is Professor of Planning Theory at the University of Amsterdam in the Netherlands. This article sets out to examine his ideas as a case study of procedural theory, for this purpose it will concentrate on his book *Planning Theory* (Faludi, 1973).

Faludi recognises that planning theory can be concerned with widely varying things and that there is a need to specify the area he wishes to deal with. He argues that the theory of planning must be defined as the fundmanetal planning theory and is concerned with the process of planning. It is, therefore, procedural. Theories which concern themselves with the subject matter of planning; towns, social welfare, economic activity, etc., are called substantive theories and are encapsulated by the procedural theory. In real terms substantive knowledge is regarded as technical knowledge held by planning agencies about the environment in which they operate to produce change. This form of conceptualization enables procedural theorists, like Faludi, to postulate general theories of planning which seek to establish the existence of a distinctive type of thought and action without reference to any particular object which this distinctive form may be associated within the real world. Consequently, the procedural theory is essentially

*Originally published in *Planning Outlook,* Autumn 1979, Vol. 22 No. 2.

'contentless' in that it specifies thinking and acting procedures but does not investigate what is the content of these. In this respect, and in many others, procedural theory is very similar to cybernetics which can be regarded as one of its intellectual foundations. Faludi uses town planning as the basis of his work but clearly he does not regard town planning as being the only area of application of planning theory. It is accidental that in Britain (the location of the book) town planning is the only fully developed form of public planning having a full range of technical, political, educational and professional institutions. This fact often seems to lead to the transfer of experience derived from a very specialised field onto a much wider area without reflection on the interaction between the nature of the objects planned and the nature of the planning process or the historical forms in which a particular form of planning practice has developed. But this is a problem which any empirically founded general theory of planning is bound to have to face.

Faludi's View of Planning Theory

The essence of planning is rationality or the application of reason to human affairs. Rationality is presented as the method by which an intelligent human approaches the problem of taking action to secure his goals. Rationality as a style of acting generally refers to decisions being made in a particular way according to technical rules for choice between a number of different strategies. Thus there are several crucial elements in this sort of procedure; the use of quantifiable data coupled with a set of empirically established laws about the external world and the employment of formal decision rules. The use of such forms of 'instrumental rationality' produces an attitude within the actors which is abstracted from the qualitative, historically real situation they are in, in order to permit the decision to be taken objectively. Weber characterised the increasing application of this formal process over larger areas of social life as rationalisation. The spread of rationalisation was led by the growing power of the new forms of economic activity produced by industrial capitalism where greater calculability meant greater profit. Science and technology have become increasingly incorporated within the productive system not only as suppliers of the techniques employed in the material transformations performed by the productive system but also as generators and refiners of the forms and procedures of instrumental rationality. Faludi's planning theory, being principally concerned with the rationality of means, is part of the general process of rationalisation. What is clear is that Faludi does not start his analysis from the view that planning is a public activity carried out by the State and, therefore, legitimated politically, within a structural situation dominated by particular socio-economic formations to which planning responds.

Faludi conceives of planning as a 'rational process of thought and action which ultimately aims (as science does) at promoting human growth' (Faludi 1973, p. 15). This statement is what he calls a rationale which used to identify those forms of human activity to be included in the category 'planning'. The definition of human growth at first appears extraordinary but it does fit in with his general position which is to argue for more planning. Human growth is represented as the realisation of man's potency to control the world, both natural and human, through the power to dominate and utilise the resources of the physical environment and to create human institutions which can harness that potency. Human growth is said to be both a product and the process leading to the product. The power to control ourselves and the environment creates the contents of human growth, what it represents as a thing, while the act of controlling is a process of human growth. The benefits achieved are described as a widening area of choice for humans and an enhanced capacity for learning and creativity. While Faludi is not proposing an authoritarian State and clearly believes that human growth entails a release of human creativity and, therefore, freedom, he does not set out a picture of the social conditions which would allow the human characteristic he desires to promote to exist.

Faludi's main use of his definition of planning is to aid the construction of a model of planning. The model is to be the principal vehicle to develop hypotheses about planning behaviour for testing in the real world. The ultimate aim of this would be the development of a positive theory of planning. The development of theory in this respect would follow the classical lines of the deductive method. But in the immediate sense the model is also to serve as an ideal type. It is, therefore, also a normative theory which seeks to improve the quality of planning. The analogy is frequently made of the relationship of scientific method to the practice of science. The method is not what scientists do but what they ought to do — a set of best practices, similarly with planning theory. But Faludi is not examining individual human planning behaviour. His purpose is to theorise about planning as a public activity through which society decides and controls its own development in a rational way. What he sets out to do is show that because planning is a generalised pattern of thought and action it is possible to transfer a model of human rational behaviour to the area of public action and use it to construct a model of the way planning agencies act. The model of public planning agencies (in effect a model of English local government town planning departments and committees) is the central element of the theory of planning.

The purposive thinking individual surveys the environment as the area of action and as a set of constraints to action, draws from his memory of strategies and images and creates a comprehensive list of possible courses of action. From these options the individual makes a choice as to the course most likely to secure the goal he favours and implements his decision. While in the process of carrying out his decision the individual receives information from the environment (feedback) about the results of his action which causes him to continually assess his own progress towards his goal (monitoring).

Although this presentation is said to be a function of the rational individual behaving as the model itself, it derives not from any studies of psychology of thinking but from cybernetics. The simplest model and the starting point for the elaboration of a model of planning agencies is the idea of a controlled feedback system (for example, a thermostat). This system consists of three elements situated within an environment, in the case of the thermostat, the environment has only one quality—temperature. The system receives information from the environment, selects a course of action based on that information and then effects its decision in the environment (see Fig.1).

Of course, the simplicity of such a system rests on the single fixed quality of its goal (to maintain a certain temperature). The choice available to the selector is only off/on and the environment is one-dimensional. To raise the system above this mundane level it is

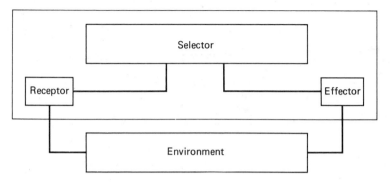

Fig. 1. A controlled feedback system.

necessary to include elements which extend the range of knowledge held by the system about its environment to give it some capacity for formulating programmes for action in the environment and to possess a set of goals to which the programmes relate. Faludi, therefore, places a box called 'memory' within his simple system. Inside the memory are the linked elements just described of image (knowledge) programmes and goals. These three elements, it is argued, form a technology for the purposive use of knowledge and are, therefore, given the title 'technology-image'. The system now appears as in Fig. 2.

Following from this basic model of the human mind certain extra refinements are introduced. The memory is split into two; the active and general memories, each with their set of images, goals and programmes. The active memory is that part of a person's knowledge which is actively engaged in thinking about the problem at hand whereas less relevant knowledge is assigned to the background general memory. The receptor is shielded by two filters, one controlling the receipt of information from the environment and thus it can be said to represent the selection principles employed to choose what information is extracted from the environment. The other controls the transmission of information from the receptor into the memory. The nature of both these filters — that is essentially what gets through to the heart of the system — are said to be controlled in turn by the technology-image and especially the goals elements. So what we see

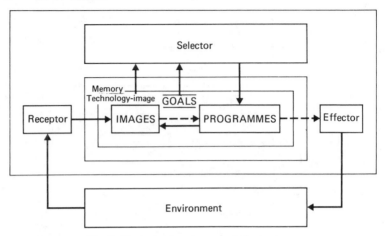

Fig. 2. The technology image and the memory.

of the world is a function of what we want to do or make happen in the world.

The image element of the memory is also refined by adding in two new features. First, the idea of a self-image is incorporated to express the self-awareness of human beings. Consequently, the model, by including this notion, allows for the fact that social interaction and experience builds up inside individuals an image of themselves and this permits them to be reflective about their own behaviour. The rest of the image is an internalised picture of the external environment. Faludi distinguishes between this present picture and that which represents the future environment projected on the basis of trends discerned in the present — this is the future image.

This in outline is the model of the human mind as a learning system which is to be made into a model of planning agencies. It is argued that this model forms the basis for many different sorts of investigation in psychological and social science. One of the obvious examples would be the work of Karl Deutsch (1963) on political decision-making.

The translation of the human mind model to the English planning system is essentially an exercise in naming the parts in accordance with standard English local government internal structures. The receptor is the survey unit which collects data and carries out research which is fed to the development plan section. The development plan section is the technology image. It holds knowledge about the environment and its future and the goals which the planning system is pursuing and from these goals develops alternative courses of action to realise them. Decisions about which course of action to pursue are taken by the political element of the system, the planning committee, which in Faludi's terms is the selector. Implementation is achieved through the effector which is identified as the development control section where applications for planning permission are processed.

Discussion of Faludi's Theory

Whether or not this picture of the English local planning system is acceptable depends on the degree to which it raises significant issues for analysis and theory building. There are a number of ways that the planning system could be conceptualised (for example as a process for managing the conflicting claims over urban space). The important question is what problems are isolated by the use of one conceptual framework compared to another. Faludi's purpose is to see to what extent planning is rational. He has, through the model, identified the various functions of the elements of the planning system so rationally, the interaction of these various elements as well as the operation of the whole system or agency can be seen. 'A planning agency is simply an organisational unit specialised for the formulation of programmes designed to solve problems in the most effective way' (Faludi, 1973, p. 84). On this definition the essence of the matter is how are problems defined and how are the best programmes formulated?

A problem is 'a state of tension between the ends pursued by a subject and his image of the environment' (Faludi, 1973, p. 82). So the question of defining the problems a planning agency sets itself to deal with is a matter of looking at the interaction between the images and goals held inside the agency and the effect of information flowing into the agency from the environment and subsequently between various parts of the agencies. For example, the effect of a change in political control of the local authority may be to alter the goals of the agency or the results of a census can indicate the image of population growth and be changed (Thomas, 1973; DOE, 1976). The precision with which a problem can be stated is a reflection of the clarity of goal statements and the accuracy of the image. Generally speaking, problems are rather ill-defined, sometimes for technical reasons — like a lack of relevant data — or at other times because vagueness is politically expedient.

Ill-definition of problems complicates the formulation of programmes by failing to provide a clear statement of what the programme is meant to achieve. In any case, the ideal of rationality sets up an impossible standard for planning in the real world when it comes to formulating programmes. The rational ideal insists that the agency must develop a comprehensive set of all possible courses of action from which the agency or at least the selector element can choose the one most likely to secure its goals. Such comprehensive formulation of programmes never happens. Faludi deals with this problem by suggesting a number of strategies an agency can use to operate in a limited mode of rationality. The effect of these strategies is to greatly cut down the area of search for possible programmes or plans. One of the strategies Faludi favours is known as mixed scanning (developed by Etzioni, 1967) which involves making fundamental decisions about the nature of the solution to a problem by working out lower-order details but returning to modify the fundamental level when difficulties occur at the detailed level, thus there is a continual oscillation between high- and low-order decisions.

The very technical nature of this discussion of planning is very useful in throwing light on some of the problems planners face. How to shorten the period of time taken to produce a plan and yet produce it in a rational way, or how to control the research activities of the planning agencies to prevent vast sums being spent in gathering data which may not be used. But the answer to such questions is only partly a technical issue (DOE, 1974). Faludi cannot offer an explanation for the products of planning agencies because he has very little to say about what planning is doing, i.e. effecting particular changes in the environment. He is concerned with explaining from a technical point of view how it is done or more precisely how it is decided how it is done.

If his work is searched for an underlying view of society, none is found. But implicitly it can be identified as a society which is pluralist in structure and exhibits a high degree of consensus. Further, more consensus will grow as rational planning becomes more widespread as the mode in which society sets about solving its problems. The spread of planning will produce a better society because it will increase the choice available to the members of society. Rationality in public decision-making must benefit society by making it possible for people to take control of their society and direct it onto chosen paths of development. This rationality the Frankfurt theorists would label instrumental reason and, according to B. Fay (1975), would be part of the positivist tradition of seeking technical control over the environment. Consequently, for these writers Faludi's planning rationality does not represent an attempt to transform society to something more responsive to human needs but rather a technology which will be used to reproduce the present structure albeit in a more efficient form. Faludi's position seems to counter these criticism in two ways. Firstly, he asserts a positive value to be derived from a commitment to and involvement in rational planning. Here his argument has a curious similarity to that put forward in defence of democracy by Duncan and Lukes (1963). The political process will be substantially replaced by rational planning as the principal means through which people communicate with each other about the society they live in. Politics appears as an adjunct to planning as a process where risk is accepted and commitment located, the politician being the person who is elected to take such risks. Being involved in rational planning, people grow by learning more about their society and becoming aware of their role in guiding society (Faludi likens this to the benefits of being involved in science). Of course, this view locates planning as one of the central modes of communication in society, yet it is a technical language dedicated not to maximising the communication between people but rather to maximising their control over the environment.

The second argument which could be adduced against the argument of Habermas (1971) and Fay (1975) stems from the initial normative definition given to planning at the outset. Planning is an activity which aims at promoting human growth. There seems to be no logical reason why planning should be dedicated to this aim. Procedural rationality can be utilised to advance any goal however questionable.

The emphasis which procedural theorists give leads to a neglect of the purpose of planning. This has two aspects, firstly the procedural theorists do not analyse the particular role which planning, as a State activity, plays in the market economy in terms of the values it pursues and the interests it protects (Kapitalistate, 1976). Secondly, the procedural theory provides no substantive basis for a critical position within the planning process itself, since the technical nature coincides with rationality of the dominant economic forces. If Faludi wishes to insist on planning having a particular goal, then it is necessary for him to specify the goal in some detail and to elaborate a planning method dedicated to achieving it. That means giving planning theory a substantive content. In fact human growth is not defined in any detail but is said to have two aspects: growth as a product and the process leading to the same product. The process argument was referred to above and relates to the positive value of people adopting a planning mode of action. The product of the process is presented in a rather vague way and seems to embrace the idea of people and society as a whole achieving greater freedom to realise an increasingly wide range of goals. Thus the range of human experience is widened and our material standards are improved but material questions are not fundamental to this argument. As Faludi says, 'The production of material goods apart, growth as a process refers mainly to learning and creativity, defined as the gaining of insights into the existing order of things, and the transformation of that order into a new one'. The new order will ensure 'the fulfilment of an increasingly diverse range of goals'. It is noted in passing that 'one could argue for a more equal distribution of economic assets within the same concept' (Faludi, 1973, pp. 40-1). But beyond this no further hint of concrete conditions for the achievement of human growth is given. However, this argument is placed within 'our present climate of pluralism' (Faludi, 1973, p. 40) and our present failure to surmount barriers to human growth, like unequal distribution of resources, is to be found in our way of doing things. What is needed is greater consciousness or societal self-awareness, which would lead to our overcoming the present constraints. This consciousness is given its fullest expression in rational planning. This position can be seen to rest firmly on a pluralist-consensus model of society; if the consciousness is there, all things become possible, real barriers to human growth in the form of entrenched class interests are discounted. Lukacs (1971) seemed to have had the same view of the power of consciousness, albeit proletarian consciousness, and G. Stedman Jones' (1971) critique of it could be transposed onto Faludi.

How does this rational planned process fit into the society as a whole? More precisely, what is the relationship with politics? Faludi presents two answers to this question. At the overall level a future image of society is put forward which is called 'The Planning Society' (Faludi, 1973, pp. 293-6). While it would be cynical to describe this as a society fit for planners, the aim is to suggest what central institutions would be necessary if planning is to be the principal mode of decision-making. Faludi is conscious of the danger that planning might be institutionalised to produce a centralised authoritarian society but he also rejects the idea of a society completely conflict-ridden. Strangely enough, conflict is seen only on an individual basis. But it is maintained that a qualified agreement exists in society which expresses itself in the belief that there does exist a public interest and that interest is mainly embodied in central planning agencies. The concern of these central planning agencies is not substantive policy issues. 'In this way the supreme planning agency would act as the guardian of the rationality of processes by which variety is articulated and choices made' (Faludi, 1973, p. 294). Beneath this central agency level conflict and bargaining would continue but within a general accord on procedures. One can only conclude that politics has been removed from its central position in society and replaced by the methodology of planning and agencies protecting that methodology. The theoretical basis for this is the theory of planning which would be 'the most fundamental normative theory of all, indicating how decisions in society ought to be made' (Faludi, 1973, p. 296). If this sounds somewhat extreme it is echoed in the recent major review of planning published by the Royal Town Planning Institute, *Planning and the Future,* which states 'Planning has a special forward-looking responsibility stretching beyond political and personal horizon' (R.T.P.I., 1976).

At a lower level where planning is concerned with substantive issues the orthodox division of labour between politics and planning, that is politicians determine the policies and planners implement them in plans, is rejected. In most cases politicians, expecially in local government, rely heavily on planners to provide them with policy options as well as information about the environment. Faludi argues that the relationship between politics and planning must be seen in terms of a distinction between decision-taking and decision-making (Friend and Jessop, 1969). Decision-taking is the final stage of decision-making when a formal binding decision is taken which commits the agency to a definite course of action affecting the environment, thus employing resource of one form or another. Politicians have the prerogative of taking decisions because of their public responsibility and accountability. However, in the preceding stages of decision-making where information is generated, goals specified, alternative programmes formulated and evaluation carried out, the politician has no superiority, rather the politician and the planner should interact freely on a basis of equality although it is an equality based on different outlooks and interests.

What seems to echo through Faludi's writing is that variety of American political thought current in the late 1950s and early 1960s which become known as the 'End of Ideology' (Seliger 1976). His work can be seen to fit into a view of society in which radical ideological politics (left or right) are said to have lost their power to mobilise support. Rational planning theory represents the technique of continuing progress towards greater benefits for all untroubled by questions of relative distributional shares. While the end of ideology may seem somewhat quaint now in the context of the USA and even more so in the politics of much of Europe, it is clear that its general notions still hold some sway in planning thought. This may be because it has been something of an intellectual backwater mostly populated by professional practitioners whose work served to legitimate their own activities. The Royal Town Planning Institute's paper *Planning and the Future* (1976), referred to above, in an outstanding example of the genre.

Conclusion

Faludi probably stands at the high point of rational procedural theory. His theory is a theory for a society enjoying high employment and steady economic growth. When both these characteristics are missing and social strains begin to appear then notions like human growth begin to look a little threadbare. In ideological terms Faludi's theory fits neatly into the structural position which planning occupies in the industrial market economies. There is nothing which challenges it by proposing that planning ought to be motivated by goals or values other than those which now operate. By elaborating the technology of planning in a non-critical way, while at the same time giving planning a central position as a mode of social communication, Faludi contributes to the attempts to depoliticise politics as well as planning.

References

D.o.E. (1974) Circular 98/74 Structure Plans, London: HMSO.

D.o.E. (1976) Strategy for the South-East. Review, London: HMSO.

Deutsch, K. (1963) *The Nerves of Government,* New York, Free Press

Duncan, G. and Lukes, S., The New Democracy, *Political Studies,* Vol. VII, pp. 156-77.

Etzioni, A. (1976) Mixed scanning: a third approach to decision-making, *Public Administration Review,* Vol. 27, pp. 385-92.

Faludi, A. (1973) *Planning Theory,* Oxford: Pergamon.

Fay, B. (1975) *Social Theory and Political Practice,* London: George Allen & Unwin.

Friend, J. K. and Jessop W. N. (1969) *Local Government and Strategic Choice,* London: Tavistock.

Habermas, J. (1971) *Toward a Rational Society,* London: Heinneman.

Kapitalistate (1976) Focus Issue: The Urban Crisis and the Capitalist State, No. 4-5.

Lukacs, G. (1971) *History and Class Consciousness,* London: Merlin Press.

R.T.P.I. (1976) *Planning and the Future,* London.

Seliger, M. (1976) *Ideology and Politics,* London: George Allen & Unwin.

Stedman Jones, G. (1971) The Marxism of early Lukacs, *New Left Review* **70.**

Thomas, M. J. (1973) Public participation in East Oxford, *Journal of the Royal Town Planning Institute,* **59,** No. 4

Towards a Combined Paradigm of Planning Theory?

A Rejoinder by Andreas Faludi*

Thomas' critique of *Planning Theory* ranks among the most thorough, competent and fair essays written on my work. It gives me the welcome opportunity to take issue with two strands of critcism voiced against it:

(i) that it depoliticises planning,

(ii) that it fails to locate planning in its historical context.

Both are inspired, amongst others, by works emanating from Germany and France, i.e. the positivist debate in German sociology and the revival of Marxist social science and its application to urban phenomena and to planning issues generally.

Thomas draws on both these strands. My procedure will be to (a) analyse his paper, pointing out certain shortcomings in his argument, and (b) pursue the more fundamental issue raised by the existence of at least two paradigms of planning theory: the political-economy paradigm inspired by Marxist analysis on the one hand and the decision-making paradigm which can be said to form the basis of my work on the other. In so doing, I shall refer to some German literature which I explored on behalf of a research team comparing local planning in Leiden in the Netherlands and in Oxford in England.[2] This literature shows researchers starting from the political-economy paradigm attempting to incorporate elements of the decision-making paradigm. Recently a more evenly balanced combined paradigm is being advocated.

*Originally published in Planning Outlook, Autumn 1979.

Shortcomings of the Critique by Thomas

I said the critique by Thomas was thorough, competent and fair, but it still has shortcomings. In saying so, I am aware of the fact that he is unlikely to accept my rejoiners. He draws on the Frankfurter Schule, amongst others. I find myself increasingly in agreement with the philosophy of critical rationalism. Frisby (1972) was not the only one to comment on the so-called positivist dispute between these two camps as representing a dialogue of the deaf, saying that '. . . the dispute has developed between groups with such divergent assumptions that it is difficult to see how an exchange could take place.' I am aware of the possibility that, in the eyes of Thomas, my efforts to combine the two paradigms might therefore simply serve as further evidence for my ideologically distorted views, rather than as an attempt to reach out beyond my own initial position and to encompass an awareness of others. Perhaps we are not writing rejoiners for the benefit of our opponents after all, but for our own benefit and that of our intellectual kinsmen.

Be this as it may, the rules of the game compel me to take issue with certain of the interpretations which Thomas gives of my work. These concern my view of substantive knowledge; of rationality; of society; and of politics. I shall leave until later his various comments on my procedural planning theory.

(a) Substantive knowledge

Thomas characterises my view of substantive knowledge as follows:

> In real terms substantive knowledge is regarded as *technical knowledge*. . . . Rationality as a style of acting generally refers to decisions being made in a particular way according to technical rules of choice. . . . Thus there are several crucial elements in this sort of procedure; the use of *quantifiable data* coupled with a set of *empirically established laws* about the external world.

Now, I totally agree that these elements are contained in my view of substantive knowledge, but there is more to it. Indeed, as Thomas himself explains later on, the 'technology image' held by the planning agency consists of **three** elements.

Thus Thomas has chosen to high-light particular aspects of my view of substantive knowledge and to ignore others, in particular the normative dimension which is encapsulated in the 'goals'-element of the technology image. Otherwise, he might have refrained from identifying it with technical knowledge. He might also have noticed that the concept of filters being 'set' by the technology-image ('. . . in particular its images and, even more important, the goals built into it. . . .': *Planning Theory*, p. 66) takes account of something that should be close to his heart: the relationship between 'Knowledge and Interest', which is the title of a famous essay by Habermas (1970). However, this would not have fitted his view of me as firmly based in the positivist camp. That it is in the latter camp that he sees me becomes evident where he characterises my concept of rationality as instrumental.

(b) Rationality

The criticism of certain types of rationality as instrumental, and thus narrow, is another favourite theme of critical theorists. As Thomas has it:

> Science and technology have become increasingly incorporated within the productive system not only as suppliers of the techniques employed . . . but also as generators . . . of the forms and procedures of 'instrumental rationality', Faludi's planning theory, being principally concerned with the rationality of means is part of the general process of rationalisation. . . .

However, nowhere do I talk about the rationality of means nor about instrumental rationality. Goals can also become the object of deliberate choice, in particular in the form of planning which I describe as normative (see chapter 9). Thomas might perhaps have linked this to my concept of human growth, which he discusses at some length, calling it 'extraordinary'. He might have noticed the following passage and perceived the parallels which exist with the ideas on which he seemingly draws:

> So, the rational planning process leads to growth in a narrow sense. But we must not be satisfied with this narrow view of growth. Goals may very well change, even whilst the planner is engaged busily in identifying the means for their attainment. . . . Nevertheless, even planning efforts that lead to no action may still result in human growth. This is because the rational planning process forces one to make assumptions explicit about one's self, one's environment, and how one relates to it, and it to one's self. . . . Ultimately, because in planning one must reflect one's goals, it also increases awareness of oneself (*Planning Theory* p. 50.)

(c) Society

Thomas complains that, if 'the work is searched for an underlying view of society none is found, . . .' Fortunately, he has no difficulty in finding it himself later on, i.e. in the Epilogue on 'The Planning Society'. There, my view of society is described as 'qualified holistic', using a terminology derived from the classic work by Meyerson and Banfield (1955). Thomas takes note of this and comments in passing that 'conflict is seen only on an individual basis', even though in my description I refer to my 'awareness of the existence of divergent views and interests' without tying these to individuals. Towards the end he states that my theory 'is a theory for a society enjoying high employment and steady economic growth'. For this he adduces no evidence.

(d) Politics

Thomas is concerned about planning invading the realm of politics:

> The political process will be substantially replaced by rational planning as the principal means through which people communicate with each other about the society they live in. . . .
> Of course, this view locates planning as one of the central modes of communication in society, yet it is a technical language dedicated not to maximising the communication between people but rather to maximising their control over the environment.

Later on, he repeats the same point with respect to my outline of the functions of a central planning agency in a 'planning society':

> One can only conclude that politics has been removed from its central position in society and replaced by the methodology of planning and agencies protecting that methodology.

He then goes on to describe my views on the relationship between planning and policy in a perfectly adequate manner, but for no particular reason he locates them at 'a lower level', i.e. beneath central planning. Also, he concludes that this latter, correct, description of my view echoes '. . . that variety of American political thought . . . which became known as the "End of Ideology".' No further explanation is given as to why this should be the case.

Now, as to this whole debate I can only say that I pre-empted it in an easily identifiable section headed 'Politics and Planning' (pp. 100-3). There I argue for planning and politics as **complementary** to each other. There can, therefore, be no question of one replacing the other. Also, I reject the idea implied in Thomas' position of political and planning choices being in some way different. In my inaugural lecture at Delft University of Technology I refer to the work of another political scientist, Van Gunsteren, who has concerned himself with the nature of political responsibility:

> He claims that it can only be determined through people in concrete situations, talking to each other. With this, he describes how political responsibility is form- ed. But he leaves out the rules for deciding whether a decision is responsible. Ra- tional planning provides the grammar for saying whether the decision-maker has discharged his responsibility properly . . . (*Planning Theory and the Education of Planners;* see Faludi, 1978.)

Political and planning choices are one and the same in the sense that all public choices have an element of both. There is no methodology of planning, therefore, which might conceivably replace politics from its central position in society, nor are there any higher-level choices made by central planning agencies which I would describe as being beyond politics. Planning and politics entail each other, on whichever level.

The Political-Economy and Decision-Making Paradigms of Planning Theory

Thomas charges me with committing the eternal sin of not being 'critical':

> . . . the procedural theory itself provides no substantive base for a critical posi- tion within the planning process itself since the technical nature coincides with rationality of the dominant economic forces. If Faludi wishes to insist on plan- ning having a particular goal then it is necessary for him to specify the goal in some detail and to elaborate a planning method dedicated to achieve it. That means giving planning theory a substantive context.

The answer to this challenge on the lines of the argument above is that I do not even pretend to provide a substantive basis for a critical position, nor do I therefore wish to insist on planning having a particular goal. Such arguments I prefer to leave to citizens meeting in the public arena. The only claim is that, in arguing rationally about the choices with which they are faced (whether they draw on expert advice is neither here nor there for the purpose of this argument), issues of a political nature will be raised more pointedly, which is one of the reasons why I claim that rational planning promotes (not ensures, achieves, and the like, but opens up avenues for) human growth. It eludes me once again, therefore, why rational planning should be labelled technical.

The reason for this can again be found in *Planning Theory*. In the chapter on 'The Rationale of Planning Theory' I refer to two German authors, Grauhan and Strudelt. In terms which should please Thomas, they argue that a purely procedural definition of rationality is inadequate: the goals of rational choice must themselves be rational; they must contribute to 'self-enhancement', a concept which I equate with human growth. This is a dynamic concept and must be measured in terms of 'the potentialities realisable at any given time in history' (quoted on p. 49).

Now, I interpret this as indicating a **direction of search** implied in the very concept of rational planning, a search, however, which will result in different conclusions, depending on the case at hand. To this I agree in *Planning Theory,* and this agreement still holds. Pronouncements as to the substantive goals of planning can only be made when referring to **specific cases.** Any general discourse about planning must keep to generalities such as 'self-enhancement' or 'human growth', which are indications only. Thomas himself proves my point. He formulates his critique of my position without ever going so far as naming a single substantive goal of planning. Nothing would be further from the truth than to suggest that there is no difference between Thomas and myself. The real difference seems to lie in our respective perspectives on planning. He likes to see planning as nothing but a reflection of a particular phase in the development of late capitalism, and it is this type of analysis which he seeks in vain in *Planning Theory*:

> Faludi's planning theory, being principally concerned with rationality of means is part of the general process of rationalisation. What is clear, is that Faludi does not start his analysis from the view that planning is a public activity carried out by the state, and therefore, legitimated politically within a structural situation dominated by particular socio-economic formations to which planning responds.

Now this is very true but less fatal to my planning theory than Thomas would think. There are two aspects of planning which this sort of debate constantly confuses. One is the process by which decisions are arrived at which is what I am concerned with, and another one is the issues which become the object of public planning by virtue of the State—with a bow to my critics, I write State with the ominous capital 'S' which seems so dear to their hearts—being given powers to regulate them. Had I made it the object of my analysis to explain why certain powers, e.g. in the field of sanity legislation, housing, town planning, social legislation, economic planning, etc., have been given to public agencies, I might have come up with very similar conclusions as my critics. The simple point is that this is not my object of study.

How could I separate out these two points? The answer lies in what I said before about the goals of planning in specific circumstances. These are determined amongst others by what public authorities can do, by the powers which are vested in them. I need not go into the reasons why they exist, because I do not see why there is a need for me to make pronouncements on the specific ends of planning in a treatise concerned with planning as a **general** approach to decision-making. Arguments are needed, not about specific ends, but about how such ends can be related to decision-making in matters of policy. This is what I attempt to do, and these are the grounds on which I prefer to be judged.

Now, it is, of course, possible to take exception to the usefulness of theories concerned with the organisations and procedures of planing. A cogent way of doing so would be by showing that organisations and procedures have no significant impact on the outcomes of planning. If research into the role of planning as a social and political activity could demonstrate that planning is completely circumscribed by the political and economic processes in the society of which it forms part, then there would indeed be no immediate justification for enquiry into the organisations and procedures of planning.

This issue has been debated most extensively in the German planning literature. This debate is couched in terms of the 'political economy' and the 'decision-making/action' paradigm of planning theory. The difference between them, and their possible convergence have been described by Naschold (1972) and Grauhan (1975).

According to Naschold, decision-making theories take as their domain (as I do) the intended and actual decisions of individuals and groups which are analysed for their determinants and effects. This is combined with a theory of social differentiation according to which social development is characterised by increasing complexity and a growing differentiation into relatively autonomous subsystems. Planning is seen as being concerned with creating connections between the subsystems, whose reconciliation is regarded as the function of the political system. Under this paradigm, reform intentions extend only so far as the elimination of short-comings within the structure of the existing system, to which a certain basic optimality is ascribed.

The political economy paradigm has its foundation in analyses of late capitalism. This paradigm identifies contemporary planning explicitly as one aspect of the growing intervention of the State in the continuing conflicts of interest which characterise capitalist societies. Accordingly, planning is aligned with the mutually contradictory functions of the State, namely the maintenance of the forces of production and the stabilisation of the tensions brought about by the accumulation of capital. Moreover, it can be understood more clearly in the economic context of the system of production and its relationship with other forms of State activity than through the logic of the planning process itself.

In comparing the two approaches Naschold suggests that the decision-making paradigm suffers from two major shortcomings. First, by emphasising rationality in planning the decision-making theorists assume a fundamental consensus of interest—or, if conflict is acknowledged, it is assumed to be capable of resolution through rational decision-making. Second, this position limits the concern of planners to the production of plans and the organisation of the planning process. In turn the political economy paradigm is being criticised according to Naschold, for its rejection of the idea of achieving even marginal reforms through improved decision-making in planning. To my mind this reveals an important difference between the two paradigms in terms of scale of application.

The decision-making approach is more concerned with specific plans and projects and with ways of improving the processes by which they are formulated and implemented. In contrast, the political economy paradigm is concerned with the impact of planning on the structure of society as a whole.

Evidently, my work has been undertaken in the belief that questions internal to the process of planning do form a valid field of study. A number of arguments can be put forward in support of the emphasis on procedural questions.

First, it is possible to argue that whatever the political system, there will always be procedural and organisational problems to overcome. In socialist as in capitalist states, in federal as in central administrations, the problems of uncertainty about the future, information overload, and of relating knowledge to action are characteristic of organisational behaviour and present similar procedural difficulties. Organisations and procedures are developed to resolve conflicts and to implement solutions within the overall political structure. In this sense, procedural questions can be seen as ubiquitous, and to an extent independent of the political system.

A second reason for the choice of a procedural focus is the belief that local authorities and other factors in the planning process are hampered in their activities by organistional and procedural inadequacies, and as a result do not make the most of their opportunities, even within the existing system.

A third reason for focusing on decision-making in planning is that it is possible to see a certain measure of convergence between the two paradigms. Naschold already argues that studies of planning systems, following the decision-making paradigm, may be of considerable theoretical and empirical importance, and analyses of planning in capitalist societies should not ignore them. Consequently, they should be 'assimilated' into the political economy paradigm.

Other recent work in Germany points in the same direction. Research into local politics has attempted to interpret relations at the micro-level in terms of the macro-level principles of the political economy of late capitalism. The findings of the study group which undertook this research have been published in two volumes edited by Grauhan (1975) and include papers by Everts, Bauer, Väth and Siebel cited below.

The investigation was concerned with testing both the empirical relevance of Marxist theory in explaining the realities of local politics and planning, and its practical relevance to those concerned in a professional capacity with improving decision-making in the local planning field.

The context of planning activity as defined within the political economy paradigm was described by Everts. According to his analysis urban areas can be considered as localities in which production, exchange and consumption relations are determined by capitalist investment strategies and supported by the State in its role of providing the conditions for the accumulation of capital. This results in deteriorating living conditions for the workforce as the means of subsistence purchased out of wages become scarce and more expensive, while the political institutions which are intended to provide the means for supplying the additional requirements of city life fail to do so because of the financial plight of urban areas. In this sense, the areas of social reproduction (housing, recreation, etc.) are the setting for the continuing conflict between the forces of labour and capital over the creation and distribution of surplus value.

This analysis was criticised by Bauer, who suggested that it was impossible to relate conceptual analysis of development within capitalist society to empirical observations of their manifestations at the local level. Rather, he identified a number of other areas of application for theories following the political economy paradigm which included investigations of the links between forms of social development, and analyses of whole historic epochs which aim to define general principles for the practice of political action. These areas of application are distinct in important respects. Bauer suggested that general analysis can only occur after the event and should be strictly separated from empirical research relating to day-to-day politics since it is impossible to analyse the latter for its basic economic determinants with the result that analyses of local politics are likely to remain incomplete. Consequently, research into local politics which aims to be empirically meaningful should confine itself to seeking explanations of local political conflict in terms of conflicts of interest between empirically observed classes and class factions. This approach includes analyses of the organisations and procedures of conflict management and necessitates resource to theories usually associated with the decision-making paradigm.

The practical relevance of the arguments of Bauer and Väth has been reflected in further research on the work situation of practising planners. Siebel identified 'pluralist enclaves' in the hierarchical structure of planning organisations which operate around communalities of interest both within and outside the planning field, but which are ultimately controlled by the administrative hierarchy, often through financial constraints. This situation is inherently unstable, oscillating between the tendency towards hierarchical internal organisation and a degree of organic pluralism in planning administration.

Conclusion

A general conclusion to be drawn from these examples of German research is that action under planning is not completely structurally determined, but rather that there exist, albeit limited, areas within which planning can operate to achieve change. Hence theories which follow the political economy and the decision-making paradigms of planning may not be necessarily exclusive. My work is being undertaken in this belief, the emphasis being on the decisions and actions of participants in the 'planning process' but with the awareness that these are set within a framework which is determined by macro-level forces and which frequently limits their freedom of action.

One might even think in terms of a combined paradigm. Recent discussions in Germany seem to point in this direction (see Fürst and Hesse, 1978). Certainly for the purpose of explaining the reality of planning, both should be drawn upon. Reforms of planning, what

I have termed 'meta planning' in *Planning Theory*, must also take cogizance of both paradigms. Only for the purpose of theory building does it seem possible to isolate particular aspects of planning such as the organizations and procedures of decision-making. But then, isolating particular aspects of realtiy, catching them in the net of specific theories, is a precondition of theory-formation anyway. Obviously, there are nets of various types catching fish of various sizes. Thomas and his like seem to aim for the big catches, i.e. the structural conditions in society which set the parameters of planning. I am quite content with the small fry of decision-making theories, knowing that they will be of more immediate application to the practice of planning. But there seems little reason why we should not sit side by side.

Notes

1. Based on: A. Faludi (1978) *Beyond "Planning Theory"*, Paper delivered to the 18th European Congress of the Regional Science Association, Fribourg, Switzerland, August 29 to September 1, 1978.
2. See: Department of Town Planning, Oxford Polytechnic, and Planning Theory Group, Delft, University of Technology (no date) *Leiden-Oxford: A Comparative Study of Local Planning in the Netherlands and England,* Project Paper I: *The Conduct of Comparative Research, Oxford.*

References

Faludi, A. (1978) *Essays in Planning Theory and Education,* Oxford: Pergamon.

Frisby, D. (1972) The Popper-Adorno controversy, *Philosophy of the Social Sciences,* Vol. 2, pp. 105-19.

Fürst, D. and Hesse, J. J. (1978) Thesen zur Distanz zwischen der 'lokalen Politikforschung' und dem kommunalen politisch-administrativen System, *Politische Vierteljahresschrift,* Vol. 19, pp. 296-315.

Grauhan, R. R. (1975) *Lokale Politikforschung* (2 vols.), Frankfurt: Campus.

Habermas, J. (1970) Knowledge and Interest, in: *Sociological Theory and Philosophical Analysis* (edited by Emmet, D. and MacIntyre, A.), London: Macmillan, pp. 36-54.

Meyerson, M. and Banfield, E. C. (1955) *Politics Planning and the Public Interest,* Glencoe, Ill.: the Free Press of Glencoe.

Naschold, F. (1972) Zur Politik und Okonomie von Planungssystemen in: Fehl, G. *et al,* (red.), *Planung und Information,* Berlin: Bertelsmann,

PART TWO

Planners as Urban Managers

Introduction by the Editor

During the late 1960s it became increasingly popular to think of town planning as 'urban management'. Three strands can be identified in the development of this notion: the introduction of the 'systems approach to planning' (McLoughlin, 1969; Chadwick, 1971), changing perspectives on urban sociology (Pahl, 1970) and the growth of applied management techniques to local authority service provision (NB government reports on management and staffing of local authorities - the Maud, Mallaby, Bains and Paterson reports; Stewart, 1971; Eddison, 1975). The system of town and country planning established since the 1947 Act was overhauled by the Town and Country Planning Act, 1968 which established a two-tier approach of broad strategic structure plans supplemented with geographically specific local plans.

The notion that town planning is urban management is consistent with a simple model specifying that the last 100 years has seen rapid growth in various processes of 'management'. Ownership and control of industry on the one hand and actual production processes on the other are overlain with complex organizational management systems so that some theorists claimed the age of a 'managerial revolution' whereby management acquired powers separate from those of notional owners - i.e. the shareholders (see Galbraith, 1967). Radical commentators, too, argued that the whole of an individual's life was increasingly managed and controlled by others over whom he or she had little or no control (Marcuse, 1964).

This kind of framework, albeit more rigorously expressed, led urban sociologists in particular to describe town planning as 'urban' management. The 'urban managerialist' thesis derives in particular from the writings of Ray Pahl, particularly the essay in *Whose City?* (1970), entitled 'Urban Social Theory and Research'. In this he

41

suggested that urban sociologists should concentrate on 'the social and spatial constraints on access to scarce urban facilities as dependent variables and *the managers or controllers of the urban system,* which I take as the independent variable' (my emphasis). Clearly Pahl was not suggesting that 'urban managers' operate in a completely autonomous manner, rather that this was a fruitful approach to the analysis of urban issues.

Town planners, and other departments of local government, were conceptualized by Peter Norman as the most crucial actors affecting change in the (inner) city. He argued that if we know which department does what, when and how, we shall best be able to 'arrive at an understanding of how the social character of the inner city is changing and why' (Norman, 1971, p. 362). Town planners and state bureaucrats clearly affected other people's life chances if only because 'the complexity of the industrial city places considerable power in the hands of bureaucratic officials' (Lambert, 1970).

Increasingly, too, *planners thought of themselves as 'managers'.* Traditionally, officers of the local authority are the 'administration'. But one of the urban managers' more progressive and persuasive prophets, in arguing that the local authority should 'govern' not merely 'administer', believed that 'new *management* processes are required to establish support and develop a governmental perspective' (Stewart, 1974, my emphasis). And town planners in particular? At least one voice proclaimed that the town planner was 'the master-allocator of the scarcest urban resources: land, capital and current expenditure on the built environment and the services which are offered to the community' (Eversley, 1973).

The notion that industrial management had become autonomous and separate from ownership, however, was itself increasingly criticized after the late 1960s. Critically, it was far from proven that management did constitute a separate power and interest group apart from shareholders (Nichols, 1969). Directors often are major shareholders and are also very highly paid (Brown, 1968). Blackburn (1972) referred to an Oxford Institute of Statistics survey which found that directors of companies had the *largest average holding* of all groups of shareholders. If anything the only differences between firms run by owners and those run by professional managers, he argued, was that the logic of the latter 'more exactly reflects the rationality of the market':

> The spread of budgeting in the business world has helped to re-establish and clarify the importance of the profit objective. A recent survey of more than four hundred companies established that more than 96% of these engage in comprehensive planning for defined short-run profit objectives, and that of these about nine-tenths specify the objective concretely, in writing. (Chamberlain, 1962, quoted in Blackburn.)

Blackburn thus argued that in aiming at 'fair' profit as opposed to such short-term maximisation the modern capitalist was acting *precisely* according to the dictates of the market, particularly in the context of an international economy. For few firms are safe from takeover and finance capitalism demands acceptable performances from those managers who do not own large amounts of capital, or else they will become unemployed.

Thus, on two counts the notion of autonomous industrial management is severely undermined. First, many directors *are* significant owners; second, if they do not produce the goods for those who *do* own, 'professional' managers no longer get the income and status their position normally grants them. They must make *profits,* and such profits on every occasion represent either the direct expropriation of surplus value from labour, the historical accumulation of surplus invested and objectified in plant infrastructure and capital goods, or the ability of landowners to extract rent for the use of that land. Such reference to land is an appropriate point to cut short this discussion of managerialism in industry and return to the 'urban managers'.

Although Pahl's original formulation did not intend the term 'urban manager' to mean only local government employees, that was the way the term came to be used (Norman, 1975). In that context it is important to dispel any notion that 'urban managers' represent an homogeneous group. As in industry the structures of command in the UK are hierarchical, bureaucratic - at the apex, today, we have the chief executive officer, in close contact with senior councillors. Then there is an array of departmental heads, senior, middle and junior management, which tails off with a variety of 'urban clerks' like the inverviewer who meets housing applicants or the planning technican who files applications for development. At every level powers of discretion are passed down; every level has an area of discretion, but this is defined by those above. The flow of power is *down* the hierarchy, the responsibility-to is *up*.

Discretion is defined, crucially, by national legislation and centrally determined fiscal policy. Ironically, the literature on planning theory contains little or nothing about the relationships between income and expenditure, i.e. it has no material basis whatsoever.

Gordon Moore, the Chief Executive Officer of Bradford, had argued in 1974 that 'The idea of the authority producing an annual report for its "shareholders" — the ratepayers — has much to recommend it'. This, perhaps, could give a fiscal basis to urban management. However, the payment of rates can hardly be the equivalent of *owning* something: ratepayers receive services not dividends — they are customers rather than shareholders. They cannot as such get profit, nor do they derive control. Those who profit, as usual, are the owners of property, capital and land.

This, essentially, is the message spelt out by the readings in this section. In the first paper, Ray Pahl reconsiders his earlier views on 'urban managers' and comes to the conclusion that, although it was wrong to suggest that urban managers were an independent variable, it is still useful to see them as a focus for analysis. Chris Pickvance, on the other hand, shows that over the key issues of high-rise housing and inner London employment, the urban managers had remarkably little influence. Thus, by inference, Pahl's focus on urban managers, albeit redefined, could still be criticized for drawing attention away from crucial influences — in Pickvance's paper these were central government and national changes in the nature and location of employment.

The other two papers in this section consider important aspects of physical planning of current relevance. Martin Boddy examines in some detail the ill-fated Community Land Act which was the most recent attempt at positive state intervention in the land market. He shows that, in practice, very little control was achieved and goes on to argue that even the total nationalization of land, *on its own,* would be insufficient basis for land-use planning. Finally, in this section, John Lambert looks at the relationship between post-war planning and the so-called inner city crisis. Do inner city problems represent a 'failure' of the planning system or, as Lambert suggests, can we not learn more about the nature of planning under capitalism by recognizing the relationship between state activities and capital accumulation? The inner city problem, he claims, can be seen partly as a result of a planning system specifically operating, not in the 'public interest', but in the interests of capital.

References

Blackburn, R. (1972) 'The new capitalism'. In Blackburn, R. (Ed.) *Ideology in Social Science,* London, Fontana.

Brown, M. B. (1973) 'The controllers of British Industry'. In Urry, J. and Wakeford, J. (1973) *Power in Britain.*

Chadwick, G. F. (1971) *A Systems View of Planning,* Oxford: Pergamon.

Eddison, T. (1975) *Local Government: Management and Corporate Planning* (2nd edn.). London: Leonard Hill.

Eversley, D. F. C. (1973) *The Planner in Society: the Changing Role of a Profession,* London, Faber.

Lambert, J. R. (1970) 'The management of minorities', *The New Atlantis,* Vol. 1, No. 1.

Marcuse, H. (1964) *One Dimensional Man,* London, Routledge & Kegan Paul.

McLoughlin, J. B. (1969) *Urban & Regional Planning - A Systems Approach,* London: Faber.

Moore, G. (1974) 'The chief executive role', *Municipal Journal/Municipal Engineering Supplement,* 29 March.

Nichols, T. (1969) *Ownership, Control and Ideology,* London: Allen & Unwin.

Norman, P. (1971) 'Corporation Town', *Official Architecture and Planning,* Vol. XXXIV.

Norman, P. (1975) 'Managerialism: Review of recent work'. In Harloe, M. (Ed.) *Proceedings of the Conference on Urban Change and Conflict,* Centre for Environmental Studies, London p. 14.

Pahl, R. F. (1970) *Whose City?,* London: Longmans.

Stewart, J. (1971) *Management in Local Government: A Viewpoint,* London, Charles Knight.

'Urban Managerialism' Reconsidered*

RAY PAHL[†]

The previous two chapters (of *Whose City*?) have raised issues of allocation and accessibility which deserve further discussion. The notion that there is a redistribution of real income as a result of the allocation of public resources and facilities is becoming understood.[1] At the same time many cling to allocation according to need, as part of the trappings of 'the Welfare State' as a type of society, and professional groups claiming special expertise in the determination of and provision for such needs have grown in power as the resources they allocate increase.

Research on Urban Managers in Theory and Practice

Whilst, as I have argued in Chapter 11 in particular, a focus on these urban managers or gatekeepers is a useful research strategy, and whilst an exploration of their implicit goals, values, assumptions and ideologies may provide a valuable approach for students exploring the role of professionals in bureaucracies, such an approach lacks both practical policy implications and theoretical substance. Practically, the implication is so often that there is need for more sensitivity and more resources: basically, the planners, social workers, housing managers and so forth are very often trying to turn the taps of their resources to favour the most disadvantaged; but either through a mistaken belief in the validity of their data, a lack of awareness of the

*I have received very generous, pertinent and detailed comments on an earlier draft of this chapter from Michael Harloe, John Lambert, David McCrone, Rosemary Mellor and Chris Pickvance. Some of their criticisms were so fundamental that they must be faced in later work. Hopefully, the open sharing of ideas amongst us may enable some advance in sociological analysis of the urban question to be achieved collectively.

†Originally published in 1975 as Chapter 13 of *Whose City?*, Harmondsworth, Penguin.

unintended consequences of their actions or simply through human error, the results of their activity fail to improve, and possibly add to, the plight of the poor. Sometimes, it is true, they are carrying out basically inequitable government policies, often with reluctance, and knowing that this is against their own values, if not their professional training. Generally a lack of resources inhibits the full development of their programme, plan or provision and the central government is accused of having the wrong order of priorities, or private employers and enterpreneurs are accused of putting private gain above public interest. Thus, in practical terms, the implications turn out to be remarkably similar: researchers show that the area of operation of the professional allocator is far more complicated than his training and policies suggest.[2] Wiser, more sensitive and better-trained urban managers, supported with more resources, is inevitably the policy conclusion. As with industrial relations there is a permanent plea for 'better communications'. Since that is an inherent problem in large-scale bureaucratically organized societies, there is no reason why every research worker should not discover the point for himself.

I consider that this emphasis on the local gatekeepers is perfectly valid and I consider further that it is part of the sociologist's general responsibility to explore, expose and to demystify the workings of our institutions, which must not become 'iron cages' or reified structures which dominate us. We should not be surprised to find that within local government structures there are conflicts, feuds, factions, cliques, cabals and all the strains and tensions common in bureaucracies.[3] In particular, we should not be surprised that individuals and professional groups often dress up their plans for personal and collective career advancement with altruistic and professional ideologies, emphasizing the needs of the clients as a basis for their own expansion. Some may believe that with different relationships of means of production different motivations and a different 'human nature' may emerge. Until such time comes, it would be unwise for us to expect that local government bureaucracies would operate very differently from other types of bureaucracies.

That there may be some differences between urban managers and, say, industrial managers would be hard to deny. Despite the attempts, no doubt well-intentioned, of those who seek to make local government 'more efficient' by introducing management consultants, operational research and other aids from the world of profit-maximizing, not all those in local government are concerned with providing efficient services at least cost to the rates. Those who believe in public service, who believe that the library service, for example, has always too little money and too few clients, would claim that more money spent is not profligate but rather a form of community investment in the good life. Similarly, those responsible for education, health services, the personal social services and the like would rarely consider their task solely in terms of efficiency, but would also be concerned with equity or even equality. Local government's search for a collective managerial ideology and identity is certainly an interesting research field, but it needs to be related to a broader intellectual context.

This brings me to the second weakness in the approach — that of theoretical substance. The focus on urban managers or gate-keepers 'allocating' indirect wages and controlling access to scarce urban resources and facilities in 'an urban system' is useful, but too much should not be built upon it. Certainly the danger of reifying concepts such as 'allocative structures' should be avoided. Recent research in Britain has focused on the urban gatekeepers, largely because the research has been heavily on the side of the lower participants who may have suffered at the hands of insensitive local officials. It is understandably very easy for the researcher to view the situation through the eyes of disadvantaged local populations and to attribute more control and responsibility to the local official than, say, local employers or the national government. Following Gouldner's scathing discussion of this issue, it does seem likely that it is easier for sociologists receiving their research funds from government departments or national research councils to combine with, as it were, the bottom and the top in blaming the middle. As Gouldner remarks, such 'a criticism of local managers of the Caretaking Establishment' and 'of the vested interest and archaic methods of these middle dogs' may lead to an uncritical accommodation to the national élite and to the society's master institutions.[4] Such is the danger, and it does seem to be the case from recent British studies that the middle dogs have been the chief target for champions of the underdog.[5]

These local studies, focusing mainly on local government officials, are admirable in enabling us to understand the workings of bureaucracies and organizations. The detailed accounts of the use and misuse of rules, the internal struggles, the confusions, decisions and non-decisions are all useful accounts of the workings of large-scale organizations and, in particular, of their relationships with those outside the organization. More of such studies are needed since they certainly add much to our understanding of the city in capitalist society. However, we must be careful lest they confuse and mystify us by suggesting that research on the sociology of the urban manager implies an understanding of an *independent* variable in the creation of the urban system. Such is the position I have adopted above in Chapter 11 and which I am now terming 'urban managerialism'. It involves *systematic* control of the *same* urban resources and facilities in *different* localities; it further implies the ineffectiveness of the elected councillors. It ignores the constraints of capitalism.

Some Paralles with the Managerialist Thesis in the Industrial Context

Turning to the industrial sphere in order to clarify the point about the inadequacy of the thesis of urban managerialism, the crucial point industrial managerialists put forward is that ownership and control have become separated.[6] Thus, even in such matters as forward planning and investment decisions it is the managers and not the shareholders, or their representatives the directors, who take the crucial decisions. Clearly, this argument applies most strongly when investment is drawn mostly from retained earnings and, in the case of public companies, assets are appropriately reflected in the quoted share price. Without the former the managers would be dependent on external sources of finance and the control that might follow from that; without the latter the company would be in danger of being taken over.[7] Managers maintain control largely because of their technical expertise in industries operating with the more advanced technologies; the logic of science and technology is said to determine the way such industries must develop. Managers thus form part of the technostructure, in Galbraith's term.[8]

Further discussion of managerialism in the industrial context would be misplaced here. Even those who would hold to a thesis of industrial managerialism — and this is hard to sustain in the light of Nichols's attack — would be even more pressed to develop a thesis of urban managerialism.[9] Certainly the professional officers of a local authority can manipulate their elected councillors by withholding information or presenting it selectively and by other means. Also, to some degree and in some cases, they have control over income from rates. Further, they can influence the scope and range of central government legislation by informal pressure exerted by their most senior professionals and also through their various associations and institutes. However, at best, they only have slight, negative, influence over the deployment of private capital, and their powers of bargaining with central government for more resources from public funds are limited.

Indeed, it is evident that far from there being a clear-cut relationship (as I argue on pages 201-211) (of *Whose City?*) between the managers and the managed in an urban system—taken to mean a local configuration of social, economic and political structures — the whole notion must be seen as extremely problematic. Unless one assumes a relative amount of autonomy within local configurations, life chances would be solely determined by national decisions and there would be no variation in access to resources such as housing or education, from one part of the country to another (holding position in the occupational structure constant).[10] It is well documented that there is, however, considerable variation in the level of services and accessibility to resources between localities.[11] This must imply variations in real income in different milieux or spatial configurations. It may appear in a specific context that those controlling the local 'taps' — whether planners, housing managers or medical officers of health — are the true 'gatekeepers' and the way that they use and interpret their rules and procedures influences life chances in a fundamental way. There are recent case studies which support this argument.[12] However, if it is the case that in one area of provision the 'managers' can operate according to one set of criteria, it is equally plausible for 'managers' in a different area of provision to control their local taps according to different principles such as 'positive discrimination' or 'least charge on the rates'. Indeed, this must be partly the cause of the empirical variation in the provision of facilities which has been demonstrated.

If it is the case, then, that the existing state legislation in the fields of planning, housing, social welfare and so on permits wide discretion on the part of the local controllers, it is more difficult to see how organized, systematic and structured opposition, implying the linking and coordination of many different groups in different localities over some length of time, can emerge. If the local gatekeepers of public resources and facilities do not *systematically* work together to reinforce, reflect or recompense inequalities engendered through the productive process, then a 'pure' urban managerialist thesis could hardly be sustained.

Alternative Models of Resource Control and Allocation

In a attempt to clarify the distinctions I am making, I now set out four alternative ideal types.

(a) The 'pure' managerialist model

This assumes that control of access to local resources and facilities is held by the professional offers of the authority concerned. Such 'gatekeepers' share a common ideology (which it is the job of sociologists to uncover), manipulate their elected representatives so that the political composition of the council makes little difference to the policies pursued and, hence, there is a common impact on real incomes of the population as a whole.

(b) The statist model

This assumes that control over local resources and facilities is primarily a matter for the national government and that local professionals or managers have very litle room for manoeuvre. National legislation in the fields of housing, planning, education and so forth, effectively determines the indirect wages or real income of the population as a whole. While there may be *marginal* differences between one local configuration and another, these do not substantially affect the consumption capacities of different social classes.

(c) The control-by-capitalists model

This assumes that at either national or local levels resources are allocated primarily to service the interests of private capitalists. These may be taken to be the reproduction of a docile, well-trained and healthy labour force. If housing affects the supply of labour then resources must be allocated to ensure that the supply is adequately maintained. If growth and profits depend on some extent upon investment in education, then, again, minimal resources must be allocated accordingly. Public services and facilities are always seen as a 'luxury' according to this model. At a local level private is a more legitimate basis for the allocation of, say, central locations than public good.

(d) The pluralist model

This assumes a permanent tension between national bureaucracies, committed to obtaining and distributing larger resources (following partly their internal logic of growth), and the interests of private capital manifested through the economic pressures of 'the City', private industry and the political party representing the dominant class. Cuts and increases in public expenditure ebb and flow between different sectors as the lines of conflict shift. Similarly, local authorities are in competition with each other to get larger shares of central funds and, once funds are obtained, there is the same tension between public and private interests at a local level.

Each of these ideal-typical models produces different explanatory frameworks for answering the question 'Who gets what?' in given spatial contexts. Leaving aside for the present the difficult questions of political economy, which would have to be resolved to determine which model is most appropriate for any given society (for example, is Sweden more like model (b) or model (d)?), there remains the problem that local configurations have neither equal demands nor equal needs for national resources. Since in Britain the physical and demographic variation is considerable between one locality and another, the opportunities for *an hoc* special pleading in the claiming of national resources are very great. Given, too, that territorial justice is an elusive concept,[13] implying an ability to come to a satisfactory definition of social need by the benevolent dictator or benevolent bureaucracy at the centre, some kind of negotiating or bargaining between the centre and periphery is likely to be an inevitable element in any system. That being so the problem of ultimate allocative control remains.

Local Variations, Organized Collective Action and Urban Class-Consciousness

The very differences in local configurations, which give rise to different cases and therefore the allocation of different amounts of national resources, inhibit the establishment of organized collective responses to the allocative process across a wider area. While one local bureaucracy may have made an effective claim for more resources for local schools in the light of its demographic structure, a neighbouring authority might have less good schools but better health provision. Since people's conceptions of the provision of these services are likely to be heavily influenced by their local subjective experiences, a sense of common deprivation or 'urban class-consciousness' may not easily develop. Further, since different groups benefit at different times from different services, common urban consciousness is undermined. Sporadic protests may, indeed, develop: the mobile and the affluent may protest by moving their location; the poor may take part in rent strikes or squatting.

Taking direct action may lead to a local authority amending its housing policy or providing more pre-school playgroups but, once the particular goal has been achieved, there seems little evidence that such groups continue, aiming at broader political goals. In one recent account of a successful attempt to change a local government decision it was claimed that 'there is a chance that community power can begin to turn the scales of social justice'. The author, who led the local campaign, claimed 'We can now regard ourselves as part of a new social and political force at the local level. In time, it will have national significance'[14] These are large claims; if they are substantiated they will confirm the urban managerialist thesis by action from below. Ironically such claims could also be held to support a model of central state control, by showing how reformist demands are being met in order to preserve the system. However, it is the thesis of this paper that such sentiments must be wrong. Since different groups benefit at different times in different parts of the same city, common city or nationwide situations of deprivation rarely occur. Those who claim that they can see the development of 'urban social movements' leading to radical changes in the nature of urban society would find difficulty in getting empirical support from British experience, although there may be more valid reasons for using the term elsewhere.[15] Very rarely would situations arise in the British context where workers were *systematically* deprived of indirect wages through the administration and distribution of what is most aptly termed in France collective consumption. One example of a collective response to a widespread threat was the coordination of a whole cluster of local organizations set up to oppose the concentric system of urban motorways proposed by the Greater London Development Plan. The London Motorway Action Group appeared to be more concerned with preserving 'amenity' and protecting property values and gained its support from home owners more than from local authority or private tenants. An attempt to put forward separate candidates to oppose the two main political parties in an election, held at a time when feeling was running high, was singularly unsuccessful.

With so many local authorities, and with services provided at different levels in different historical and geographical contexts, it is hard for the academic researcher to find a clear pattern. Unlike the situation in France, with its very rapid post-war urbanization and massive suburbanization of the working class, Britain had a rather slower and more piecemeal urban development. Local authority building was more evenly balanced between the inner city and the periphery and the quality of the dwellings and level of public provision, while not exactly lavish, nevertheless maintained a modest standard. Indeed, the quality of working-class dwellings in some areas produced a sort of housing aristocracy within the working class in comparison with those in the privately rented sector. It is hard to see aggressively exploitative capitalism at work, if one considers simply the national standard and the distribution of local authority dwellings. Tenants' associations did not organize collectively to produce a national rent strike during the period when the Conservative government introduced a system of 'fair rents' for local authority housing, essentially tying them to a local free-market rent structure. Many local authorities made it clear that they were introducing this measure reluctantly and the transparency of the power situation was clear enough for the opposition to be focused at a national level where the measure was vigorously attacked clause by clause through the committee stage of the Bill by the Opposition.[16]

Similarly the activities of property speculators, whilst generating sporadic local squatting in unoccupied office blocks, did not stimulate working class collective action against the private ownership of urban land. Controlling the excess profits of property speculators became a national political issue at the end of 1973 when, amongst others, Lord Plowden, Chairman of Tube Investments, one of the largest of British industrial enterprises, wrote to *The Times* urging government action. It is significant that this pressure to take action seemed to come at least as much from the controllers of industry as from trade unionists, and was directed, evidently, against the capitalist system in housing and land and not at the capitalist systems in industry. 'The City' was seen as serving 'finance capital' at the expense of industrial capitalism.

Now whether Britain has a more divided ruling class than France, whether we have adopted a 'softer' form of capitalism and whether a French Prime Minister would own up to the 'unacceptable face of capitalism' (in Mr Heath's phrase) is in each case hard to say. One conclusion does, however, seem clear, and that is that *urban conflicts relate directly to the specific nature of the particular type of capitalist society concerned.* It is clear to me that it is *not* possible to generalize about cities in capitalist societies without making many serious qualifications. The 'urban question' will be very different in France, Australia, the United States, Germany and Britain.

Finally, it is worth remembering that by focusing attention on indirect wages and excluding the generation and distribution of direct wages the sociologist may create the very mystifictions I am at pains to describe. By focusing on urban resources and facilities and by altering urban populations to their relative deprivations in the field of consumption, attention is shifted from the main *source* of inequality in society, namely, the field of production. The work by Hindess in Liverpool shows that the extreme salience of housing opportunities for workers' life chances has made this a central feature of working-class political discussion. As Hindess puts it, 'local government is experienced not simply as providing a background but also as an external constraining and coercive organisation'.[17] In many northern cities the Labour party in control is seen as being as constraining and a coercive as the alternative. If workers are made to think that their *main interest* are in the field of consumption and if sociologists adopt a form of urban managerialism to explain the allocation of resources within an urban system, then clearly basic inequalities arising from the productive process may remain hidden.

Territorial Inequality, Political Ideology and the Power of Overt and Hidden Markets

Up to now we have noticed the tension between the national and the local and hinted at the inevitability of territorial injustice. It is now necessary to make certain points explicit: *no economy can develop in a 'spatially neutral' way.* Inevitably certain areas will have certain advantages for the production of certain goods and services; As technology develops or (but not necessarily) as markets change, certain areas grow more rapidly, while others decline. This unbalanced development follows as much from the logic of technological development as from the logic of profit associated with capitalist ownership of the means of production. As the division of labour becomes more fine, differentiation and concentration of the workforce inevitably creates a spatial form to an economy, which seems to acquire a relative autonomy of its own.

In the same way that a certain *scale* of production leads to the creation of a resource—the economies of scale—so too does the physical concentration of the workforce in cities create a resource, namely *accessibility.* As long as facilities are concentrated so that some locations are more favoured than others, then inequalities of accessibility will occur, which again are inevitably reflected in hidden or overt market structures.

There are only two ways of overcoming such inequalities: the first would be to allocate centrality according to need. Since need changes over the life cycle (being close to a primary school when under 11 is an advantage, being close when over 65 can be a disadvantage) and since the facilities are more spatially fixed than the users, then a high level of individual mobility would be necessary. However much this might disrupt social relationships and draw families apart, it would have to be insisted upon in the interests of territorial justice. The second alternative would be to 'abolish centality'. Cities are inherently inegalitarian structures and ultimately the only way to eradicate spatial injustice is to eradicate the city. This would seem to imply a regression to a simpler mode of production and a less fine division of labour. So far I am arguing that *technology and the division of labour create inequality independently of that engendered by the capitalist mode of production*. If cities are predominantly privately owned then a *second* source of inequality, over and above that connected with accessibility, will emerge, namely differential rent. And the two aspects of inequality are interrelated. High accessibility is generally equated with high rents. But areas of very high rent are in turn created by the existence of the mass of the population that surrounds these areas. If, overnight, the city was totally depopulated, apart from those living in the area of the very highest rentable value, such high rents could not be sustained. Thus, the owners of central locations get a 'surplus rent' over and above what is required for their personal needs and the maintenance of their property. They further gain an increase in *capital* value which can be used for other purposes. I am arguing for a position which recognizes that centrality cannot be analysed as simply the basis for another commodity market.

The fundamental difference between a 'capitalist city' and a 'socialist city' appears, therefore, to be in terms of the *ownership of land and rent structures.* Hence, it is possible to postulate a 'socialist city' in a capitalist society. This would be the case if the state owned all urban land, despite the ownership of the forces of production still remaining in private hands. Apart from paying rent (however determined) to the state, private capitalist enterprises could presumably carry on much as before. Such a situation raises in acute form the relationship between the political economy and the territorial structure of the society. How would a city owned on a socialist basis interrelate with a privately owned system of production?

Under these circumstances the strong urban managerialist thesis I have discussed above would have force. Possibilities for genuine redistributive policies would emerge so that indirect wages could compensate for low direct wages. Tension would then arise between the polity and the economy as capitalists found that their control over local labour markets was thereby dimished. Indeed it is through the construction of such a scenario that the realities of power in a truly 'mixed' economy emerge. The city then becomes a short-term for the public allocation of all services and facilities (including accessibility), apart from position in labour markets. Such a situation would create enormous strain, as firms' competitive positions were undermined by state action. In such a situation the urban managers would not necessarily have any more power than at present to get information on incomes from local employers, to change the structure of local labour markets by introducing new and more flexible types of employment, to prevent closures or to affect earned incomes, hours of employment or anything else. The recent *Report of the Panel of Inquiry into the Greater London Development Plan* summarizes the situation as it exists at the present time:

> We are driven, therefore, to the view that the local planning authority can, within its area, over the long term influence only marginally the tendency of employment to contract or alter, or retain its nature. It can somewhat more effectively exercise, or fail to exercise, its power to inhibit expansion, but even here the power of the market renders less than perfect the ability of an authority to check it consistently in the long term.

Yet even in an area where the local authority *does* have the power to intervene directly in the market, as in the case of allocating land for private residential development, there is no clear evidence that there is redistribution towards the poor. Indeed the best evidence suggests the reverse. The massive study evaluating land-use planning in England since the 1947 Act concluded:

> The objectives of the planning system result in various economic and social costs being created and borne by different sectors of society. At the present time, the lower end of the private housing market (both the groups who succeed in purchasing and those who fail) seems to be bearing a high burden of real or opportunity costs. In effect, this is indirect *redistribution of income*. Unfortunately, this is in the wrong direction; in this case from the relatively less well-off house purchaser to the rural landowner. . . . Rather than contribute and be instrumental in achieving an egalitarian society, the current planning of land development has made matters worse.[19]

Similar general points can be made in relation to the urban low paid workers.[20]

In the light of this kind of evidence, it is hard to sustain the more extreme urban managerialist thesis which I advance in Chapter 10. Even when the state does make attempts to 'solve' the housing problem or to restructure the declining regions by introducing new employment through the Regional Employment Premium, it does not seem to have much success. Indeed, examples of government decisions leading to unintended consequences are unhappily only too common:

> In London the siting of the GPO Tower in an area that has long been a traditional centre for a tightly-knit community of small tailors, working largely for West-End stores, has affected the trade. Here was an area occupied by rather seedy buildings, which were perfectly adequate from the viewpoint of their occupiers, who were sometimes their owners. Some were demolished in order to make room for the Tower. Now that the Tower exists there is a large tourist interest in the area. Higher rents can be obtained from souvenir shops and cafes. As short-term leases expire, tailors are asked for higher rents, and often they cannot afford them. They move to other places, in a way that disrupts this trading community and leads to a decline in its efficency.[21]

Such examples indicate that it would be by no means certain who would lose in a genuinely mixed economy, so long as the main productive forces were outside the control of the state. Evidence from the command economies of Eastern Europe indicates that even with state control of all investment and allocations to urban resources and facilities, there still exists in such societies:

(a) hidden market mechanisms favouring those with higher incomes

(b) territorial injustice in access to resources and facilities;

(c) inequitable tax redistribution between one locality and another;

(d) all the informal operations within bureaucracies that favour those who know how to work systems and probably implying further redistribution of real wages;

(e) conflicts over the 'needs' of one socio-economic category in relation to another.

Indeed, paradoxically, if urban managerialism applies anywhere it is most likely to have relevance in societies operating systems of state socialism where the power of central bureaucracies is increased.

The Need for Comparative and Historical Analysis

It is now becoming more widely accepted by sociologists that Marx's unitary model of capitalist society is misleading, particularly in so far as it relates to the European societies of his time. By taking Britain as 'the most typical form' of capitalist society and then developing a typology which could be applied to other European societies Marx, in Gidden's view, committed the error of 'misplaced concreteness'.[22]

> The point is, that rather than being the 'type cast' of either capitalist of industrial evolution, Britain is the exception; or, more accurately, it represents only one among various identifiable patterns of development in the emergency of the advanced societies. In Britain—no doubt as the overall result of a complicated (and still highly controversial) set of specific historical antecedents—the way was paved in the nineteenth century for the mutual accommodation of capitalism and industrialism within a general framework of bourgeois democratic order. Consequently the process of industrialisation took place in an 'undirected' fashion, through the agency of a multiplicity of entrepreneurial activities in a relatively stabilised 'bourgeois society'. France in the nineteenth century, and arguably ever since, was dominated by the legacy of the 1789 revolution.[23]

It would be ironic if contemporary sociologists adopted the same error in reverse and derived a new abstract model from an analysis of the urban question in France or Italy which they then applied to the situation in Britain. Comparative analysis can do much to illustrate the *differences* between capitalist societies and the distinctive nature of British urbanism.

Giddens discusses some of the differences in the infracture and space economy between Britain, France and Germany in the nineteenth century. It is curious that Marxist geographers such as Harvey have not, apparently, recognised the relevance of the historical geography of the nineteenth century and its relationships to the political economy of early capitalism and developing urbanization in Britain.[24] As Briggs points out, 'the first effect of early industrial was to differentiate English communities rather than to standardize them'.[25] Briggs goes on to emphasize how far Manchester and Birmingham 'diverged very strongly in their economic life, their social structure and their politics' and

> Sheffield had much in common with Birmingham in its economic system, but the shape of its society and the chronology and trend of the municipal history were quite different. A full study of social structure must take account of property relations as well as income, of religion as well as economics, and not least of demography, which provides a quantitative basis for much subsequent generalization. . . .

> In the fundamental study of comparative property relations obvious points to note are the pattern of ownership of urban land, the extent of aristocratic interest (including absentee interest), the volume of industrial investment, the amount of corporate wealth and the total rateable value.[26]

Different types of corporation and sources of finance meant that 'the early- and mid-Victorian cities would confront urban problems with differing degrees of imagination and efficiency. . . . Some Victorian cities quite deliberately embarked upon large-scale programmes; others lagged behind'[27] Professor Briggs does not make it clear who is confronting and who is embarking.

It is certain that the industrial and occupational structure of cities varied greatly and that the life chances of the urban working class varied according to social, economic and political factors in the different cities. Foster's comparative analysis of Oldham, Northampton and Shields provides clear evidence of the variation in pattern and style of exploitation between towns as industrialism advanced.[28]

The growth in the scale and volume of grants-in-aid from the state during the nineteenth century was gradually to lead to a decline in provincial autonomy and the increasing dominance of the power of the state in determining appropriate levels of education, health, housing and so forth. However—and this is the point of this brief excursion into nineteenth-century history—the development of national standards of public provision during the twentieth century was grafted on to a wide variation in local infrastructure. Thus, Norwich, Bristol, Sheffield and Manchester, to take four cities at random, not only had different local economic structures but also, consequently, had different levels of indirect wages.

Then, in the twentieth century, in the same way that some cities had acquired greater growth and greater wealth in the previous century, so differential industrial and urban decay produced a pattern which increasingly has come to be seen as a national and not a local problem. Further, as Britain's competitive position in the world declined, as it lost its overseas investments, its Empire, its supply of cheap raw materials and its captive markets for manufactured goods, so that political power of its productive industry increased, forming, as it does, the foundation of our economic base. Unlike France, Britain has to import about half its food and this means that the production of goods and services for export occupy a particularly key role in political economy. The competitive arena of international capitalism puts very severe constraints on Britain's room for manoeuvre. The pursuit of what are seen by international financiers as 'too radical' measures could lead to a massive flight of capital from the City of London to money markets elsewhere and, possibly, a similar flight of skilled managerial and professional workers. If Britain cut itself off from trading partnerships with Western capitalist societies it would be likely to enter acute balance-of-payments crises if food imports were to be maintained. In this context, with continuing inflation, aided by the inevitable increase in world primary-product prices (especially oil), expenditure on urban infrastructure is inevitably seen as a 'cost' restricting our overall competitiveness in world markets.

In the light of this, it is surprising that the level of our public provision is as high as it is in comparison with, say, France. Partly this can be accounted for by the incorporation of the working class into the political process, the extension of the rights of citzenship and the reform of social security in the 1940s. However, it would also be reasonable to attribute some measure of credit to the forces of bourgeois, liberal, humanitarian reformism in the Fabian tradition for ameliorating the harsh logic of capitalist enterprise. The lower-middle-class values of decency, orderliness and 'balance', enshrined in such ameliorist pressure groups as the Town and Country Planning Association,[29] have done much to create a climate of opinion in which the small scale of our urban scene, epitomized in the New Towns, has been preserved and maintained. The fact that a unitary capitalist ruling class did not exist in nineteenth-century Britain and that while the aristocracy 'ruled officially', the bourgeoisie ruled 'over all the various spheres of civil society in reality' as Marx noted, has led Giddens to conceive of a system of 'leadership groups' to describe the situation today.[30] This pattern may serve to soften and moderate more aggressive capitalist tendencies.

There has been remarkably little research on the ideology which has produced British urbanism and on the relationship between urban allocation and the political economy of the state. Ruth Glass's survey of the nineteenth-century literature[31] and Raymond Williams's masterly work on the literary images of *The Country and the City*[32] provide valuable starting points, and detailed case studies such as that by Stedman Jones[33] or Wohl[34] are also notable. For recent years we have to rely on journalistic analyses, such as *The Property Boom,*[35] and somewhat garbled attempts to link the activities of property speculators with the housing crisis in London.[36] What is needed is a systematic socio-economic analysis of the implications of the rapid movement of capital into land and property markets.[37] The recent operations of capitalism are sucking resources out of local spatial economies in a way previous industrial investment did not. (At least it provided local employment.) Such shifting patterns of investment have led Eisenschitz to conclude that 'now the city as a physical artifact is being used in order to absorb the economic surplus and promote the welfare of the capitalist system'.[38] Eisenschitz's emphasis on the flows of investment capital is correct. As he puts it:

> To understand the relation of the city to the world and in particular the relations of areas within the city one needs to know where the surplus is generated and absorbed, and the magnitude, generation and destination of wages, rent, profits and output. Areas and land uses should be examined with regard to their relative production and consumption, and their generation and absorption of profits, relating land use patterns to economic forces. Each pattern of flows has an associated pattern of social relationships.[39]

This must be done in the context of *British* political economy, based on our distinctive infrastructure and distinctive position in the pattern of world trade in capitalist markets. Hopefully, we may be able to explicate the constraints within which the urban managers must operate and to show the relationship between access and allocation in urban and regional systems. Unless we have a clearer notion of the nature of *British* capitalist society it will not be possible to come to a sound theoretical understanding of 'the city' and the space economy. Certainly in terms of pracital policies in connection with 'the urban crisis' (variously defined) it is clear that attacks at the level of urban management may be misdirected. It is rather like the works stoning the house of the chief personnel manager when their industry faces widespread redundancies through the collapse of world markets.

Conclusions

'Urbanism', as Harvey reminds us, 'entails the geographic con-concentration of a socially designated surplus product.'[40] Cities are essentially unfair. A distinctive focus for urban sociology in capitalist society is to explore the system by which that society allocates its urban resources and facilities. I am arguing, somewhat elliptically perhaps, that British urbanism and the indirect wages generated and distributed, are a produce of *the tensions between competitive international capitalism and ameliorist Welfare-State-type ideologies.* Since the urban managers are the central mediators between urban populations and the capitalist economy and since they also serve to generate and maintain the ideology of welfare-statism, their role remains crucial in the urban problematic.[41] This *may* mean that the British urban working class suffers less naked exploitation in the area of collective consumption, and that the central government is less *dirigiste,* than *may* be the case in France. However, in making these analyses of the distinct nature of various forms of capitalist urbanism there is an urgent need to remember—as Marx and Engels first saw—that 'the housing question', and much else that is wrong in our cities, can *never* be solved while 'modern big cities' survive. Even if we had the social control and ownership of the means of production, so long as such 'modern big cities' exist, so also, if in a different form, will the inequitable generation of indirect wages continue. The search for a just city is self-defeating. As long as there are 'modern big cities' there will be a need for ameliorism and the allocation of resources by managers and gatekeepers. And, to return to Harvey, 'the reputation and significance of individual cities rest to a large degree upon their location with respect to the geogrpahic circulation of the surplus. The qualitative attributes of urbanism will likewise be affected by the rise and fall in the total quantity of surplus as well as the degree to which the surplus is produced in concentratable form.'[42] The urban managers remain the allocators of this surplus; they must remain, therefore, as central to the urban problematic.

References

1. Harvey, D., 'Social processes, spatial form and the redistribution of real income in an urban system', in Chisholm, M., Frey, A. E. and Haggett, P., *Regional Forecasting,* Butterworth, 1971.
2. See, for example, the work by Norman Dennis, *People and Planning,* Faber & Faber, 1970, and *Public participation and Planner' Blight,* Faber & Faber, 1972; and Davies, J. G., *The Evangelistic Bureaucrat,* Tavistock, 1972.

3. A good instance of this is given by D. M. Muchnik, in *Urban renewal in Liverpool,* Bell, 1970.

4. Gouldner, A. W., 'The sociologist as partisan: Sociology and the Welfare State', in *For Sociology,* Allen Lane, The Penguin Press, 1973, p. 51.

5. In addition to the work by Dennis and Davis cited above there are the Birmingham studies by Rex, J. and Moore, R., *Race, Community and Conflict,* Oxford University Press, 1967, and by Lambert, J. R. and Filkin, C. J., *Ethnic Choice and Preference in Housing,* Report to the Social Sciences Research Council, 1971, and in Glasgow by Damer, Seán, 'Wine Alley: The sociology of the dreadful enclosure', *Sociological Review* **22** (1974), 221-48.

6. These arguments are admirably summarized in Nichols, Theo, *Ownership, Control and Ideology,* Allen & Unwin, 1969.

7. See Pahl, R. E. and Winkler, J. T., 'The economic élite: Theory and practice', in Stanworth, P. and Giddens, A. (eds.), *Élites and Power in British Society,* Cambridge University Press, 1974.

8. Galbraith, J. K., *The New Industrial State,* Hamish Hamilton, 1967.

9. It is only fair to note that I have come probably as close as anyone to adopting this position in my previous work. See also Lambert, J. R., 'The management of minorities', in *The New Atlantis* **2** (1), Milan, 1970.

10. See Pickvance, C. G., 'On a materialist critique of urban sociology', in *Sociological Review,* N. S., **22** (2) (1974) 203-20.

11. Taylor G. and Ayres, N., *Born and Bred Unequal,* Longman, 1969; Davies B., *Social Needs and Resources in Local Services,* Michael Joseph, 1968; and Harvey, *op. cit.*

12. See above, the works cited in references 2 and 5.

13. See Harvey, *op. cit.,* Chapter 3.

14. Clark, G. 'The lesson of Acklam Road', in Butterworth, E. and Weir, D. (eds.), *Social Problems of Modern Britain,* Fontana, 1972, 186.

15. See *Espaces et Sociétés* **1** (1972), 6-7, particularly the introduction by M. Castells. See also Castells's books, *La Question urbaine,* Maspero, Paris, 1972, and *Luttes urbaines et pouvoir politique,* Maspero, Paris, 1973.

    For a discussion of the French work in relation to British examples, see Pickvance, C. G., 'From "social base" to "social force": Some analytical issues in the study of urban protest', paper prepared for the session on Social Conflicts in Urban and Regional Development at the Eighth World Congress of Sociology, Toronto, 1974.

16. See, for example, *Hansard,* Vol. 826, No. 10, cols. 32-160.

17. Hindess, B., *The Decline of Working Class Politics,* Paladin and MacGibbon & Kee, 1971, p. 77.

18. *Report of the Panel of Inquiry into the Greater London Development Plan,* HMSO, Vol. I. p. 79.

19. Hall, P. *et al., The Containment of Urban England,* Allen & Unwin, 1973, Vol. II, p. 402.

20. See Chapter 9 above.

21. Medhurst, D. Franklin and Lewis, J. Parry, *Urban Decay,* Macmillan, 1969, pp. 75-6.

22. Giddens, A., *The Class Structure of the Advanced Societies,* Hutchinson, 1973, pp. 146.

23. *Ibid.,* pp. 144-5.

24. Harvey, D., *Social Justice and the City,* Arnold, 1973.
25. Briggs, A., *Victorian Cities,* Penguin Books, Harmondsworth, 1968, p. 33.
26. *Ibid.,* pp. 35-6, 38.
27. *Ibid.,* pp. 42-3. See also Hennock, E. P., *Fit and Proper Persons: Ideal and Reality in Nineteenth Century Urban Government,* Arnold, 1973.
28. Foster, J., 'Nineteenth-century towns: A class dimension', in Dyos, H. J. (ed.), *The Study of Urban History,* Arnold, 1968.
29. Foley, D., 'Idea and influence: The Town and Country Planning Association', in *Journal of the American Institute of Planners,* **28,** (1962), pp. 10-17.
30. Giddens, A., 'Élites in the British class structure', in *Sociological Review* **20** (3) (1972), pp. 345-72.
31. Glass, R., 'Urban sociology: A trend report', in *Current Sociology* **4** (4), 1955.
32. Williams, R., *The Country and the City,* Chatto & Windus, 1973.
33. Jones, G. Stedman, *Outcast London,* Clarendon Press, Oxford, 1971.
34. Wohl, A. S., 'The housing of the working class in London 1815-1914', in Chapman S. D. (ed.). *The History of Working Class Housing,* David & Charles, 1971; also the forthcoming book by Professor Wohl.
35. Marriott, O., *The Property Boom,* Hamish Hamilton, 1967.
36. Counter Information Service, *The Recurrent Crisis of London,* 1973.
37. Gibbs, R. and Harrison, A., *Land Ownership by Public and Semi-Public Bodies in Great Britain,* University of Reading, Department of Agricultural Economics and Management, 1973.
38. Eisenschitz, A., 'Planning and inequality', mimeo, Architectural Association, 1973.
39. *Ibid.,* pp. 73.
40. Harvey, *Social Justice and the City, op. cit.,* pp. 246.
41. I am grateful to Michael Harloe for pointing this out to me.
42. Harvey, *Social Justice and the City, op. cit.*

Physical Planning and Market Forces in Urban Development

CHRIS PICKVANCE*

According to the conventional interpretation of post-war urban development in Britain physical planning is the determining factor and hence physical planners must shoulder the blame for 'failures' such as 'soulless' housing estates, high-rise flats, or the decline of inner-city areas.[1] The aim of this article is to show that the scope of planning powers and the way they have been exercised are quite inconsistent with this interpretation, and that the determining factor in urban development is the operation of market forces subject to very little constraint.

We shall first examine the powers of physical planners and how they are used, and then make a detailed analysis of two cases—high-rise housing and the decline of employment in London—to illustrate our argument that physical planning has little influence on urban development when compared with market forces.

The Scope and Use of Physical Planning Powers

The Town and Country Planning Act 1947 gave counties and county boroughs the task of preparing development plans which would lay down the proposed uses of land within their area, and the task of 'development control', i.e. the issuing of 'planning permissions' for the development of that land. Under the 1968 Town and Country Planning Act a new tier of plans was added known as 'structure plans' which are intended to set out the guidelines for the preparation of

*Originally published in slighly different form in *National Westminister Bank Quarterly Review,* August 1977.

The published version of this article contained a considerable number of editorial changes. The present version is the original version submitted for publication. The only changes made are in notes 3 and 15.

69

'local plans' (which correspond to the previous development plans) and are prepared by shire or metropolitan county authorities. The practice of local plan preparation and development control at district council level, however, remains largely unchanged, and this will be our main concern.

The question we need to examine is to what extent the existence of the system of development plans and development control leads to a different allocation of land from a 'free market' or 'non-planning' situation. If the allocation is very different then physical planning is a powerful force in urban development; but if the allocation is very similar then market forces determine land use despite the existence of the planning system.

The essential point about local planning authorities is that they have no 'positive' powers to ensure that the developments (industrial estates, housing, etc.) set out in a plan will take place. Their powers are 'negative' powers - they have the ability to *refuse* permission for development which does not conform to the plan.

An important consequence follows from this which is not generally recognized. If the planning powers involved in plan preparation and plan implementation (i.e. 'development control') are essentially powers to prevent rather than powers to initiate, then the actual development which does take place depends on the initiators of development or 'developers' (of industrial, residential, commercial property, etc., and who may be public or private sector agents), and not solely on the preventers of development, the physical planners.

So far we have implied that the negative powers of physical planners to prevent housing development in one place or industrial development in another necessarily leads to a different pattern of urban development from the pattern under the non-planning alternative. But a moment's reflexion will show that this is not always the case. For example, in city centre business and financial districts most planning authorities would not consider any other sort of development besides offices. In other words, certain types of land use are seen as 'logical', 'sensible' and 'financially sound'. In city centres it is seen as 'illogical' to zone land for uses which are not the most profitable and which do not bring in the highest rates income.

It is in ways such as this that market forces directly influence development plans so that the allocation of land in those plans may be very similar to a free market allocation, rather than being quite different as the idea of planning might imply. When this is the case planning may be described as *trend planning* since the development plan merely reflects market trends in the allocation of land. In trend planning the negative powers of physical planning are not used to intervene on market trends. Clearly, to the extent that physical planning is trend planning it does not lead to a pattern of land uses different from that which would occur in a non-planning situation.

The importance of trend planning in Britain can be seen from the way in which flexibility in planning has consistently been treated as a virtue. Flexibility means that plans can be amended and adjusted to correspond to changes in market forces. The flexibility of the current system can be seen from the fact that, following the 1971/72 period when house prices rose dramatically, planners designated large amounts to additional land for housing with the result that in 1973 a government-commissioned study showed that in four counties in the South East between 54 and 66% of permissions granted for residential development were on land not designated for housing development one year previously.[2] This study thus disproved the view current when it was commissioned, that planners were holding back land for housing development.

The converse of trend planning is *interventive planning,* i.e. planning which uses negative powers to zone land for purposes other than those which would have come about in a free market situation.[3] The classic example of this in Britain is Green Belt policy which has undoubtedly prevented continuous urban development (as well as leading to longer commuting journeys). The creation of New Towns also involved intervention on market trends. However, what is striking about these examples of interventive planning is how exceptional and untypical they are of planning in Britain since the war. They are in fact both products of the immediate post-war Labour government which was notable for its very strong policy of intervention on market forces. To argue that subsequent governments had been interventionist to the same extent is untenable.

In brief, in my view, the negative powers of physical planning since the war have most often been used to carry out trend planning as opposed to interventive planning and to that extent the physical planning system itself can clearly not be the main determinant of the pattern of post-war urban development as the conventional wisdon claims. In order to determine what is, we need to look at the actions of the public and private sector developers who, unlike physical planners possess the *positive* powers to implement developments.

In 1947 when the post-war British planning system was created it was assumed that local authorities (and new towns and other public agencies) would themselves *initiate* development as well as control it. As Hall has written:

> They would be almost wholly responsible for the urban renewal programmes in the older parts of the cities and for the construction of new and expanded towns of all kinds in the countryside. The negative powers of control would be needed merely to control *the minority of developments that would still be carried out by private agencies.*[4]

In practice because of the rapid rate of population growth which increased the amount of development needed, and the return of a Conservative government in 1951 wedded to the promotion of private enterprise, a totally different situation emerged. Private sector developers carried out the majority of development although public sector involvement in house-building and urban renewal remained important. The London New Towns which were originally intended to absorb most of the population 'decentralized' from London finally contained only 7% of the dwellings built in the South East. The balance was made up mainly of private housing estates, and to a lesser extent of overspill council estates.

Thus the conventional wisdom which treats physical planning as a prime cause of urban development (confusing the physical planning and development functions) and private sector development as a minor factor is doubly mistaken. This view corresponds to that intended by the framers of the Town and Country Planning Act 1947 but not to the actual process of urban development since the war.

Let us now turn to two case studies: high-rise housing development, and the loss of jobs from London, which are currently cited as two self-evident examples of physical planning failure.

1. *High-rise housing*

We have seen that there is an important distinction between negative planning controls exercised by local authorities and positive development powers which may be implemented by private or public sector institutions. In the case of high-rise local authority housing clearly what is being attacked is the role of local authorities as developers and not their physical planning powers. The accusation thus appears simple: local authorities built high-rise flats in the 1960s out of ignorance, stupidity or possibly both; and the 'failure' of this type of housing can be taken as symptomatic of public sector development. However, a closer examination shows a more complex picture in which local authorities are subjected to constraints from central government.

It is frequently assumed that high-rise housing was an inevitable response to the need to rehouse slum-clearance households at high densities on inner city sites, and that local authorities had little alternative but this form of construction. But the facts suggest otherwise. As Stone has shown high buildings have to be spaced well apart in order to allow adequate daylight and this destroys any simple proportional relation between the number of stories and density, measured in terms of rooms per acre. For example, he points out that

> the effect of increasing the number of storeys arranged in parallel blocks (street formation) from two to twenty is only to double, approximately, the number of rooms per acre.[5]

Thus some gain in density can be achieved but much less than might be expected. However, this gain in density is bought at a higher unit cost. Stone shows that the overall cost (including land, infracture, construction garaging, and maintenance) of building in 15-storey blocks is 50% higher than that of building in 2-storeys, outside London and Scotland. Whether the net result is cheaper development depends on the assumptions made about the cost of the land saved. Stone argues that only in the centres of large conurbations are land values high enough for high-rise building to mean a net saving *to the local authority*—and even there lower density development further from the centre is a much cheaper option. But he concludes that looked at in *national resource terms* in the long run the land saved is farmland, typically worth about £200 an acre in 1964. Clearly building high is an extravagent way of saving land.[6]

If the savings from high-rise building are by no means clear-cut is there a more effective explanation of the rise of this type of building in the 1960s? In fact there is. It lies in the graduated subsidies paid by central government to local government for building higher blocks of flats. For example, in addition to 'expensive site' subsidies which are clearly relevant to high-rise building the Housing Subsidies Act 1956 provided extra subsidies for building over 6 storeys, and the same practice was continued under the Housing Act 1961.[7] Only in the Housing Subsidies Act 1967 (*before* the Ronan Point disaster of May 1968) was this extra subsidy ended. In the same year a housing-cost yardstick was introduced and an announcement made that from 1969 Parker Morris standards would have to be met.[8] Table 1 shows the way in which the building of high flats responded to the removal of this subsidy and the introduction of the cost yardstick—the figures dropping sharply after the peak of 1966.

TABLE 1. *Tenders approved for flats of 5 or more stories in Local authorities and new Towns in England and Wales*

Year	Absolute number	Percentage of all dwellings (including houses)
1956	8011	6.6
1957	10,009	8.7
1958	11,369	11.1
1959	15,109	12.7
1960	15,685	14.2
1961	17.109	16.5
1962	18,891	18.2
1963	29,500	23.5
1964	35,454	24.1
1965	34,953	21.5
1966	44,306	25.7
1967	39,309	23.0
1968	21,570	19.9
1969	13,340	13.5
1970	9740	9.8

Source: Department of the Environment, *Housing Statistics*

The connection between government subsidies and local authority high-rise building is thus fairly clear. But the question remains why the extra subsidies for high flats were made available in the first place. The answer to this appears to be partly that high flats were seen as potentially a cheaper form of housing (a hope which as we have seen proved to be unjustified) but more importantly as part of a desire to introduce technological innovation into the building industry.[9] This involved the encouragement of prefabrication of materials, more on-site mechanization, better coordination, and standardization of design—in a word, 'industrialization'. According to this argument high-rise housing was necessary to provide the scale of operation and opportunity for use of standard designs to justify the introduction of new techniques. Thus the main beneficiary of high-rise housing was intended by central government to be the building industry, in the first place, with subsequent benefits in lower costs to the public purse. But the latter did not occur, with the result that subsidies for high-rise housing primarily helped the building industry to adopt new technology with probable benefits to it in other areas of construction such as offices and hotels.

Thus the conventional wisdom which attributes to physical planners the responsibility for high-rise housing is doubly mistaken. Firstly, because physical planners are not involved in decisions about what type of housing is built in areas zoned for residential use, as long as certain standards are met. Secondly, because when we look at local authority involvement in high-rise housing *as developer* we find that the subsidy structure imposed by central government in order to aid the private building industry was a very strong constraint on local authority freedom of action. Thus we are very far from a situation in which local authorities act freely imposing ill-considered housing design preferences at all costs on the public as the conventional wisdom would suggest.[10] Rather the demands of the private building industry and central government measures to meet them were the primary factors.

2. *The decline of employment in London*

As a second case study we may take the falling level of employment in London, and in particularly inner London, which, as in the case of high-rise housing, is blamed conventionally on 'the planners'. Let us examine this argument by seeing how physical planning powers can affect employment.

There are two main ways:

(a) through the granting or refusal of planning permissions (a local authority power), and

(b) through the granting or refusal of Industrial Development Certificates (IDCs) for manufacturing expansion or of Office Development Permits (ODPs) for office building (central government powers).[11]

Local authorities are responsible for drawing up plans and granting or refusing planning permission for land uses such as industry or commerce which involve employment. In most cases they do not wish to place unreasonable limits on land zoned for uses leading to employment since this would be to deny any interest in local prosperity and a high rates income. The unwillingness of one local authority to see employment going to another and the competition between towns and districts for employment is at the origin of the centralized Industrial Development Certificate scheme set up in 1945. This was designed to prevent local authorities in prosperous regions from attracting still more manufacturing industry, and give the 'assisted areas' a better chance. Similarly the introduction of Office Development Permits in 1964 was designed to regulate centrally the freedom of local authorities to offer planning permission for office development. In this case the concern was with the distribution of offices *within* the same region.

How can this combination of central and local physical planning powers have brought about the decline in employment in London? In order to answer this queston it is necessary to distinguish the four components of employment decline and then ask how physical planning could affect each one. These are

(a) a decline in employment in existing firms,

(b) the closure of existing firms,

(c) the outward movement of existing firms, which is partly counterbalanced by

(d) the opening of new firms or arrival in London of firms previously established elsewhere.[12]

Firstly, a decline in employment in existing firms is quite clearly outside the scope of the influence of physical planning powers. For planners to have this type of effect would require degrees of intervention in the running of firms, in the hiring and firing of employees which are non-existent in this country.

Secondly, the closure of existing firms which is the largest source of decline in employment quoted by Gripaios is equally beyond the scope of current physical planning powers. These powers simply do not allow such drastic intervention.[13] The decline in employment due to closures must thus be due to a series of decisions by private and public sector employers in response to market and central government pressures—for example, the decline in dock employment due to containerization and the shifting pattern of port use, or the decline of jobs in sugar-refining due to the shift from cane sugar to sugar beet as a result of EEC membership. These are the types of pressure which lead to the closing down of existing workplaces. Broadly speaking they can be described as the rationalization and restructuring of British industry with government help to strengthen the competitive position of each industrial sector in world markets. This rationalization and restructuring has spatial consequences: districts within London whose advantages led to the establishment of firms there seventy years ago lose their attractiveness today when motorway links are more important for transport, and 'greenfield' sites can be found on favourable terms in New Town and small and medium town fringe locations.[14]

If the first two components of employment change are beyond the influence of physical planning powers then the alleged impact of the latter must operate on the remaining two components. We will first examine the possible influence of physical planning on the discouragement of new firms from establishing in London, and secondly its possible influence on the encouragement of outward movement.

Physical planners might discourage new firms either through the refusal of planning permission by local authorities, or by the refusal of IDCs or ODPs by central government. The first possibility is extremely unlikely since as we have seen local authority planners at the behest of the local council typically try to *attract* employment by the granting of planning permission rather than seeking to deter it by refusal. They have little reason to want to 'lose' jobs to neighbouring authorities.

The second possibility, that it is through the refusal of IDCs and ODPs that physical planners discourage new firms, has apparent plausibility. IDCs and ODPs are intended to improve the inter- and intra-regional distribution of jobs at London's expense and must thus surely have been used to obstruct efforts to attract employment by local authorities within London. The great surprise is that the potentially strong power of the two schemes to prevent office and manufacturing development in London has never been used. This can be seen from the percentage of applications for IDCs or ODPs which could potentially be refused, but which are in fact approved.

In the case of IDCs the percentage of applications *approved* in the South East and Midlands, the regions from which diversion of industry was being sought, was of the remarkable order of 85% in the 1950s and 75% in the 1960s when a more 'active' regional policy was being pursued.[15] This is far from the blanket prohibition which the IDC system is often assumed to involve. Similarly when one turns to the ODP system one finds that the rate of *approvals* for office development in central London has been in the 67-88% range in all but three years of the 1965-1975 period. (The exceptions were 1965/6 26%, 1972/3 49% and 1974/5 51%.)[16] The true figure is even higher since many of the applications which are refused are resubmitted successfully. Thus the effect of this potentially powerful planning control has in practice been very limited. It is sometimes argued that the existence of the two systems of control is itself a deterrent and therefore the rate of applications approved is a poor guide to their real effectiveness. However, a recent enquiry among 100 firms to discover whether any had themselves been deterred by the IDC system failed to find a single case. The hypothesis therefore remains unsubstantiated. Our conclusion regarding the effectiveness of the IDC and ODP systems in discouraging new firms from London is supported by a recent Government report which concludes that

> IDC and ODP controls do not appear to fulfill a very useful function. They do not seem to inhibit much development in London. . . .[17]

In sum it would seem that neither central nor local government planning controls have had an appreciable effect in discouraging *new* employment in London. What seems far more likely is that London locations as such have become decreasingly attractive compared with other locations and that this has been the main factor in discouraging new employment from London.

Finally, when we consider the fourth component of employment decline, that due to the out movement of existing firms, the evidence leads to the same conclusion. Office decentralization from central London has been a sizeable trend ever since the 1950s—before even the Location of Offices Bureau started operation in 1963. But this trend has has not been due to physical planning controls forcing offices to move out of central London since no such powers exist. The principal cause of the out-movement of offices is the substantial savings in rents, wages and rates when more routine office functions are moved from central London.[18] Unlike the case of regional policy where very large subsidies are paid to induce firms to move to the assisted areas (currently totalling some £500m per year), *no* government incentives have been necessary to encourge offices to move from central London. For this reason the term 'policy' to describe office decentralization is something of a misnomer. As a recent government report concluded,

> The objective of decentralizing office employment from central London is being achieved by market forces.[19]

The movement of manufacturing firms from London is also independent of physical planning controls for the same reason as offices. Controls which force manufacturing firms out of London are simply non-existent. (Of course the movement of these firms is dependent upon the 'receiving' local authorities giving planning permission for the resiting of these firms.) As in the case of offices it is likely that lower operating costs in locations outside London are the main explanation of the outward movement of manufacturing firms— although the realization of high land values in the original site may sometimes play a part.

To conclude our examination of the thesis that physical planning is the cause of the decline of employment in London we may quote from the Layfield Panel's report on the Greater London Development Plan. The context is different—the Panel is reporting on the GLC's desire to *maintain* London's population or at least slow down its decline—but the theme is the same.

They write:

> We are driven, therefore, to the view that the local planning authority can, within its area, over the long term, influence only marginally the tendency of employment to contract or alter, or retain its nature.[20]

This corresponds precisely to the argument of this section.

Conclusion

The aim of this article has been to demonstrate that the conventional wisdom which accords an omnipotent role to physical planners in urban development in Britain is based on a complete misconception of the scope of physical planning powers. These powers are limited in nature and weak in their application due to the prevalence of trend planning. It follows that market forces are correspondingly powerful and that these are the main determinants of urban development.

Secondly, it was shown that the conventional wisdom confuses physical planning powers with local authority initiation of development. Our examination of high-rise housing, a local authority-initiated development generally regarded as a disaster, showed it to be less a result of local authorities acting on their own in some inevitable blundering bureaucratic fashion than the outcome of the role they were obliged to play by central government in its attempt to provide the conditions for technical innovation in the building industry.

Thus rather than supporting the statements that 'physical planning has failed' and that 'local authority development is inevitably a failure', our analysis leads to the conclusions that

(a) physical planning has for the most part been too weak to have any effect, and that

(b) local authority development is constrained by a variety of economic, political and financial pressures which frequently hinder its success.

We shall not conclude with any detailed recommendations for the strengthening of central and local physical planning powers, or for the removal of constraints from local authorities. This would require a much more elaborate discussion of particular issues and areas. Our aim has been less ambitious—to show that the post-war British experience does not justify the jettisoning of physical planning and the restriction of local authority development activity. The evidence suggests rather that it is the largely unrestricted operation of market forces (in land, property, finance, etc.) which has been the prime determinant of urban development and that if the latter is deemed a 'failure' then there is a *prima facie* case for interventive planning on a much larger scale than has been tried in the past twenty-five years.

Notes

1. C. Booker, 'Physical planning: another illusion shattered', *National Westminster Bank Quarterly Review,* February 1977, pp. 56-64.
2. Department of the Environment, *Housing Land Availability in the South-east,* HMSO, London, 1975.
3. [Since writing this article I have come to think that the distinction between trend and interventive planning is not entirely satisfactory. While the distinction makes clear that physical planning may simply reproduce market trends, it overlooks the fact that some degree of 'intervention' is not only compatible with, but also necessary for the functioning of land markets at a certain stage of capitalist development. At the simplest level landowners will see the advantage of intervention in the form of land use controls to avoid negative externalities, e.g. to prevent a neighbour building an abattoir next door.]
4. P. Hall, *Urban and Regional Planning,* Penguin, 1974, pp. 122-3, emphasis added.
5. P. A Stone, *Urban Development in Britain: Standards, Costs and Resources 1964-2004,* Volume 1, Cambridge University Press, 1970, p. 106. I have relied entirely on this source for the discussion of the costs of high-rise housing.
6. P. A. Stone, *op.cit.,* p. 157.
7. Under the 1965 Act those were as follows: Dwellings up to 3 storeys £22.05 (per annum for 60 years), 4 storeys £32, 5 storeys £38, 6 storeys £50 plus £1.75 per storey above six. Under the 1961 Act extra subsidies above basic level were paid as follows: up to 3 storeys nil, 4 storeys £8, 5 storeys £14, 6 storeys £26, plus £1.75 per storey above this. See P. A. Stone, *op.cit.,* Appendix 13.
8. E. Gittus, *Flats, Families and the Under-Fives,* Routledge, London, 1976, pp. 150-4.
9 R. McCutcheon, 'High flats in Britain 1945-71', in *Political Economy and the Housing Question,* Conference of Socialist Economists Housing Workshop, London, 1975, and E. Gittus, *op.cit.,* pp. 134-9.
10. Research in fact suggests that while 'high living' is unacceptable to many households with young children, it is by no means unpopular with households with children over 5, or adult households without children. See I. Reynolds and C. Nicholson, 'Living off the ground', *Architects' Journal,* 20 August 1969, pp. 459-70.
11. For the sake of argument we will assume that it is both local and central government physical planning which is being attacked when 'the planners' are blamed for the fall in London's employment.
12. Some idea of the relative importance of the last three of these components can be gained from an article by P. A. Gripaios who states that in inner South-east London between 1966 and 1974, 28,000 jobs were lost due to closure of existing

82   C. Pickvance

firms, while 11,041 jobs were lost through firms moving away from Greater London, while 894 were gained through openings. ('A new employment policy for London?', *National Westminster Bank Quarterly Review,* August 1976, pp. 37-45.) The Department of the Environment's *Strategic Plan for the South East: 1976 Review* (HMSO, 1976) states that for London as a whole 'total closure of larger firms' account for 44% of jobs lost, and 'firms moving out' 27% (p. 36).

13. It may be objected that urban renewal is a cause of firm closure and it is indeed true that several local authorities have recently admitted that their own urban renewal policies have contributed to the loss of jobs via the demolition of small and dilapidated premises, through this is often only a precipitating cause of a fate which was inevitable sooner or later given the marginal existence of such firms. However, urban renewal—though only a minor cause of job losses—is an example of local authority-initiated development, rather than of physical planning powers alone, our chief concern here.

14. The connection between the changing needs of industry and the fortunes of 'older' and 'newer' urban areas is clearly made in *The Costs of Industrial Change,* National Community Development Project, London, 1977.

15. B. Moore and J. Rhodes, 'Evaluating the effects of British regional economic policy', *Economic Journal* **83** (1973) 87-110. The percentages refer to the estimated employment in projects approved. In the absence of precise data for the 1950s, and 85% figure is based on the authors' comment that there was a 'significantly lower rate of refusals' then than in the 1960s (*op.cit.,* p. 109). [Since this article was written new data has become available which shows that between 1950 and 1959 the approval rate varied between 77% and 98%. See C. G. Pickvance, 'Policies as chameleons: an interpretation of regional policy and office policy in Britain' in M. J. Dear and A. J. Scott (eds.), *Urbanization and Urban Planning in Capitalist Societies,* Maaroufa, Chicago, 1979.]

16. Department of the Environment, *Office Location Review,* 1976, Appendix F. The percentages refer to the gross area of the projects approved. The figures for the rest of Greater London are somewhat lower-within the range 41-72% apart from 1965/6 (26%).

17. Department of the Environment, *Strategy for the South East: 1976 Review, op.cit.,* p. 55.

18. J. Rhodes and A. Kan, *Office Dispersal and Regional Policy,* Cambridge University Press, 1971.

19. Department of the Environment, *Strategy for the South East: 1976 Review, op.cit.,* p.11.

20. Department of the Environment, *Greater London Development Plan, Report of the Panel of Inquiry,* Volume 1, HMSO, 1973, p. 79.

Planning, Landownership and the State

MARTIN BODDY

> . . . the problem arises from the existing legal position with regard to the use of land, which attempts to preserve, in a highly developed economy, the purely individualistic approach to land ownership. (Uthwatt Committee, 1942, quoted in Cullingworth, 1976, p. 124.)

The basis of 'land use planning' might conventionally be characterised as state intervention in the private land market. The state can seek either to curtail the right of control which private landownership confers or to itself take over these rights through public landownership. This chapter explores the crucial relationship between landownership and control of land use, examining the extent to which effective land use planning can be achieved. It does so by focusing on the abortive Community Land Act 1975 (CLA) posing two questions in particular: what if the CLA had been fully implemented in its original form; and what would be achieved through full land nationalisation?

The Labour Government's land legislation in 1975 was an immediate political response to the early 1970s property boom. Popular reaction to the boom in house prices and land prices, property speculation and commercial redevelopment schemes demanded a legislative response. The price of housing land doubled in 1972. This pushed up the cost of public housing schemes and contributed to the massive rise in the price of owner-occupied housing which almost doubled between 1971 and 1973. Speculative office development funded by banks, pension funds and insurance companies threatened to engulf city centres, making fortunes for developers such as Harry Hyams of Centre Point fame. The property boom was blamed for diverting investment away from industry, and the feeling that these fortunes were unearned and undeserved as office blocks stood vacant while the housing crisis deepened, fed popular criticism of the land

and property system. There was mounting concern and indeed political action, much of it at a local level, centring around the spatial impact of redevelopment and land use change and the conflict between the needs and desires of the local community and the imperatives of the property market. The response and analysis of these issues by the 'broad left' was, as Massey and Catelano (1978) have pointed out, confused. But many sections of the Labour movement and Labour Party at local and national levels increasingly came to see private ownership and control of land as the root of the problem and demands for land nationalisation grew. The legislative response of the Labour Government elected in 1974, however, fell far short of total land nationalisation, amounting to the gradual nationalisation of development land over a period of years.

Although it was introduced in the specific context of the early 1970s boom, the CLA was the third major legislative attempt by post-war Labour governments to tackle the land problem—and the third to be dismantled by a returning Conservative government (see Cullingworth, 1976, chapter VII). First, the Town and County Planning Act 1947 nationalised future development rights and their associated values; development or change of use was controlled by the requirement for planning permission from a local authority; and development gains resulting from the granting of planning permission were taxed at 100%. A Central Land Board (CLB) had the power to buy land compulsorily at existing use value, primarily to try and prevent owners overpricing or witholding land. Today, the development control system survives but the development charge and CLB were abolished by the Conservatives. Second, the Land Commission Act, 1967 reintroduced a tax on development gains, set initially at 40% in an attempt to maintain the flow of land onto the market. It also set up the Land Commission with powers to acquire development land, compulsorily if necessary, and intended to play a substantial role in the supply of development land nationally. The Land Commission and the development gains tax were removed in 1971 by the Conversatives who had returned to power in 1970. Finally, the Community Land and Development Land Tax Acts collectively referred to hereafter as the Community Land Scheme (CLS), taxed development gains at up to 80% and empowered local authorities in England and Scotland and a special Land Authority for Wales (LAW) to buy development land at market price net of Development Land Tax (DLT). After a transitional period, initially thought of as around 10 years, all development land was to be provided by local authorities and LAW which would buy land at existing use value. The CLA was repealed by the Conservatives in 1980, although LAW was retained, and DLT remains for private land sales, set at 66.66%. Thus the Labour Party has had a long-standing commitment to land reform, although the form that this should take has been the subject of considerable internal debate within the Party and the wider Labour movement. But in 1975, more so than 1947 and 1967, this political commitment to reform was called forth by the state of the land and property market. Without the excesses of the property boom, and popular response to this, it is unlikely that the party leadership would have pursued what was on the face of it such far-reaching legislation as the CLS. Indeed, once the immediate issue subsided with the slump in the land, property and housing market in 1975 to 1976, government commitment to the CLS evaporated and, even before the Labour government fell, there was little intention or expectation that the legislation, which never developed beyond its initial 'transitional' phase, would be fully implemented. Whatever the long-term commitment within the Labour Party to land reform, for the leadership the CLS appears to have had a largely symbolic political function in the circumstances of 1974/5.

But before looking in a bit more detail at the CLS itself it is worth clarifying the nature of the land problem. There are in fact two related issues bound up in the land question: first, the allocation of land for different uses and second, the distribution of increases in land value; and related to these issues are, respectively, state intervention in land use and taxation of increases in land values. Three examples will help.

1. In the absence of any planning or zoning regulations land would be allocated among competing users by pure market mechanisms, i.e. by the ability of different users to pay. Ability to pay, and outbid competing users, would relate to the revenue which alternative uses— agriculture, housing, industry, offices—could earn on different sites. Landowners would benefit from rising land prices as, say, demand for housing on the agricultural urban fringe grew, or city centre land

prices were bid up by demand for offices. Landowners thus make capital gains. On grounds of fiscal equity it might be argued that such gains should be taxed on an equivalent basis to other forms of personal or corporate income, or capital gains. Alternatively, it can be argued that such gains are not earned by the individual owner but arise from general urban growth and development, and reflect activity on adjacent sites and the relative location of different parcels of land. Being in a sense 'unearned', such gains should be taxed at 100%, to be returned to the 'community' which in effect created them.

2. The introduction of negative land use controls, as in the 1967 scheme, complicates matters. Zoning controls the land use of particular sites, hence it can limit the revenue that can be earned and, therefore, the price a user is prepared to pay. The same acre of land might fetch £X as agricultural land, £10X for housing and £15x for warehousing. Zoning thus affects the price a landowner can obtain. It also raises the issues of 'compensation and betterment' which have taxed policy-makers and legislators since before the last war. Should landowners be compensated where permission for a higher value use is refused and should owners whose land increases in value simply because it is rezoned for a higher value use benefit personally from this 'development gain'? The Uthwatt Committee decided in 1942 that 'It is only if all the land in the country were in the ownership of a single person or body that the necessity for paying compensation and collecting betterment on account of shift in value due to planning would disappear altogether' (HMSO, 1942, p. 13). In the absence of outright nationalisation, rejected by the committee, compensation has never been introduced but, as noted earlier, the 1947, 1967 and 1975/6 legislation did tax development gains to varying degrees. They did not, however, tax increases in land values without change of use, which have remained subject to the general tax system.

3. Finally, one might envisage a system of land use allocation divorced from market mechanisms: 'under a system of well-conceived planning, the resolution of competing claims and the allocation of land for the various requirements must proceed on the basis of selecting the most suitable land for the particular purpose, irrespective of the existing values which may attach to individual pieces of land' (HMSO, 1942, quoted in Cullingworth, 1976, p. 129).

The Community Land Scheme

The CLS explictly addressed both aspects of the land question, land use and land values. The twin aims of the scheme as set out in the White Paper (Department of the Environment, 1974) were:

— to enable the community to control the development of land in accordance with its needs and priorities, and
— to restore to the community the increase in the value of land arising from its efforts,

or, in short, 'postive planning' and 'public profit'.

In theory The CLA empowered local authorities in England and Scotland and the Land Authority for Wales to buy development land for disposal to private sector developers for housing, industry or commercial uses. 'Community land' was specificially defined as land acquired and then disposed of to the private sector. Land could be acquired from landowners willing to sell, or compulsorily using CPO powers in theory slightly stronger than were available under the Planning Acts in that objections on the grounds that public acquisition was unnecessary were invalid. Authorities could also, under the CLS, fund site preparation and infrastructure works before bringing sites they acquired onto the market. Under the CLS all land for industrial and commercial uses was disposed of on a leasehold basis so that over the years public ownership of freeholds would build up. The freehold of housing land could be transferred to individual housebuyers.

In a critical 'transitional' period, local authorities were *empowered* but not *required* to buy and sell development land; eventually all development land was to pass through the hands of the authorities. During this transitional period authorities paid landowners full market value less the owner's liability to DLT; but they sold land at full market value, thus benefiting financially to the tune of the owner's tax liability. Eventually authorities were to pay current use value for land benefiting in effect from a 100% tax on development gain. The scheme was financed entirely by local authorities borrowing, a new loan sanction 'key sector' being established for this purpose. Throughout the life of the scheme, authorities had to obtain permission to borrow to buy each individual site, although a more flexible system giving authorities greater discretion had been envisaged and would have been introduced had the scheme lived longer.

The CLS was essentially a land-trading exercise. Authorities were expected to break even or make a profit over a relatively short time period, thus the scheme did not constitute any form of subsidy to cover high land prices or the costs of reclaiming derelict inner city land. 'Positive planning' was to be achieved in two respects. First, by identifying and acquiring development sites, assembling sites in multiple ownership using compulsory purchase powers where necessary, and carrying out site preparation and infrastructure works, local authorities were to initiate and stimulate development in accordance with the planning framework. Second, freehold ownership of land was to give authorities greater power to control the form of development than was possible under the planning acts. 'Public profit' was to be generated by land trading and, specifically, buying net of DLT and later at current use value.

In practice   Except in Wales the CLS fell far short of expectations and contributed little in the way of positive planning, public profit or land supply. Only 473 sites totalling about 3500 acres were bought by English local authorities in the first three years (1976/7 to 1978/9). One government estimate in 1976 has suggested 13,000 acres would be acquired over this period. Total housing land acquired in three years was sufficient to replace only about 5% of land used for new private housebuilding during that period, representing a negligible contribution to the supply of housing land.

A number of specific factors combined to limit the scale of activity. Lack of central government financial commitment to the scheme was the main factor. Grant (1979) has estimated that the total value of development land transferred annually from agricultural use at £1300m, yet only £31m was allocated to the scheme in the first year and £77m in the second. Furthermore, following the December 1976 public expenditure cuts the scheme was a relatively uncontroversial target for the axe, the allocation for the second year being halved to £38m. But even this low level of resources was not fully taken up. Lack of finance placed the emphasis firmly on the rapid and profitable turnover of sites, and led to tight Department of the Environment (DoE) control. The DoE, in an attempt to ensure the profitability of the scheme nationally, failed to allocate to local authorities the total loan sanction available. And local authorities were unable, for a variety of reasons, actually to spend all the money they were allocated. The reasons are complex and discussed in detail elsewhere (Boddy, 1978; Barrett *et al.,* 1979; Sawyer and Barrett, 1980), but four main factors were apparent.

1. Borrowing permission granted in one financial year lapsed at the year end if an authority had not been able to complete a purchase. Inexperience led to many authorities applying for and being granted borrowing permission for sites they could not buy before the permission lapsed.

2. All land owned by builders and developers or which had planning permission on the day the Land White Paper was published (12.9.74) could be registered as 'expected', putting it effectively beyond local authorities' powers of acquisition. This severely restricted authorities' opportunity to buy development land, particularly that on which quick and easy profits could be made since much of this land was already in builders' landbanks and/or had planning permission.

3. There was little financial incentive for local authorities to operate the scheme. An authority retained only 30% (latterly raised to 50%) of any surplus generated on its land account, to be used in place of other borrowing. All the authority gained, therefore, was the annual interest saved through not having to borrow this amount of money.

4. The CLS was in a sense stable-door legislation prompted by bolting land and house prices and property speculation but launched into a spectacular slump. The situation could hardly have been worse for a scheme emphasizing rapid trading profits. Landowners were hanging onto land in expectation of both rising profits and repeal of the CLS, while the market among builders, developers or industrialists for any land authorities did buy was particularly sluggish.

These various factors help to explain the very slow start made by the CLS. By the time the Conservative Government returned in 1979 there were signs that activity was picking up to some extent. By this time the scheme had become established as a useful and relatively uncontroversial addition to local authority powers and finance given that there was little if any expectation either in the Labour Government or the Department of the Environment of its full implementation, involving the duty of authorities to acquire all development land and pay current use value. Thus by the time it was repealed the CLA bore little resemblance to the scheme as originally envisaged at the time of the White Paper.

What if it had worked?

The fate of the CLS, in its first three years as much as its actual repeal, prompts the question, what if it had survived and been fully implemented? Four points are worth making.

First, local authorities would still have been selling land on the private market. The CLS placed authorities, as traders, between landowners and developers. The scheme thus *depended* on the continued existence of a healthy and profitable private development market and on the maintenance of market prices of development land for its successful operation. The need for profit was actually built into the scheme since it was designed, after an initial 'pump-priming' injection of funds, to be self-financing. The 'public profit' element was to come from authorities buying at current use value and selling at a market price. They would be encouraged therefore to sell to the highest bidder. Furthermore, they would be encouraged by the pursuit of profit (albeit public) to allocate land for uses which would maximise the revenue obtainable from, and hence pay the highest prices for, particular sites. To the extent that 'positive planning' cut across such aims, market price and public profit would be reduced. The twin aims of the CLS were thus in basic conflict.

Second, under the CLS, authorities would still have been buying land on the private market. The price paid would be current use value. But this is still a market value, even though it eliminates development gain due to the granting of planning permission. For current use value is the market price of a piece of land given its current planning permission or its existing use, whichever yields a higher value. So the price of housing land or the price of land with permission for offices would continue to rise with market forces. Thus, for example, derelict and vacant land with permission for industrial use, or land with old and vacant office buildings on it, would be valued not at zero as their current use might suggest but at their value as industrial or commercial land. This is the price an authority would have to pay—and recoup when selling the land. So high value office land would tend to be resold for office use to recoup the purchase price. Even when purchasing at current use value, market imperatives would influence land use. The 'system of well-conceived planning' envisaged by the Uthwatt Committee in which land use would be determined 'irrespective of the existing values' would not have been attained.

Third, the scope of the CLS would have remained narrow compared with full land nationalisation, due to the way in which 'development land' was defined. Only land needed for development within a ten-year period was covered by this definition, precluding long-term land-banking by local authorities. Many categories of land were 'expected' including in addition to land owned by builders and developers or with planning permission on 'White Paper Day', land owned by industrial undertakers, charities, the Church, Crown estate and statutory undertakers. Although it is unclear what this designation would have meant in practice, it is unlikely that local authorities would have had the duty to acquire 'expected' development land, or even automatically have been given the power to acquire it compulsorily. Agricultural land was 'exempted' under the Act, denying authorities any power to acquire it compulsorily. Yet it is the agricultural sector where many new problems and issues arising out of the private land ownership are starting to emerge and to which, significantly, the pension funds and property companies are increasingly turning as an avenue for investment.

Finally, 'positive planning', one of the twin aims of the scheme, was *planning* nevertheless. Sites could have been assembled and brought onto the market. But if private construction and development interests were unwilling to proceed, then development itself would not have occurred. The scheme still relied on the private sector to implement local authority development plans. Positive implementation of local authority plans would involve authorities in the development process itself: the provision of roads, schools and leisure facilities, and the production of housing, industrial and commercial premises for sale, lease or rent. Existing local authority housebuilding schemes or factory-building programmes are in a sense more positive planning than would necessarily have been achieved through the CLS. Thus, even if it had been fully implemented, the CLS would have remained subject to market imperatives, unable to sever completely the link between land values and land use, and restricted in scope by the narrow definition of development land embodied in the statutes.

Land Nationalisation

The CLS was not, then, land nationalisation. The aim of this final section is not to rehearse the arguments for and against nationalisation of land but to spell out some of its implications. The argument follows in part the conclusions of Massey and Caletano (1978) in their analysis of capital and land. Land is, under capitalism, a necessary condition of production and it is not reproducible, i.e. it is not the product of labour. Thus ownership of land may give considerable economic and political power based on the ability to levy rent from the land user, the producer of surplus in the economy. The historical emergence of capitalism in Britain has, furthermore, resulted in predominantly private ownership of land. So any attempt to limit private rights over land will meet considerable opposition, as seen in the battle over the CLS. Indeed, different fractions of capital itself, particularly finance capital but to a lesser extent industrial capital, have a considerable economic stake in private landownership.

They do not, however, by and large depend for their existence on private landownership. For it must be recognised that private landownership is not fundamental to a social system which is, like Britian today, structured around capitalist commodity production. It is in a sense technically unnecessary. This is because private landownership is not essential to the appropriation of the surplus by the exploiting class (the bourgeoise) from the producing class (the proletariat); put another way, it is not essential for the realisation of private profit and capital accumulation. Landownership is not, therefore, the basis for fundamental class antagonism or the primary contradiction between labour and capital. Under capitalism the crucial relationship is private ownership and control of the means of production. This contrasts with feudalism where the surplus was appropriated by the exploiting class by virtue of their ownership of land; private landownership was the crucial relationship. Land nationalisation under capitalism would not therefore necessarily strike at the basic economic relationship between capital and labour. It is not necessarily a socialist reform. It could equally be argued that private landownership is dysfunctional for industrial capitalism: it creams off surplus in the form of rent and may, as in 1972/3, destabilise the legitimacy of the existing, predominantly capitalist, social order.

But, as Massey and Catelano point out, land nationalisation would not represent a technical solution to the conflict between private land-ownership and either the working class over the use of, say, inner city land, or industrial capital over investment and in the economy and the division of the surplus. For the state does not have a technical, rational 'managerialist' role. It cannot be seen as some sort of neutral manager standing outside of the processes of capital accumulation and the production and distribution of the surplus within the economy. Following nationalisation, the allocation of land among competing users, the price charged to users on different sites and the distribution of any charges levied for the use of land would be the out-come of political class struggle. The role played by the state as land-owner would reflect its role in the wider social structure. In practice, the allocation policies of the state could mirror the outcome of the present mix of market and development control or could be operated to the benefit of industrial capital rather than for any socialist ends.

> Total land nationalisation is therefore not an aim to be fought for as an end in itself; nor is it an issue which can be ignored by the working class as a problem internal to capital. It must be fought for, but in the knowledge that its primary effect will not be to end the struggle over land related issues, but to change the conditions of that struggle . . . 'the land problem' though once again changed in form, would still result from the continuing problem of systems of landowner-ship within a capitalist social formation (Massey and Catelano, 1978, p. 190.)

Total land nationalisation would eliminate private gain from land-ownership and resolve the problems of 'compensation and better-ment'. But without accompanying changes in the development and construction industry the state's role would be simply the efficient supply of land to private builders and developers albeit with greater control over the *form* of development. As with the CLS, bringing development sites onto the market is not the same thing as actual development. Effective control over land use and the production of the built environment would probably necessitate restructuring of the construction and development industries rather than land nationalisation in isolation. This might involve the extension of local authority direct labour organisations and/or nationalisation of a section of the building and construction industry; and a significant extension of the state's role (national or local) as developer and landlord of industrial and commercial premises, rather than purely as the freehold landowner, funded by capital from the pension funds and insurance companies. Obviously such structural changes could only come about in the context of a radical shift in political power—they might, for example, be feasible in the context of the introduction of something along the lines of the Benn-Holland 'Alternative Economic Strategy'. But the point is that just as land nationalisation is not, from a socialist viewpoint, an issue to be fought for as an end in itself, neither is it an issue to be fought for in isolation from the struggle for changes in the structure of the construction and development industries and the financial institutions. More generally, the foregoing discussion demonstrates that landownership is not, in itself, an effective basis for land use planning, but must be placed in the wider context of economic and political relationships.

References

Barrett, S., Boddy, M. and Stewart, M. (1979) Implementation of the Community Land Scheme, School for Advanced Urban Studies, *Occasional Paper* 3.

Barrett, S. and Sawyer, G. (1980) Local authorities and the supply of development land to the private sector, School for Advanced Studies, *Working Paper* (forthcoming).

Boddy, M. (1978) 'Community Land Scheme is dying of neglect', *Roof,* May 1978, 78-80.

Department of the Environment (1974) *Land,* Cmnd. 5730, London: HMSO.

Cullingworth, J. B. (1976) *Town and Country Planning in Britain* (6th edn.), London: George Allen & Unwin.

Grant, M. (1979) Positive planning and the Community Land Act, paper presented to the British Sociological Association Urban Studies Group, Warwick University, April 1979.

HMSO (1942) *Report of the Expert Committee on Compensation and Betterment (The 'Uthwatt Report'),* Cmnd. 6386, London: HMSO.

Massey, D. and Catelano, A. (1978) *Capital and Land,* London: Edward Arnold.

The Inner City:
Planned Crisis or Crisis of Planning?

JOHN LAMBERT

I.   It is too soon to assess whether the rediscovery of urban poverty in the 1970s and the promulgation by the Government of an Inner City crisis will prove to be a major turning point in Urban Policy and Planning or a minor episode in the unfolding tale of Britain's industrial decline. The Labour Government's 1977 proposals were not such as to spark off political controversy and the threat of repeal if and when government changed hands. Rather it was a case of the Conservative opposition at the time arguing that too little was being proposed too late and that theirs were the more radical proposals for tackling the crisis. In Mr. Peter Walker the Conservative Party had one of the 1970s' most persistent advocates for inner city policies. It was after all his conversion early in the 1970s somewhere on the streets of Liverpool 8 (Shelter, 1972) to the cause of a new 'total approach' to urban problems which led to the Inner Area Studies of Birmingham, Liverpool and Lambeth (DOE, 1977a) and the reports on Sunderland, Rotherham and Oldham (DOE, 1973b), which provided his Labour successor at the Department of the Environment the research basis for the review of urban policies in 1975. In 1979 Mr. Walker was still arguing that the Inner City constituted "the most serious social problem facing British Government" (Walker, 1980).

The Labour Government's policy proposals contained in Cmnd. 6845, *Policy For the Inner Cities* (DOE, 1977b), called for a long-term commitment to the problems of the inner city. Unable to provide a substantial expansion of public funds for the task the government proposed some modest extension of local authority powers in selected areas to do with industrial development, called for the 'bending' of main programme spending by local authorities to give it an inner city

95

dimension and offered new administrative relationships—partner-ships—between government departments, local authorities and Area Health Authorities to achieve improved coordination of services and expenditure to inner areas.

The change in government in 1979 did not mean any immediate changes: the commitment to administrative and planning solutions re-mained. Partnerships have been supplemented by Inner City Develop-ment Corporations to attract an enhanced level of private investment to aid industrial devleopment. The *concern* for the Inner City as a policy area continues although the new economic strategy has dimin-ished very greatly the amount of money going to all local authorities' main programmes. The Conservative Government's Housing and Planning Acts which became law in 1980 represent a marked limita-tion in local authority powers and extend the scope for the Secretary of State for the Environment to determine the pattern of local authori-ty expenditure. In 'Enterprise Zones' the government is hoping to find the means of attracting and focusing industrial development in ways that are consistent with the thinking of *Policy for the Inner Cities.* But writing in 1980 as the recession deepens and unemployment rises, it is clear that there is little sign of a restoration of health in any part of the economy let alone in the Inner Cities. But the Government would ap-pear to remain committed to policies seeking to favour the inner cities when the long looked for recovery in the economy occurs or when the much talked-about U-turn happens in the Government's economic strategy.

But if there was something of a political consensus as to the nature of an urban crisis in the 1970s requiring a new direction of policies, what is of greater interest and the focus of this article is the critique of Planning which is contained in the White Paper and the Ministerial statements which preceded its publication. These and developments in the first phase of implementation of the new policies provide a good basis for analysing the position of Planning as a developed institu-tional and professional practice in the 1970s.

What I want to argue in this article is that there is to be found in the researches and reviews carried out for Government in the early 1970s, a radical analysis which nonetheless generated conservative proposals. The logic of the analysis required policy measures consistent with a model of planning practice that, following McKay and Cox (1979), may be termed *positive planning*. The political conjuncture imposed another logic for a milder merely *regulative planning*. Yet the social conditions of urban Britain in the 1970s—especially in the large cities in regions thought of as prosperous but also in the cities and towns of the traditionally depressed regions—can only be explained by reference to the relationship between market forces and state intervention which emerged in the post-war period. In a very real sense, I believe, the contemporary crisis of the inner city needs to be seen as a *planned* crisis. Yet that crisis and the nature of Planning which is revealed by it indicates clearly that conventional and contemporary modes and techiques of Planning cannot provide the means of solving the problem: and that poses a problem for the profession, especially that part of it which has grown within central and local government administrations. For these planners the condition of the inner areas and the processes creating urban and regional underdevelopment present a challenge which is critical. Shall planners and Planning continue to be in a subservient position within the political apparatus, or is there an active politically engaged role and form of Planning? Any past claims planners and Planning may have made for their being outside, above, or in some way neutral about politics must finally be buried. Hereafter whose side *is* Planning on? Crisis, literally, means turning-point or moment of decision—the Inner City problem provides then a crisis for Planning.

II.   The radical analysis and critique of Planning is not the most obvious aspect of *Policy for the Inner Cities*. Part of its conservative character and its plausibility as something which was non-controversial and part of a political consensus rests in a fairly conventional argument that in no small measure the conditions of the inner cities were due to past policies and that 'it should be possible now to change the thrust of policies which have assisted large scale decentralisation' (Cmnd. 6845, para. 24). So policies in the past which have encouraged new investment in the depressed regions will be refocused to aid the inner areas of cities. In particular the White Paper draws attention to three features of Planning which have contributed to the decline of the inner areas:

(i) Slum clearance and redevelopment policies have got badly out of step. The bulldozers have done their work but the rebuilding has lagged behind. . . . Whatever the explanation there is a wide extent of vacant land in some inner areas . . . there is much under-used land and property. . . . The opportunities offered by redevelopment to create public open space have not been taken (para. 12).

(ii) The effect of New Town and Regional Policy has been an imbalanced out-migration and in future the effects of New Towns on city regions need to be taken into account. The mismatch between population and number and kinds of jobs must be tackled (paras. 66-69 and Annex 17/19).

(iii) In the process of comprehensive redevelopment and in planning generally 'non-conforming uses' have been discouraged yet these, it can now be seen, are what gives an area an economic base of diversity and soundness (para. 46).

The other feature of the White Paper is its commitment to the belief that 'Local Authorities are the natural agencies to tackle inner area problems. They have wide powers and substantial resources' (para. 31) that 'A great deal can be done within the resources already available (para. 42) and 'Generally the initiative must rest with the local authorities. . . . The emphasis throughout is on coordinated action by local and central government' (para. 43). Moreover, 'Most of the proposals in the White Paper can be implemented administratively and do not need new powers' (para. 97).

Now this emphasis on technical failures and technical and administrative remedies is attractive politically. It suggests that without major reforms changes can be effected. What Planning has done, a reformed Planning can remedy.

However, as can be shown by scrutinising the three features referred to, it is not a strong position to maintain when the evidence is:

(i) that local authorities quite simply do not possess the powers to effect the kind of balanced and coordinated slum clearance and redevelopment programmes referred to here (see English *et al*, 1976; Lambert *et al.,* 1979);

   (ii) that New Towns and other features of Regional Policy have been of minor significance in determining the rates of decline of inner city employment or the destinations of inner city out-migrants (see Thrift, 1980); and

  (iii) that the influence of local authority controls on non-conforming uses has been marginal in the extreme (see Paris, 1977).

As Pickvance has cogently demonstrated, although

according to the conventional interpretation of post-war urban development in Britain physical planning is the determining factor and hence physical planners must shoulder the blame for failures such as 'soulless' housing estates, high rise flats or the decline of inner city areas;

this is based on

a complete misconception of the scope of physical planning powers. These powers are limited in nature and weak in their application (Pickvance, 1977).

He shows that local authoritiy development (often confused with local authority planning powers) is likewise constrained 'by a variety of economic, political and financial pressures which frequently hinder its success' and he quotes the significant finding of the Layfield Panel's report on the Greater London Development Plan:

We are driven . . . to the view that the local planning authority can, within its area, over the long term, influence only marginally the tendency of employment to contract or alter or retain its nature, (DOE, 1973).

This line of argument, it might be supposed, would do severe damage to the policy assumptions and direction of the White Paper. Nonetheless, scrutiny of the White Paper can find due recognition of this view. It can be found quite clearly expressed in a speech delivered in Manchester in September 1976 by Mr. Peter Shore, Labour Secretary of State for the Environment in charge of the Cabinet review of urban policies. It was the Minister's first major speech to signpost the direction the review was taking, and it is safe to assume that in it are reflected not so much Mr. Shore's personal views but those of his Ministry officials and advisers in the process of formulating government policy proposals. It is a speech which contains more than simply 'we got it wrong in the past, we can get things right if we change direction now', but a rather more complex analysis which scrutinises they very nature of Planning and the legacy of the post-war Planning system to urban Britain of the 1970s.

III. Mr. Shore started conventionally enough by noting that the combination of 'a declining economic and industrial base' and 'a major and unbalanced loss of population over the last decade and a half' had brought changes and problems to large cities such as to lead 'many people to seek urgent shifts of policy by central and local government to avert this crisis'. Then having sketched some of the basic evidence he said:

> It is easy enough to chart what has happened but of course more difficult to identify the complex interaction of factors which as led to this decline. Partly it has been due to conscious decisions by individuals, and to conscious dispersal by government, but partly to social and economic developments which have been both unanticipated and unplanned. (Shore, DOE, 1976, p. 2.)

In the *unanticipated* category, Mr. Shore put population growth rates. Certainly government planners in the late 1960s, responding to forecasts of sustained population growth in the period through to the year 2000, gave a boost to the scale of New Town Development and sponsored studies like that of Severnside to cater for the expansion. Those forecasts did not match actual trends in the early 1970s and certainly it would have been consistent with those earlier forecasts to anticipate no major changes in the population levels of urban areas.

In the unplanned category, Mr. Shore put 'a voluntary movement of people much greater than was anticipated by the Planners'. He contrasted such movement with that which was part of 'planned efforts to decentralise and decongest the inner city'. Clearly Mr. Shore is referring here to Planners and Planning associated with his Ministry and especially those concerned with the New and Expanded Towns programme.

Then—still apparently developing this idea of unanticipated and unplanned social and economic developments—the Secretary of State continued:

> Alongside this exodus of people from the inner areas has been a major shift in the factors affecting industrial location. Road haulage has taken over from rail almost completely so far as secondary and tertiary industries are concerned, and with the building of inter-urban motorways, peripheral locations have appeared to offer substantial advantages on transport grounds alone. If one adds to that the relative ease with which it has been possible to develop purpose-built factories on green field sites, or to acquire advance factories developed on such sites by public bodies, in comparison with the difficulty of assembling land and obtaining planning permission in inner areas, it is small wonder that most industrial development has taken place outside inner areas. . . . (p. 3).

Now the transfer from road to rail and the building of the motorways was hardly unplanned! And the relative ease of green field site developments still required planning permission. What Mr. Shore is drawing attention to here is the separate and competitive operations of different sorts of Planners in different Ministries and local authorities. This becomes explicit later in the speech when Mr. Shore developed the argument that:

> if we are to attract industries back to these (inner) areas we also have to look closely at the operation of our planning mechanisms. The post-war system of land use planning and development control has been a great success and has rightly earned Britain a high international reputation in this field. Nonetheless, I think we must recognise that the system has introduced distortions which have strongly favoured development in peripheral sites at the expense of the inner areas (p. 6).

Problematic land assembly, cumbersome development control procedures and zoning are singled out for attention. The adequacy of incentives of industry and of population dispersal policies are likewise named as in need of review. But Mr. Shore defends 'his' Planners from the blame for creaming off mobile industry from the inner cities. Clearly it is the relationships between different parts of the 'system' that is the focus of attention.

The ideas being developed in this speech would seem to owe a lot to the critique of the post-war planning system provided by Peter Hall and his associates in *The Containment of Urban England* (Allen & Unwin, 1973). There it is argued that the *aims* of the post-war planning system were

(a) to promote regional balance by diverting industry and population from the relatively prosperous Midlands and South East to the depressed regions;

(b) to control the growth of large cities, especially London, by preventing development on agricultural land, at their peripheries and by defining green belts across which population and industrial movement would be effected;

(c) to permit the replanning of old cities by planned relocation of populations and firms to new towns to create the space for publicly controlled inner city rehabilitation; and

(d) to favour the development of strong service centres with neighbourhood planning to promote a style of post-war development in sharp contrast to the ribbon development of sprawling dormitory suburbs which was a feature of 1930s planning and urban development.

The *means* for achieving these aims lay in the elaborate development control machinery of the Town and Country Planning Act 1947 linked to detailed Development Plans indicating where future development would be permitted. Comprehensive Development Areas for replanning urban areas were included in the legislation. The New Towns Act 1946 and the Location of Industry Act 1946 completed the triad of new powers whereby Central and Local Government would thereafter plan and control urban development. It was an assumption of those responsible for the post-war *system,* Hall argues, that the public authorities would be the major initiators and executors of urban development.

The *results,* Hall demonstrates, were quite different: the assumed coordination of Development Plans by a strong Planning Ministry never developed; New Towns have been few and account for a small proportion of new housing developments. Green belts and restrictions on peripheral developments in the context of increasing city populations had the effect of containing urban areas geographically but imposing high densities within cities. Industrial relocation policies were operated with considerable flexibility and discretion and contained loopholes which allowed firms to expand piecemeal and new firms and subsidiaries to develop on the new industrial estates growing up around the medium to large towns within the growing regions of Britain. The growth of population and industry was concentrating in a coffin-shaped corridor whose axis ran from Manchester through Birmingham to the South Eastern coast with the broadest tract being in the South-east around London. Regional policy at the most slowed the rate of decline in depressed regions.

What failed to materialise was a Planning *system* with coordinated and integrated powers capable of controlling the pattern and process of urban and regional development. Far from the positive interventionist apparatus that its architects hoped for, the sort of planning which developed tended to reflect and facilitate trends emanating from the private market for land and buildings whether for industrial, commercial or residential purposes. The regulation of initiatives from the private market characterised the British post-war planning system, whatever its aims.

Yet it must be acknowledged that this was a Planning system. This was the period during which Planning as a profession came of age and within local authorities the size and status of Planning departments grew and grew. To refer to developments in this period as unplanned in the way Mr. Shore and his DOE advisers suggest is misleading, for there is clear evidence that it was central government planners who were vigorous and explicit in their support for the large-scale city and town centre redevelopment schemes of the 1960s. These helped the rise and rise of the property companies and 'clean sweep' schemes whose consequences for road planning, land values, and blighting effects between central areas and inner areas hastened the conditions to which the new inner city policies were directed. But drawing attention to the diversity of powers and relative lack of central control and direction allows a line of argument—the Total Approach—which gives these planners a legitimate directive and coodinating role, to establish in the 1970s the sort of planning system which the architects of Britain's post-war system sought but which did not materialise. So when the 1977 White Paper speaks of partnerships in selected areas which 'will enable new forms of organisation to be tried and new methods of working to be adopted', when it calls for 'A new and closer form of collaboration . . . between government and the private sector' there needs to be seen in attenuated form the critique of the planning system which is present in the Minister's Manchester speech.

In addition to the mammoth Hall study already referred to, there were other studies which drew attention to the form of state intervention in urban problems on the post-war period. Most notable among these is *The Costs of Industrial Change* (CDP, 1977), an interpretation of urban problems provided by workers involved in five of the Home Office funded Community Development Projects published quite explicitly to coincide with the Government's review of urban policies. With much of it Mr. Shore's Manchester speech would be in close accord. Its conclusions and proposals are quite explicit: for a mode of planning capable of controlling the free movement of capital to wherever wages or material costs are lower and capable of imposing social and political priorities upon market forces. But the authors of the report were clear that such a planning system was quite different from the one which had been facilitating the quest for profitability among private firms by easing the movement of jobs and capital investment in the pattern of uneven development which characterises capitalist social development. The CDP authors anticipate no dramatic shift towards positive interventionist planning since political developments in the late 1960s were towards different kinds of state intervention. And it is those developments which ensured that when the government review of urban policies was completed and the White Paper was prepared, the outcome was the predominance of a conventional conservative analysis working securely with existing powers and resources entailing merely technical changes in approach. Yet the logic of the radical analysis for a different form of planning could not be entirely suppressed.

IV.   The suppressed radical critique of Planning in the new urban policies of the 1970s can perhaps be appreciated more clearly if the proposals are related to other policy measures occurring at the time. It is usual to trace the antecedents of Inner City Policies back through the Government's flirtation with an anti-poverty programme modelled on the American 'War on Poverty' (see CDP, 1977b and McKay and Cox, 1978). But it is important, I think, to relate the 1977 Inner City Policies to other developments in Planning in the late 1960s and early 1970s each of which can be seen as attempts to create a system more like that dreamed of in the immediate post-war period; each of which suffered a similar fate of transformation in the process of political policy-making and subsequent administration to lose their radical features and become devices to further the power of private investors.

The three policies to consider are; the reform of the Development Plan making mechanism of the Town and Country Planning Act 1968, the proposals for Land Nationalisation which became the Community Land Act 1975, and proposals for the National Enterprise Board.

The new system of Structure and Local Plans introduced by the

Town and Country Planning Act 1968 following the review by the Planning Advisory Group (PAG), *The Future of Development Plans* (DOE, 1965), was intended to resolve a host of difficulties which had faced Planning since 1947. It seems that PAG and the Ministry of Housing and Local Government planners were confident that the City Region would become a key unit in local Government and at that level economic and social planning issues could become integrated with land-use planning. The Structure Plan, based on a comprehensive survey of trends and needs within a large area, was to be the means of this integration. A moderately strengthened regional administration of the Central Ministry would allow these Structure Plans to be co-ordinated in a way that had been sought but never achieved for the 1947 Act's Development Plans. Conflicts between cities and counties, between centres and peripheries, cores and suburbs would thus become resolvable by a single planning unit and a mode of Planning providing a framework for detailed local plans. In the event, the new City Region never got further than being a well-received minority report of a Royal Commission on Local Government whose proposals anyway were not implemented. The actual 1974 Reorganisation main-tained many of the old divisions, and separated Structure and Local Planning functions between different tier authorities. Not surprisingly the Department of the Environment, taking over from the Ministry of Housing and Local Government the coordination of structure plans, advised Planning Authorities to limit their economic and social plan-ning efforts considerably and stay close to land-use issues. This has meant that the real differences between the old and the new systems have been marginal. With Structure Planning, the new forms of Transport Planning introduced by the Transport Act 1967 have not fitted comfortably. And the lack of coordination between Transport and Land Use planning was a major problem identified by PAG In the mid-1960s. And in general terms, the cogency of the PAG critique re-mains valid. The diversity and diffusion of powers is such as to prevent many of the aims of the planning system to be realised. Whatever advances in the detailed techniques the new system in-troduced, it could not alter the political position of planning within Local Government, nor could it escape from the complex web of

Central/Local relations which frames and limits the practical effects of the reformed system.

The Community Land Act 1975 was the legislative means whereby the Labour Party's long-standing commitment to the socialist principle of land nationalisation was to become a reality. It was to be 'third time lucky' after the failures of the 1947 proposals for a Central Land Board and the 1967 proposals for a Land Commission. Here were proposals whereby local authorities would become the sole holders of development land. The predictable political opposition was intense. The concessions made to enable its passage through the House of Commons and into Law were many: the time scale of the change got stretched; the exemptions and qualifications became more numerous. Most crucially, as committees considered and guidelines emerged, far from breaking the market in land by having a monopoly of development land, local authorities were obliged to trade profitably in land, perform the complex task of land assembly, and depend on the existing property-development industry and its insurance and pension-fund-based investment resources for actual operations. Moreover, the Act was in design extremely costly in public expenditure terms, for it required the purchase at market values of development land by local authorities. In the event, its passing into Law coincided with a major economic crisis for government entailing severe cuts in public expenditure. So although in preparation for the Community Land Act's complex administrative and financial duties, local authorities geared up to perform quite new tasks, in the event very little happened. The actual impact on the scale, pattern and nature of urban development has been slight. The needs and the task identified with the Labour Party in the 1970s remain to be tackled.

A similar story can be told more briefly about the National Enterprise Board. As advocated by the Labour Party in opposition, it was the outcome of the failure of the 1964 National Plan machinery and the inadequacies of the Industrial Reorganisation Corporation. As the authors of the Community Development Project report, *The Costs of Industrial Change,* argue:

If introduced in their full original form, the proposals should have enabled the government to begin to exercise some real control over economic development, in contrast to the 'voluntary' planning framework which, to date, has failed. In particular, it could have intervened to control the activities of some of the major firms. . . . Planning agreements, intended to make leading private sector firms and public corporations more socially accountable would have covered such areas as forward investment programmes, manning levels, job creation and location, technological development, export programmes, and pricing policies. In other words, the combined system would, for the first time, have begun to offer a public enterprise system with some power, but at the same time be accountable to workers and others whose livelihoods depended on or were affected by it. (CDP, 1977, p. 94.)

But such proposals never became policy and practice. The Labour Government ducked from the political opposition entailed in further nationalisation, endorsed an enfeebled version of planning agreements, and provided limited funds on narrow commercial terms to a small-scale National Enterprise Board.

The present government's strategy . . . regulates the N.E.B. and planning agreements system to subserviant roles in the *Attack on Inflation* and the *Approach to Industrial Strategy* (the 1974 Labour Government's two key White Papers on Economic and Industrial policies). The aim of present policies is to ensure the adequate competitiveness of British firms, and to restore their profitability: to these ends public expenditure is being reduced so that resources can be channelled into private industry. The reassertion of the importance of high profits for a 'vigorous' private sector, and the choice of basically voluntary planning machinery based on the National Economic Development Council, means that the government have clearly opted for capitalist solutions to capitalist difficulties. (*Ibid.,* p. 94.)

It is to this policy and political context that proposals for a 'Total Approach', for improved coordination and a long-term commitment to the inner areas need to be related. Such proposals *derive* like those of the three areas sketched above from a radical socialist critique of the Planning System which emerged in the post-war period. Yet is was a critique whose proposals were *politically* doomed. The reality of the policy proposals were for very mild sorts of change.

Yet the point must be stressed that this failure to develop a positive planning system does not signify the absence of any planning system. It requires a careful analysis of the *form* the quite massive extension of State intervention took in the 1960s and 1970s.

This period saw a very significant restructuring of welfare whereby state expenditures in the firm of welfare services were reduced in favour of special subsidies to industry and individuals to aid industrial recovery. Corporate taxes were reduced, unemployment levels were stimulated to assist modernisation, rationalisation and higher productivity. Social security benefits were selectively improved to help this process. Forms of investment were subsidised; public expenditure was geared to reducing the wage levels paid by individual firms by the collectivisation through state expenditure of the *reproduction* costs of the labour force. Family and Educational and Industrial Training/Retraining expenditures are examples of these trends. The 'social wage' was seen as a means of limiting demands for rises in the 'workplace wage' so that reduced or stabilised labour costs could aid competitiveness, productivity and profitability of firms. A kind of division of labour was worked out between the State and Private Industry. But Investment capital was left free to seek out—as investment must in a free enterprise capitalist system—the most or the most securely profitable opportunities. That freedom has not been a 'natural' or a 'chance' phenomenon. It has been fought for and won politically, it has been aided and abetted by a planning system reflecting that kind of political victory. The nature of the victory is clear in the political defeat of measures entailing a different sort of policies and a different sort of Planning. The social conditions of the inner areas of British cities in the 1970s—the outcome of the interplay between the freedom of investment capital to seek out profits and of state intervention to facilitate that search—is in this sense a Planned crisis. The conditions reflect alternatives and choices which were not pursued—and options and priorities which were pursued, implemented and administered by a system of state planning.

V.   Those social conditions in the inner cities demanded political attention in the early/mid-1970s. A fiscal crisis faced local authorities in these areas as demands for the social provision of housing, health, education and other social services increased, yet the sources for them were diminished. Social tensions—especially in those cities where the presence of ethnic minorities (another example of the consequences of planned urban development) provided scope for racist propaganda, policies and parties to proffer a sort of explanation for the conditions of poverty and decay—threatened law and order. So a policy response was necessary even if the political context ruled out radical policy alternatives.

The new policy proposals suggested that the crisis could be averted by means of a long-term commitment to new techniques of distributing resources. So Central Government promised to provide local authorities with inner city problems a more favourable share of government resources for the authorities main programmes of social expenditure by means of the Rate Support Grant (RSG). Local authorities in selected areas were asked to prepare programme plans providing for a redirection of existing services towards the needs of inner areas; a claim on a limited amount of government grant over and above RSG allocations—the Urban Programme—to aid such schemes was the means of encouragement. In some of these authorities the Government was offering a closer working relationship—'Partnerships'—in the formulation of plans and programmes, with the lion's share of Urban Programme funds going to these selected authorities. 'It is the intention to seek lessons from the progress of the partnerships and to monitor action in the inner areas. It is hoped to publicise the results so that other authorities may benefit' (Cmnd. 6845, p. 101). For the Partnership and programme authorities, some new powers enabling expenditure on industrial improvement areas and other aids to industry were brought in in the *Inner Urban Areas Act, 1978.*

In the first years of the new policies some interesting features emerged to cast doubt on the feasibility of the new policies:

(i) Careful scrutiny of RSG settlements in the period 1976-1980, during which it was claimed that the inner areas were being favoured, demonstrate the claims to be spurious. There were authorities included in the Inner City Policies framework which had received less than others not so included. There was, it is true, a general trend towards larger proportions of RSG being allocated to Metropolitan District and London Boroughs as against County areas—but within these broad categories the formula used to allocate the grant was incapable of discriminating systematically in the way the White Paper claimed had been the case and would be the case as part of the Government's long-term commitment. The complexity of RSG settlements was such that what sounded like a straightforward policy assertion was in reality something technically beyond the competence of the DOE (Centre for Institutional Studies, 1978).

(ii) The fruits of the first attempts at Partnership planning reveal all of the constraints that exist to inhibit the unified coordinated approach sought by the new policy. The published programmes—basically indications of priorities for expenditure on inner area projects to be funded by the Urban Programme—displayed a quite astonishing profusion of disparate entities, a veritable 'shopping list' of different departments' different priorities. Given the variety of departments and organisations brought together under the Partnership umbrella, such diversity is hardly surprising, since each interest around a largish table competing for fairly limited resources would be working hard to see that no one got too much and no one went away empty handed. But any notion of a strategic use of resources or of debate to fund priorities to further the social, economic and physical regeneration of cities appeared to be impossible. So what sounded in the White Paper like a plausible reform in administration to forge a new coherence in resource allocations, in practice proved far more problematical (see Hall, 1978).

(iii) These Partnership Plans displayed greatest uncertainty about the most fundamental of the White Paper's assumptions that it will be possible for authorities to utilise their very considerable existing resources on housing, education, social services, environmental health, etc., in ways which help inner areas by redirecting policies and programmes to that purpose. Some of the non-partnership programmes were quick to point out that in the three-year period for which they were encouraged to make inner area programmes, they were quite unable to see how they were going to be able to maintain existing programmes let alone 'bending' them to an inner city bias. Perhaps the most revealing critique, however, of the viability of this White Paper idea—again a plausible proposal apparently entailing no great technical or administrative problems—appeared in an article prepared for *Social Trends 1980* published in 1979 by two staff members at the Department of the Environment (but writing, of course, in their personal capacities) (Allnutt and Gelardi, 1979).

These authors describe very clearly a great difficulty facing local authorities seeking to implement the Government's 'Policies for the Inner City'.

> If public authorities, local or central, have as one of their objectives the alleviation of inner area problems, it is necessary to monitor changes in those areas so that policy may develop to meet new situations and the effectiveness of components of policies affecting inner areas may be judged . . . the proper basis for such monitoring is a plan which defines and describes—with some quantification—the area concerned, describes and quantifies existing policies in relation to the area, and assesses the changes that can be expected in the area given those existing policies. The plan would then go on to assess which policies needed strengthening or modifying. . . . In turn this would lead to the setting of strategic objectives and hence to the formulation of a programme of expenditure and activities for the coming years (p. 49).

This seems like a very clear statement of the sort of planning entailed in the White Paper, and as the authors continue:

> The preparation and monitoring of such a plan would create considerable demands for data as well as skilled interpretation and planning (p. 49).

However, leaving aside the question of who is to perform that skilled interpretation and planning which the authors do not pursue, the article makes clear that existing data sources are highly unsuitable and render this sort of planning impossible:

> The absence of any extensive quantification of the past level of, and existing plans for, expenditure and activity in the inner area makes it very difficult to develop clear objectives related to the possible uses of the available urban programme and other resources. Furthermore, if inner area expenditure cannot be identified, the efficiency with which it contributes to alleviating the area's problems cannot possibly be assessed. If measurement and projection of the area's situation is not achieved, the action programme section of an inner area plan becomes a list of projects which cannot be put in the context of demonstrated need to revise or supplement existing spending programmes because the scale and effect of these programmes has not been assessed (pp. 49/59).

Clearly these authors are writing from the experience of having to try and make sense of the plans submitted by the Partnership authorities. No one at the Department of the Environment should have been surprised by these rather fundamental shortcomings which appeared so soon in the life of the new policies. The DOE-sponsored Inner Area Study of Liverpool documented clearly the near impossibility of area accounting and area management due to deeply entrenched political resistance to such moves toward positive discrimination. So what Allnutt and Gelardi are proposing raises many issues posed by the more radical features of the other policies attempting more interventionist planning whose fate in the 1970s I have referred to. For what these authors are drawing attention to is not merely a lack of data but the absence of any tradition in professional practice to enable any group of planners to carry out that skilled and difficult interpretative task necessary to define tangible objectives for a policy for the inner cities.

A similar tale could be told about the new powers extended to local authorities in the Inner Urban Areas Act 1978. There is very little in the past practice of any department of local government to enable them to start on the work of economic or industrial regeneration in partnership with small, medium or large firms in the private sector. These new powers depicated as a modest extension to the scope of the Urban Programme entail a far more radical shift in focus for local government than is suggested by the White Paper.

In all these ways the new approaches proposed in the White Paper have in practice and reality proved far more problematical than appears to be the case. For even these modest-sounding measures to begin to engage with the processes of economic regeneration in inner areas, quite definite new practices sanctioned by political approval are necessary. There are no easy technical solutions to the conditions of inner urban areas. Nor is it simply a case of political backing for one set of planners to have free rein to coordinate, integrate or unify existing disparate issues. What I have tried to indicate in this section is that the experience of the first years of the new policies has underlined the strength of that analysis found in Mr. Shore's speech, found in Labour Party proposals in the early 1970s, found in the reports of the Community Development Projects and to a lesser extent in the Inner Area Studies that the problems of the inner areas reflect deep-seated structural features in the organisation of British society, economy and government.

VI. So what is the role for Planners and Planning in the future of the inner areas? Is it the case as argued recently that what is needed is a new political programme based on intervention by planners for problems whose nature is understood and for which solutions exist if only the politicians would allow the technocrats freedom of movement (Jacobs, 1978). Or is it that the technocrats of planning in their present institutionalised practice are inextricably part of an existing political programme which sustains some interests, areas and neighbourhoods as privileged over and against others which are impoverished?

If the latter is the case and the instances to which I have referred in this essay have sought to indicate that such *is* the case, then the inner city poses a crisis for planning. As Thompson and Thornley write:

> There is a powerful tradition which holds that the (town planning) profession is concerned only with the regulation of controls and rules for the location, appearance and use of land and buildings. This regulatory role is impartial and apolitical: intervention in the distribution of social services and economic resources between areas or groups is not the business of the town planner (Thompson and Thornley, 1980).

They go on to show how legal powers, extensive though they may seem, reinforce 'this constrained, apolitical perspective'. But, they argue, the interventionist assumptions of inner city policies are such as to impel planners to a more directly involved role. They indicate something of the way this would bring new tasks, entail new relationships and put planners into a more conflictual and overtly political environment. They provide a very useful overview of the kind of work the new policies have brought to the planners. Yet, they suggest, planning is the one profession with some claim to undertake the synoptic, interventionist coordinative task. They see 'intervention and promotion at the local level' being a new challenging dimension for planning in the future,

> but it must be related to a strategic overview of the economic and other planning priorities at national, regional and city level. This is one of the synoptic skills which planners should particularly be able to offer and a skill which correlates closely with their efforts in the field of information and advocacy. The task of developing a common strategic overview involving several tiers of government at national and local levels is a formidable one. No one is better equipped than the planner to perform this task, and without it the hard work and enterprise already devoted to revitalisation at the local level will lose much of its direction and much of its impact. (*ibid.,* p. 93.)

What I have been trying to indicate in this essay is that indeed the task is a formidable one and that the Inner City policies need to be seen as one fairly mild effort to induce a state of planning in contemporary Britain. Only if we understand that this new direction for planning is not merely a matter of demonstrating the scope and need for rational policies aimed at universally agreed goals will the nature of Planning as an activity become clear. This new direction for Planning has to confront an old style of Planning which was and is a powerfully effective means of state intervention to facilitate the primacy of free enterprise market capitalism in its quest for secure profitable business. The conditions of inner urban Britain in the 1970s as they have been since the onset of industrialised urbanism in Britain have reflected the social character of the British economy. That alternative policies and practices have been advocated but defeated politically in the course of recent decades underlies the social nature of the processes at work. These sustain an overall pattern of *uneven* economic development within which phases of relative prosperity followed by impoverishment have been the fate of different regions and areas. State involvement in dealing with the consequences of this uneven development has entailed a complex apparatus of planning; but state intervention in a capitalist society also serves to facilitate the process of capital accumulation and that means ensuring that investment is free to search out profits wherever they may occur. The scale of the task that Thompson and Thornley define is the more complex since the intervention they describe seeks to coordinate these two contradictory features of state policy, for there can be no strategic overview which can effect change without a break with what Paris has termed 'the dominant tendency' in the processes of urban change 'the search for private profits through the constant movement of capital between sectors and locations' (Paris, 1978). That 'dominant tendency' is well served by the existing planning system and by the political predominance of the tendency through the institutions of the State. The political and economic context limits the scope and autonomy of planners to devise, let alone implement, new policies. For Planners the implications of this for practice extend beyond the uncertain boundaries of the Inner City.

References

Allnutt, D. and Gelardi, A. (1977) 'Inner Cities in England', in *Social Trends 1980*, HMSO/CSO

Centre for Institutional Studies (1978) *Rate Support Grant Changes and Consequences 1974-75, 1977-78*, London: CIS.

Community Development Project (1977a) *The Costs of Industrial Change*, London: CDP.

Community Development Project (1977b) *Gilding the Ghetto*, London: CDP.

Department of the Environment (1973a) *Greater London Development Plan Report of the Panel of Enquiry*, Vol. 1, p. 79, London: HMSO/DOE.

Department of the Environment (1973b) *Making Towns Better:* (i) *The Sunderland Study*, (ii) *The Rotherham Study*, (iii) *The Oldham Study*, 3 vols., London: HMSO/DOE.

Department of the Environment (1977a) (i) *Unequal City: Final Report of the Birmingham Inner Area Study*, (ii) *Inner London: policies for dispersal and balance*, (iii) *Change of Decay: Final Report of the Liverpool Inner Area Study*, 3 vols., London: HMSO/DOE.

Department of the Environment (1977b) *Policies for the Inner Cities*, Cmnd. 4845, London: HMSO/DOE.

English, J. *et al.* (1976) *Slum Clearance: The Social and Administrative Context in England and Wales*, London: Croom Helm.

Hall, P. *et al.* (1973) *The Containment of Urban England*, 2 vols., London: George Allen & Unwin.

Hall, P. (1978) 'Spending priorities in the inner city', *New Society*, 21/28 December, pp. 698-9.

Jacobs, R. (1977) 'Save our cities', *International Journal of Urban and Regional Research*, **1**, 322-6.

Lambert, J. *et al.* (1979) *Housing Policy and the State*, London: Macmillan Press.

McKay, D. and Cox, A. (1978) 'Confusion and reality in public policy: the case of the British urban programme', *Political Studies* XXIV (4), 491-506.

McKay, D. and Cox, A. (1979) *The Politics of Urban Change*, Chap. 2, London: Croom Helm.

Paris, C. (1977) 'Small firms', *New Society*, 15 December 1977, p. 793.

Paris, C. (1978) 'The parallels are striking'—Crisis in the Inner City, GB 1977. *International Journal of Urban and Regional Research*, *2*, 160-169.

Pickvance, C. G. (1977) 'Physical planning and market forces in urban development, *National Westminster Bank Quarterly Review*, August, pp. 41-50.

Shelter (1973) *Another Chance for Cities*, Liverpool: Shelter Neighbourhood Action Project.

Shore, P. (1976) *Inner Urban Policy:* text of a speech delivered at Manchester, 17 Sept. Press Notice 835, London, DOE.

Thompson, R. and Thornley, A. (1979) 'The planner as Catalyst', in Loney, M. and Allen, M. (eds.), *The Crisis of the Inner City*, London: Macmillan Press.

Thrift, N. (1979) 'Unemployment in the inner city', in Herbert, D. T. and Johnston, R. J. (eds.), *Geography and the Urban Environment*, Vol. 2, *Process in Research and Applicants*, Chichester: John Wiley & Sons.

Walker, P. (1979) 'A Conservative View' in Loney, M. and Allen, M., (eds.), *The Crisis of the Inner City*, London: The Macmillan Press.

PART THREE

Capitalist Urbanization and the State: Marxist Critiques

Introduction by the Editor

The readings in this section take us from the more empirical concerns of Part Two and move us towards a theoretical respecification of the nature of town planning as it has developed under capitalism.

The extract from Jon Gower Davies' book is included as much to set the mood for subsequent theoretical papers as for its forceful rejection of conventional planning wisdom.

Edmond Preteceille's paper, translated from the French by Martin Boddy, seeks to explain the connections and contradictions, over time, between capitalist urbanisation and urban planning. Although it is written with France specifically in mind, the general categories of analysis are applicable to all capitalist social formations; in particular it is important to consider his emphasis on the *use* to which plans are put rather than on their explicit content. His concern to stress the political dimension of planning and his insistence on regarding all planning activities as being irretrievably linked to political relations are useful correctives to the view that planning is somehow separate from politics and political relations. Some terms and expressions used in this paper may need clarifying, particularly the Marxist categories of analysis. 'Fractions of the capitalist class' refers to different interest groups which, together, comprise the class of all capitalists; thus, for example, major financiers, owners of manufacturing firms and owners of shipping companies, whilst all being capitalists, may have different interests at particular times. 'Reproduction', of both capital and labour, refers to the process of creating anew but in identical or similar form. 'Use value' is the intrinsic usefulness of commodities; in Marxist terms 'value' is measured according to the labour invested in their production. 'Exchange value' may be more or less than use value according to the market relationships extent in particular circumstances. The 'organic composition of capital' is the

relationship between actual living labour power and capital investment used in the production of commodities (somewhat perversely
high 'organic composition' means a relatively low proportion of
actual living labour). 'Contradiction', in the Marxist sense, means a
state of tension or antagonism between different aspects of a relationship rather than that two or more phenomena are mutually exclusive.
'Social formation' can almost be used synonymously with the term
'society' but in the Marxist use it emphasises the interrelationship
between economic, politic and 'social' phenomena typically treated
separately by bourgeois social science. Finally, the term 'derogation'
refers, effectively, to the practice of waiving rules in certain circumstances.

Readers interested in a fuller account of the above terms and their
place within the wider body of Marxist theory are recommended to
read basic introductory texts such as Fine (1975), Mandel (1969) or the
excellent short and topical introduction to Marxist economics by
Harrison (1978).

During the late 1960s and 1970s there was a rapid growth of Marxist
analysis concentrating on cities in capitalist social formations. Much
of the analysis came from France, particularly inspired by Manuel
Castells' powerful critique of bourgeois 'urban sociology'. Town
planning and the role of the state in urban development were central
recurring concerns. One major problem to be confronted in studying
this now very diverse literature is that of the relationship between
general theory and specific studies. Castells, in particular, often treats
France as a 'typical' capitalist society. However, there are important
differences between capitalist *nations* in terms of: pre-capitalist social
relations 'carried over' into more fully developed capitalist relations;
the state 'form'—centralism, federalism, etc.; relations to dominant
international capitalist relations and so on. The development of state
planning has varied tremendously and different sorts of agencies, at
different levels of government, can all be said to be state planning of
one sort or another. Much debate concerns the *necessity* of urban
planning for capitalist social relations and the *necessity* of state intervention. Castells, in my view, overemphasizes and overgeneralizes
from the French case whereas experience in the USA, or Australia for
example, is quite different. Thus, in the latter, there has been very

little central control of city development. Indeed, one of the major (unsuccessful) attempts at intervention by the 1972-5 Whitlam Labour Government, *opposed* by conservative forces, was the development of federal policies for Australian cities.

One attempt to develop a theory of urban planning under capitalism was in the paper by Roweis and Scott (1977). They sought to locate planning in a discussion of modes of production and the development of relations between modes of production and the state. In particular, they focused on the 'urban land nexus' and emphasized the importance of town planning in 'smoothing' the contradictory effects of uncontrolled capitalist urban development. The major criticism which can be applied to the paper is its tendency towards a functionalist exposition, implying that 'planning' somehow 'emerged' to fill a 'gap' and solved contradictions rather than merely modified their form. An emphasis on sound historical analysis, however, and a rejection of the ideologies of dominant 'planning theory' are two great strengths of this paper.

I am delighted to include the recent paper by Susan and Norman Fainstein in this reader. They put forward a critical analysis of planning in the USA informed by Marxist theory. They confront the thorny question of general theory and specific analysis and conclude with an attempt to reconcile theory and practice. It will be instructive for readers to compare their conclusions with those of Kraushaar and Gardels in their paper in Part Five, noting the different emphases given to class analysis, class struggle and urban planning.

The chapter from Cynthia Cockburn's book, *The Local State,* is included to illustrate the growing emphasis, in studies of planning, on the need for an understanding of the State in capitalist society. Her book is particularly important as it was the first attempt to bring a Marxist analysis to bear on the activities and organization of local government, and merits reading as a whole. When published it was very controversial and despite protests from some in Lambeth, fortunately, the book went ahead and was, on the whole, well received.

The papers in this section, hopefully, will encourage readers to investigate further in the developing field of urban political economy. During the 1970s there was a vigorous debate over the nature and content of urban analysis, involving both non-Marxists and various neo-Marxist and Marxist perspectives. This debate continues, particularly within the pages of an excellent journal, the *International Journal of Urban and Regional Research,* edited by Michael Harloe (now at the University of Essex) which readers are recommended to consult.

The field is now truly international and is a major concern of scholars associated with the Research Committee on the Sociology of Urban and Regional Development (a committee of the International Sociological Association). The part president of the committee, Ray Pahl, and its current president, Manuel Castells, have been major figures in the development and internationalization of discussion. Their work and some of the seminal texts are noted in the guide to further reading (below, pp. 309-312).

There is one point in particular that I should like readers to bear in mind whilst reading the contributions to this Part. Unlike conventional planning theory which tends to view town planning as an autonomous force 'modifying' urban development, I wish to stress the interrelationship between capitalist urbanization and town planning, i.e. state planning as it has existed in one component part of capitalist urbanization, spawned by the explosive relations of capitalist competition, thus fulfilling an *integrative* role (modifying the worst excesses) and an ideological role (as outlined in my introduction to Part One).

References

Fine, B. (1975) *Marx's Capital,* London: Macmillian.
Harrison J. (1978) *Marxist Economics for Socialists: A Critique of Reformism,* London: Pluto Press.
Mandel, E. (1969) *Introduction to Marxist Economics,* London: Merlin.
Roweis, S. and Scott, A. (1977) 'Urban planning in theory and practice: a reappraisal', *Environment and Planning A,* Vol. 9.

The Oppression of Progress

JON GOWER DAVIES*

Part of the ideology of the planning profession casts the planner in the role of the natural enemy of those nineteenth-century robber-barons who, under the banner of *laissez-faire,* raped the fair countryside, spewed forth the unzoned filth of our industrial cities, and trampled underfoot the weak, the defenceless, the economically, politically, and socially impotent members of our society. It is, of course, because of its antagonism to *laissez-faire* that planning has often beeen associated with socialism.

Yet in many ways, planning departments are the natural heirs of nineteenth-century entrepreneurs. The profit motive which drove railway companies and commercial developers to destroy large numbers of the dwellings of the poor in order to use the land for new track and stations, or for new offices and shops, may seem to be far removed from the 'public interest' motivation of planners. Yet the veto on redevelopment schemes, whether undertaken for reasons of profit or for reasons of public interest, lies where it has always lain: with the possessors of large amounts of wealth, power and influence.

Furthermore, of course, development plans often do little more than accept the location of 'big' industries and commercial concerns: the plans are drawn *around* them. Even when redevelopment of, say, city centres is deemed desirable, the emphasis is often on 'coopera-tion' with commercial interests, and this cooperation frequently takes the form of the local authority using its powers of compulsory pur-chase to make land available to firms and companies that might other-wise go elsewhere. The need to maximize rateable values leads to the elimination of the 'small concern' and of city-centre housing and to the encouragement of alternative (highly profitable) uses such as huge

*Originally published in 1972 as Chapter 28 of *The Evangelistic Bureaucrat,* London, Tavistock.

office blocks or luxury hotels. The uprooted shop-owner either moves into the 'house-shops' of the outer mixed-use area, or gives up altogether. The dispossessed owner-occupier may find himself rehoused miles from his work, with the concomitant increase in travel costs and housing expenditure, and the amount of social disturbances that such a move involves.

In the circumstances planning becomes a highly regressive form of indirect taxation, with those who have least suffering most, and those who have a lot being given more. When, for example, Newcastle Central Station was built, many poor families living in tenements on the land needed for the station were simply dehoused: they vanished back into the remaining old rookeries, there to further increase the overcrowding. The justification for this (not that any justification was ever offered to the persons who were dehoused) was the old one of 'technical progress' and the benefits it conferred upon 'society'. Precisely the same rationale underlies schemes such as Rye Hill.

There is nothing 'progressive', either for the poor who used to live where the station now stands or for the owner-occupiers in Rye Hill who stood to lose their houses, in a technology which they could not afford to use or to enjoy. 'Society' is not an undifferentiated social system; nor is it a disembodied 'general will'. At any one time, it is a specific structure in which men are ranked and rank each other according to their possession of amounts of cash, status and power. British society is highly inegalitarian in the way it distributes these items: 47% of our people in 1964 had a total after-tax income of less than £1000;[1] and in 1959-60, 88% of our people on average held, 'fortunes' of £107—as compared, for example, with 5% of our population who had average fortunes of £15,200.[2] When, in the name of progress, a radical technology is intruded into such a conservative socio-economic system, then 'progress' becomes oppressive.

The planning system relates to the people it is meant to serve in exactly the same way as the educational system relates to the people *it* is meant to serve: it complements and reflects the class structure, giving most of those who already have a lot and giving least to those who need most.

As an example of the regressive effect of planning schemes, consider the plan announced on 28 November 1968 by Northumberland

County Planning Authority to build a ring road through Whitley Bay. The local paper carried interviews with two persons concerned, one an owner-occupier; and the other the head of Scottish and Newcastle Breweries, who owned a public house in the path of the road. The owner-occupier (a lady) said:

> I am so desperately worried that I will be lumbered with this house indefinitely that I have come out in a nervous complaint caused by tension.[3]

The Breweries chief took a much more phlegmatic view. He said:

> If the ring road meant demolishing entire properties as large as his own, it would be a very expensive business. He added, however, that he had seen this sort of plan in the early stages before, and he would start getting concerned about it when it actually came about.[4]

The Breweries chief was not too worried—either because the Breweries could easily absorb any 'loss' it might have to carry, or because the planning authority might eventually be put off the scheme because of the very high expense involved in acquiring commercial properties such as public houses. Neither of these two considerations could be applied to the owner-occupier. The Planning Acts, and the inegalitarian socio-economic systems they serve, pillory the 'small' man. This is why public inquiries are so often the scene of the final despairing outburst of the expletive personality: neither the law nor the policy gives scope for alternative more 'constructive' stances: 'It's no use, we can't do anything, what's the use.' What is the use? The only answer is General Ludd.

Planners solve these moral problems of their profession in two ways. On the one hand, they cling to the legal fiction that they themselves do not 'make decisions', and that democracy functions so as to ensure that the 'general will' sanctions the chosen policy. On the other hand, by according technology an independent authority of its own, they escape having to face up to the socio-economic consequences of their activities. (There is even a statement that it is the job of sociologists to 'do something about' this problem, as if economy, property and society were somehow unconnected.)

The independence of technology is often used to justify particular schemes; thus in Rye Hill part of the justification of the attempt to compel the use of modern domestic equipment was simply that it was modern! Technology, of course, is a trollop, flaunting one finery today and another tomorrow: the architectural journals are a gallery of gimmickry, an endless procession of instant obsolescence. Consequently there is no end of modernism; and if an item of domestic equipment is today held to be *desirable and a proper object of compulsory consumption* simply because it is modern, then politics cases to be viable, economics becomes unnecessary, and discourse is monopolized by men whose authority lies in mere mechanical aptitude!

The ideological functions of an 'independent' technology are made quite clear in such statements as 'Nearly all the new roads and buildings added to urban areas in the last twenty-four years will be obsolete by the year 2000.'[5]

Such statements terrorize 'laymen' and silence them; often, this is precisely what they are meant to do. Yet the more important political consequences of such claims lie in the tacit definition of 'the problem' as being a technology one when it is, in fact, an economic (i.e. political) one. Houses may be built or modernized for a 'life' of 30, 40, or 60 years; but the 'life' is not something implicit in the fabric or in the modernity of the domestic equipment: it is determined by its cost and its price. This, in turn, is ultimately a political decision: if, say, in ten years' time any of the houses we build today *are* in fact regarded as undesirable, then they can be thrown away, or we can learn to live with them. Either way, the decision is a political-economic one. *All* our houses are throwaway houses; and architects are wasting their time anxiously looking for 'the answer' in some arcane branch of technology. The more conservative the political economy, the greater the anxiety and the repression surrounding the production and consumption of the fruits of technology. Architecture is impossible not because of the constraints of technology; these are minor compared with the constraints implicit in, for example, a method of financing local authority house-building in which 70% of the revenue on any one house goes to pay off the interest (50%) and principal (20%) of the money borrowed to build it. The constraints are financial not technical.

Yet the planning profession persist in defining the problem as as technical one. They thereby maximize their professional problems and inflict them upon the consumers of the commodities they provide. They also act as props of a highly inegalitarian society.

Consider, for example, the August 1968 issue of *Architectural Design,* an issue which is devoted to 'The Architecture of Democracy'. A proper title for this issue would be 'The Architecture of Deprivation' or, even better, 'The Architecture of Fascism', for what it describes are the attempts of affluent people to get poor people, in particular American Negroes, to learn to live with the fact of their poverty. One article, entitled 'Squatter Inspired',[6] describes the production of prefabricated boxes masquerading as houses for American Negroes. The authors state that the boxes were first used for Venezuelan squatter families, and apparently see nothing incongruous in the fact that they are recommending them for use in the richest country in the world. Indeed, they claim that their 'houses' will

> Infuse an element of freedom and independence into the slum to recapture, in part at least, the spirit of the frontier that has largely vanished from the society of the United States.[7]

Whether in Newcastle or in the USA such styles of thinking make technical 'progress' the tool of political oppression. If planners and their colleagues in related fields are to be able to make a legitimate claim of being liberators rather than oppressors, then they must transfer the zeal with which they pursue that latest in technical gimmickry to an analysis of the society in which they function and in which they market their wares. The sloppy thinking that characterizes so many planning documents reveals just how committed to the *status quo* our planners have become. Brave words about 'affluence' and 'modern image' become so much hot air when confronted by the reality of a socio-economic system which must be changed before planning can become either possible or desirable.

Notes

1. *National Income and Expenditure,* HMSO, 1966.
2. *The Economist,* 15 January 1966.
3. *The Journal* (Newcastle), Friday, 29 November 1968.
4. *Ibid.*
5. Professor Jack Napper, addressing a conference sponsored by the National Provincial Bank, at Newcastle-upon-Tyne University, 16 October 1968.
6. Squatter Inspired', by Ian Terner and Robert Herz, in *Architecural Design, op.cit.*
7. *Ibid.,* p. 370.

Urban Planning: the Contradictions of Capitalist Urbanisation

EDMOND PRETECEILLE*

The critique of capitalist urbanisation often proceeds by denouncing anarchic urbanisation.[1] A standard theme of urbanism is the notion of the State restoring order to spontaneous urbanisation. Certainly the daily experience of the contemporary city for millions is of disordered suburbs with poor services, inadequate transport and housing which is too expensive, too small and too noisy. But this disorder is not really so spontaneous, for today the urban crisis and urban pathologies arise as the effects of political processes. Is this then to say that the State pursues a conscious strategy on behalf of the dominant fractions of the capitalist class? State intervention is sometimes seen as complete *laissez-faire* and sometimes as authoritarian, the latter realising a monopolistic strategy. It is the state intervention which has come to be called urban planning.

The law requires that all towns of any size produce plans which zone each parcel of land for different uses both qualitatively in terms of type and quantitatively in terms of height and form of permitted structures. For a long time the idea of an absence of urban planning prevailed, despite the fact that the first relevant law was passed in 1919. This naive idea conceived of a period to the end of the 1950s in which planning was absent or ineffective, followed by the period in which the land laws were elaborated, and later a return to the free capitalist urbanisation seen as appropriate to France. This view is, however, dispelled by precise historical study which shows that many urban plans existed prior to 1959. For Paris alone 138 commune plans

*Originally published in French in *Economie et Politique* **236,** March 1974; English translation by Martin Boddy, used in this reader, published in *Antipode,* Vol. 8, No. 1, March 1976.

were approved from 1919-1950, the 'Prost' plan was approved in 1939, PADOG in 1960, while the legal framework was well developed before the land laws. And there appear to be many exceptions to the period characterised as one of 'free development', such as the state planning agency decisions, while in the period of 'liberal politics' supposed to follow it, private ZAC's developed out of the land laws themselves.[2] 1968-1972, seen as a period of retreat from planning, saw just as many plans approved, which moveover, related to previous legislation rather than to the land laws.

So while one can sense that the urban crisis is an aspect of the general crisis of State Monopoly Capitalism (SMC) the forms of State intervention in urbanisation appear to be expanding. If urban planning is a reality what are its actual characteristics? Or is it merely a smokescreen, obscuring practices which serve the interests of private capital? These questions are important both to theory and to politics, but it is necessary to extend the analysis of the urban crisis, as an aspect of the crisis of SMC, both into the directly experienced effects—aggravation of the conditions of reproduction of labour power—and also into its causes. Merely denouncing the ill effects of the monopolies is inadequate. The gulf between the general analysis of SMC and its crisis, and the particular problems of urban politics causes severe problems for democratically elected bodies involved in the administrative process of urban planning and also, more generally, problems for those struggling against monopoly power and those concerned with the conditions of existence of the workers. It is also relevant in defining the form of democratic urban politics, in the context of the Common Programme. In an attempt to advance the analysis necessary to reply to these questions we go here to discuss the place of planning in capitalist urbanisation; in subsequent work we will study the underlying mechanisms specific to the SMC phase and the relations between urban planning, political struggles and democratic perspectives.

The nineteenth century city was intimately linked to rapid capitalist industrialisation which concentrated 'free workers' into cities and thus gave concrete expression to the opposition between town and country, which is an important aspect of the social division of labour. But we must go beyond this and examine the role of the city in terms of accumulation of capital and the reproduction of labour power.

Urbanisation, Production, Circulation and Exchange

Until now, urban economics has studied the economic role of cities in terms of the many advantages a particular enterprise can obtain from its urban location. The town is taken as a given, exogenous object which is independent of production itself, as a 'factor' or 'block of factors' of production. Capitalist urbanisation cannot be conceived either as given, or simply as an induced effect (as proposed, for example, by economic base theory), even though a city might exist before the development of the capitalist mode of production (CMP), and be favourable to it. To grasp the true nature of the links between urbanisation and the development of social production one must abandon the viewpoint of the single enterprise and consider production as a whole. The concentration of different units of production in space is linked to the development of the social division of labour, and leads to the development of a particular form of social cooperation between the units of production. However, this is different from that developed in industrial production with the technical division of labour. Despite anarchy in the social division of labour, urbanisation produces a new, socialised productive force, distinct from the productive forces dominated by capital within each unit of production. This difference explains why bourgeois economics views the social productive forces as external effects, contributing to the valorisation of capital.[3] They are not productive forces which can take the commodity form. It is important to study the social productive forces as integral with the range of productive forces which operate to give value to capital. Their effects vary with the general economic conjuncture and the evolution of the rates of profit in different sectors.

The concrete aspects of the socialised productive forces arising out of urbanisation are many. Most important is the concentration in space of a large number of workers, whose collective productive force is greater than the sum of their separate, individual productive forces. Also significant are the development of transport, and other aspects which diversify and are transformed with the general evolution of the productive forces. Multiple relations of interdependence between units of production, an actual form of the social division of labour developing in the production of a given commodity, are also of importance. Because of the available means of transport the socialisation of production can today transcend a particular urban region and take the form of exchange at the international level. In considering cooperation linked to the social division of labour in production one must also note the significance of the diverse means of production—the public services such as water, electricity and transport networks—which industry finds readily available in urban areas.

The circulation of capital is closely linked to urbanisation. The spatial concentration of units of production and population affects commodity production in two ways: firstly, it facilitates the social division of labour which tends to reduce the indirect costs of circulation from the point of production as a whole; secondly, it tends to raise the average rate of profit by increasing the rate of circulation of capital. Thus capitalist urbanisation carries to a new level tendencies already characteristic of cities in precapitalist social formation.

When classical urban economics considers the diseconomies of urban growth it treats them as autonomous phenomena to be matched with remedies. But 'economies' and 'diseconomies' of agglomeration are two aspects linked to the same process of urbanisation; urban development, expressing the growing socialisation of the productive forces, is not linear but must be analysed as a contradictory process marked by the principal contradiction of the mode of production. The analysis must therefore consider the dominant relations of production and their effects.

The capitalist enterprise gains certain advantages from urbanisation, benefiting from the effects of these socialised productive forces which are costless to it. But production implies also the reproduction of the forces of production. Certain elements of this can be controlled by the enterprises—e.g. the maintenance and development of cooperation between units of production—but always within the limits of commodity relations and profit maximisation, the latter making cooperation inherently unstable. Other elements cannot be controlled by any enterprise alone, such as the concentration of workers, and most of the concrete supports which ensure the socialisation of the productive forces—transport, roads, water, gas, etc. These concrete supports are also use values appropriated as means of production or supports of circulation and exchange, and of the production and reproduction (maintenance) of these use values, organised into particular units of production working to produce and maintain the public services. Urbanisation is characterised by the spatial juxtaposition and articulation of all these elements to form complex use values. Each element has an individual use value as a means of production, but spatial organisation produces the new, complex use value. This later is significant because production and circulation imply the simultaneous appropriation of different elemental use values in a single location.

The production of complex use values itself implies particular forms of cooperation between the units of production producing or constituting each element. The existence of these complex use values is accompanied by the social appropriation of a part of urban land, as shown by the importance of publicly owned land. Thus private, anarchic appropriation of space which is a fundamental characteristic of capitalist urbanisation due to the nature of the dominant social relations of production cannot develop without its opposite, the social appropriation of space. Similarly the anarchy of capitalist production cannot develop without simultaneous development of the socialised production of the concrete supports of the productive forces of urbanisation. The socialised character of urbanisation predates the CMP, but the scale of accumulation is different. If initially there are supports in existing cities, bequeathed by previous modes of production, the incessant desire to give value to capital and the search for profit urged on by competition between capitals is such that these use values, which are costless to capital, are rapidly used up, in the manner of air, water and nature in general. Though the capitalist discounts the effects of this accelerated appropriation of urban use values they rebound onto him. Concentration which fails to assure the expanded reproduction of the use values constituting the forces of production leads to congestion and paralysis. Having devoured the resources of urbanisation capital complains of diseconomies, urban anarchy and pathology.

Urbanisation and the Reproduction of Labour Power

The wild growth of the urban population, unfurling of the suburbs in anarchic urbanisation, is the direct effect of the evolution of the productive forces and the accumulation of capital. If during this process an already large mass of population is reorganised then the pursuit of accumulation necessitates that the reproduction of this labour power be assured. The essential characteristic of this population, free workers, is their possession of merely their own labour power. The separation of the means of production from the workers essentially removes from the workers any possibility of ensuring their subsistence by direct appropriation of nature. Once again it is the development of the social division of labour in urban agglomerations which tends to assure the production of use values necessary to meet social needs, in an autonomous specialised manner. Bourgeois economics recognises this positive aspect in its treatment of the 'advantages of the city for final consumption'. But this division of labour and production of necessary use values operates under the domination of capital, a process whereby value is given to different capitals. And the search for profit produces anarchy in the social division of labour, a deformed, mutilated response to social needs, only those commodities which allow the realistion of surplus value with a sufficient rate of profit being produced and circulated. Two insufficiencies arise: firstly, a quantitative lack of certain use values; secondly, a lack of quality in the social conditions of the reproduction of labour power which capitalist production of goods alone cannot remedy. The evolution of social needs resulting from the development of the forces of production is in effect transformed by a complex growth in the conditions socially necessary for their reproduction, and a socialisation of consumption which parallels this.

Urban space, which constitutes the social space in which labour power is reproduced, must ensure the arrangement of the necessary elements: thus housing must be linked to water, electricity, gas and sewerage nets, to roads and mass transport, to schools, shops, recreational and medical facilities, and above all to employment. This implies that the arrangement of urban space must ensure the spatial articulation of these use values to form complex use values. These are partly linked to the complex use values necessary for production and circulation. Added to these aspects concerned with the everyday reproduction of labour power are those concerned with its reproduction in the social formation as a whole. Education, research, means of information, cultural and artistic activities are all of importance in the city. But this importance is not spontaneously acquired. Urbanisation must ensure conditions favourable to the development of these social processes: so how is this done under the omnipresent domination of the search for profit?

Contradictions of Capitalist Urbanisation and State Socialisation of The Appropriation of Space

In sketching out the analysis of the productive forces of urbanisation it has been indicated that these particular forms of socialisation of production imply a set of concrete supports, organised in space, as being necessary to their development. Rapid development of economic activity means that urban use values left by previous modes of production quickly become inadequate. The crucial concern for both production and circulation is therefore that of the expanded reproduction of the urban use values necessary as general conditions of production. But this expanded reproduction runs up against obstacles which stem from the very nature of the relations of production.

These use values are consumed by each unit of production as external conditions, quasi-natural 'factors of production', but their renewal is not provided for in the cycle of rotation of capital itself in the manner of purchased raw materials or labour power. Each capital does not concern itself with preventing the deterioration of these conditions, but instead augments its production or benefits from a differential surplus profit. Urban economics is concerned with these matters in a purely external manner, as in the question of locating an enterprise in space given a heterogenous distribution of necessary factors which are taken as given and fixed; but roads, railways, water supplies, etc., can all be constructed, maintained, exploited. One might think that the development of the social division of labour would produce a spontaneous solution through the development of specialised units of capitalist production: in classical economics all demand will present the opportunity for capital to produce a supply, provided the demand is important enough. However, there are several reasons why they are not produced or are produced only partially.

Firstly, relating to the strongly socialised nature of the production and consumption of these use values, they cannot enter naturally into the cycle of commodities; their indivisible character and the actual mode of their realisation prevent them circulating as simple fractional quantities of exchange value—the case of roads is typical of this. Certainly the possibility of their circulating as commodities varies—it is easier in the case of water, electricity or gas than for roads—depending on how far consumption can be individually quantified. But it always remains partial because an important part of the use value, the network can only be realised collectively.

Secondly, relating to the role of these elements as essential supports of the socialisation of production and the development of circulation, their production strictly as commodities subordinates their use value to the rules which govern the valorisation of capital.

Thirdly, relating to the organic composition and speed of rotation of capital in these sectors, the organic composition of capital in producing, for example, transport is high, due principally to the importance of fixed capital constituted by the infrastructure—roads, bridges, tunnels, stations, etc. The mass of value (labour time) embodied in these products which constitute the fixed capital is enormous, and the period of rotation of this capital is considerable. The growth of urbanisation strongly contributes to the increase in the organic composition of capital as a whole, through the mass of urban infrastructure it necessitates. It therefore contributes to the tendency of the average rate of profit to fall.

Lastly, the problem of land must be considered. The production of urban use values uses much space, and what is more, organised space. The obstacle of landed property is already important in the fragmented, limited appropriation of space by capital, but it becomes enormous in the appropriation of continuous areas, essential for the various infrastructures, and the limited number of possible locations can give rise to considerable monopoly rent. Thus state intervention is necessary to allow social appropriation of essential land; one might note that it was in the actual case of infrastructure—transport and public facilities—that legislation on expropriation was first constituted.

In parallel, the reproduction of labour power requires the existence of general social conditions which ensure the distribution of the necessary use values to the labour force. This implies the existence, and thus reproduction, of these use values such that their spatial organisation constitutes a social space accessible to the labour force. Certain use values are linked to those which relate to production and circulation—one cannot, for example, classify the elements of a road net into those useful for accumulation and those useful in the reproduction of labour power. Other use values, by contrast, are specifically concerned with the reproduction of labour power. As in the preceding section, a first level of socialisation exists which relates to the specialised production of each element. The reasons behind the form of socialisation are, however, different and more complex. Why should the State take over part of the supply in response to social needs, and have a social policy? The answer is two-fold and contradictory, being partly a response to the class struggle and partly to certain needs of capital itself, with regard to the reproduction of labour power. Thus we have the growth of state education, the public health service and hospital facilities as examples of phenomena which cannot be reduced to their strictly economic aspects in contributing to accumulation, although the reduction in the direct cost to capital of the reproduction of labour power through socialised provision of certain necessary elements is always important, and although capitalist economic relations are manifest in many different forms.

Beyond this first level of socialisation which principally manifests itself in state politics of collective facilites,[4] one again encounters the problem of expanded reproduction of complex use values organising the social space of reproduction, as urban growth occurs. Again this requires a socialisation which concretely ensures the necessary cooperation in the process of production of collective facilities as well as coordination with capitalist production and circulation of use values which constitute that part of workers' consumption based on the commodity mode.

For these various reasons then, capitalist urbanisation is seen to develop many-sided state intervention in diverse forms, which are historically variable relating to the social formations, and tend towards a state socialisation of the production of the different urban use values. At the first level state socialisation concerns each particular use value. But beyond state intervention in particular production processes, the expanded reproduction of complex use values formed by the spatial articulation of particular elements and units of production requires in turn the organisation of a superior form of cooperation. This cooperation affects the formation of complex use values and results in a coordinated set of several processes.

Though the development of the social division of labour implies certain forms of social cooperation, its major characteristic in the CMP is above all anarchy, the clashing together of social production in many private processes dominated by the law of accumulation of capital, and in which the relations between these processes take the form of simple relations between objects, i.e. circulating commodities. Capitalist appropriation thus consists of a multitude of private capitalist processes of appropriation of space, each particular process determined by the particular relations of production, i.e. the rules appropriate to the process whereby each capital or fraction of capital is given value. Capitalist commodity production is dominated by, and oriented to the realisation of surplus value through the search for profit, even though it may respond to social needs. The search for maximum profit by each capital, competition between capitals, imposes a form of appropriation of space in which cooperation, and the form of complex use values are only considered in terms of the extent to which they permit, or are necessary to, the expanded reproduction of capital—and not in terms of their use values. This is the fundamental contradiction of capitalist urbanisation: between the necessity for an increasing socialisation of the appropriation of space for the expanded reproduction of the productive forces, and the private capitalist appropriation of space dominated by the multiple needs and conflicts in the valorisation on different capitals.

The actual forms of this contradiction can best be understood by examining different elements of the expanded reproduction of the productive forces: three of the most important are developed here.

Land ownership is reproduced in a particular form by the CMP as private appropriation of a means of production and as a source of rent. It forms a sharp contradiction which affects production more than the circulation and realisation of urban use values. Land ownership affects both value (exchange) and use value. In the case of value, it intervenes in the distribution of surplus value by allowing the levying of different forms of urban rent (differential, absolute, monopoly) which bleed off surplus value going to direct accumulation. In the case of use value it intervenes as a relation of production in defining the conditions of real appropriation of space, considered as a means of support of production. Its effect is particularly felt, negatively, in the development of cooperation in the case of use values where space is important in constituting the complex use values which relate to the organization of space. In this respect the CMP encounters an obstacle which is aggravated by the overlaying of inadequate forms of land ownership on the social formation, which operate only according to economic determinations. In the structure as a whole, land ownership is a major obstacle to the socialisation and appropriation of space, whether capitalist or not, and this is probably one factor explaining why urban planning developed so early, and before economic planning. One should not, however, always see land ownership as the principal cause of urban problems. The obstacle of land ownership is also reproduced by capital in the private appropriation of space, dominated by the search for profit. Though capitalist appropriation of space may represent a degree of socialisation superior to previous modes, which leave behind certain actual forms of land ownership, it is now itself in contradiction with the new degree of socialisation required by the development of the productive forces.

The organisation of social space or reproduction of labour power around housing immediately encounters shortage of public finance allotted in this use, which markedly impoverishes this space, making the collective facilities available to the workers and their households highly inadequate. But beyond this general insufficiency it encounters the divergent rules which govern the valorisation of different fractions of capital, whether devalorised or not, ensuring the production and circulation of the different use values constituting this social space which tend on the contrary to result in specialised monofunctional zones.

In the organisation of space in urban agglomerations the competition among the different types of appropriation of space, appropriation of urban use values which can actually be realised at different points in space, is regulated by the maximum level of ground rent possible, in the form of the price of land. This leads to the selection of types of land use in terms of their capacity to pay rent and thus in terms of the mass of profits realised, which leads to a growing segregation in urban space. This results then in a rapid growth of repeated journeys, especially in the case of the separation of workplaces from workers' residential areas, and tends to produce a general saturation of roads and transport which ends up endangering the very realisation of the use values expected in particular locations.

Urban Planning in Practice, and Contradictory Tendencies in State Intervention

Social relations of production, i.e. the social relations of each process whereby urban elements are produced and circulated, have been proposed as determinants of urbanisation. State intervention operates precisely upon these relations of production and circulation. In fact, state intervention is always present in these relations in the form of the judicial code which both reflects and supports them. Thus the first type of state intervention takes the form of juridical intervention in the relations of production. The state operates a juridical definition of the conditions under which the different social agents can appropriate urban space, by defining land regulations and thus the type of construction and use possible on a piece of land. Before planning of this type exists the only objective characteristics are physical (the nature of the land and its location) and social (proximity to other activities or facilities) which together determine possible social land uses at a given moment; urban jurisdiction then defines these socially possible uses. The process whereby each particular element is produced is thus partially orientated to the complex use value as well as to the particular use value. The complex use values result from the organisation of the element in space relative to other existing use values, or to those which may exist in the future.

This right of intervention is not limited to reflecting and codifying existing social relations, for in socialising them it modifies them, as shown in judicial orders which take into account future urbanisation. Again, it is not a simple juridical process: elaboration of the land laws must be concerned both with the future and with the technical tasks of conceiving the complex use values which are desirable outputs which it is desirable to control. The application of this right is itself interventionist when elaborated, implying forms of control and direction of the private production process. This interventionist right diverges, after a fashion, from the central idea of juridical ideology, namely the absolute equality of all before law, when it necessarily implies inequality of definition to differentiate the conditions under which space is appropriated. Control of the different processes of appropriation of space remains private, constrained only by the limits fixed by urban law. This can be severe and go so far as to forbid construction.

There is, however, a second type of urban planning in which the modification of the relations of production is more profound, which is linked to the realisation of public facilities. Two types of relation can be distinguished. The first is defined by complete state control of the production process (the work of production being assured by a public service, national enterprise or an equivalent). The second is perhaps more usual, but not in the case of the sectors concerning us here. It is defined by relative state control of production through its control of finance and of the circulation of the product while, properly speaking, the definition of its characteristics remains privately controlled. These two types have common characteristics which implicitly define 'public control of production': public finance, definition of principal characteristics by the State, and public control of circulation.

If in one respect production of public facilities responds to a sectoral logic relating to the economic interests and social logic specific to the use of values of the facilities, in another it necessarily relates to a logic of urban planning. Each public facility cannot be realised as a particular use value which assures in itself the formation of the complex use of values if it is inserted into the organisation of the other urban use values. A road, school, water or sewerage net gains its utility from the housing or other activities which it serves. Therefore the State can partly control the beneficial effects of agglomeration through controlling the production of public facilities. Having defined these two types of urban planning by the place of the State in the relations of production, it is now necessary to examine the different divergent or actually contradictory tendencies manifested in the movement towards urban planning. There is a profound difference between those urban use values necessary as social conditions for the valorisation of capital and those necessary for the reproduction of labour power. There are also differences within these two domains: between the beneficial effects sought by each sector of activity, between those sought by the monopoly sector as opposed to artisans of small-scale enterprise. And differences also in the arrangement of the way of life between the different classes and social levels, as a function of the links between way of life and their place in the labour process and relations to ownership of land and property.

So in opposition to a one-sided conceptualisation, urban planning is by nature many sided, contradictory, torn between different needs and without hope of a purely technical reconciliation. It stems from interests of different economic agents and social categories, diversely expressed in the political process. From this stem the divergencies, tensions and conflicts between the different participants, such as between local and central government, which are apparent in the juridical process whereby plans are elaborated. Though one accepts, however, the view set out above as to the nature of urban planning, that there is conflict if not contradiction in the types of urban use values which can be sought by the formation, one need not necessarily conclude that state intervention in urban politics gives rise to urban planning. This problem is alluded to in the debate on the relations between planning and derogation or more generally in the frequent recognition of the inefficacy or partial disregard of a number of plans after they have been put into effect.

The state intervenes in the reproduction of the structure of the social formation in the area of use values, but it also does so in the field of (exchange) value and the reproduction of the social relations of production. At the level of value, reproduction is shown in the different types of aid to accumulation and also the fluctuation between general aid to a sector of activity as a whole, and particular aid to specific projects or enterprises. In the state processes themselves the logic of reproduction of value can dominate that of use value: this is so in the political rules of public administration under which it is sought to break even financially on operations or where profitability is preached as the main guide to the efficiency of public services. This results in urban politics defined empirically as the set of state interventions in urbanisation, in an ungainly move towards 'economic realism'. This consists in accepting urban projects or modifications to projects which are directly determined by the logic of the profitability of the private capital involved and of breaking even or being profitable in the operation of some public project. This tendency is essentially contradictory to urban planning and results in the rapid deterioration of urban use values which the formation is seeking. What was said earlier about state intervention in land ownership and the ambivlence of its effects in terms of use values should be recalled and also its effects on the distribution of urban rent. The importance of indirect exploitation via taxation, the manner of appropriation of public funds, and the distribution of financial charges between local and central collectives should also be noted here.

The field of urban politics is in fact equally related to politics and ideology. The ideological aspects are familiar—urban planning projects both integration (the state, the general interest and the development of urban harmony) and reformism (changing the city to change life). The political aspect has always been presented in terms of the need of the capitalist bourgeoisie to safeguard certain alliances, e.g. with the landowners, and of the political consequences of the conditions of existence of the workers (in struggles over the location of workers' housing and the formation of 'red suburbs') which affect urban politics through the political direction of the municipalities and in other ways.

Several actual forms taken by urban politics will now be considered: management schemes, land use plans, programmes of public facilities, derogations, etc. Given our theoretical definition, our hypothesis is that urban planning is not only expressed in a single form—urban plans—but in many forms which are linked to the several types of planning defined above and to the many determinants which intervene. Inversely, a particular form such as an urban plan can be the basis of support for diverse determinations, and can differ from its apparent aim.

This leads on to two questions about actual forms: how are these diverse tendencies determined in each case; how are the different actual expressions of the tendency to urban planning articulated among them? Here two examples are taken: urban plans and the practices which they are inserted into, and the programmes of public facilities.

Urban plans define rights of land use and are essentially based in the first type of planning intervention where conditions of appropriation of space are juridically laid down but control of the process remains private. But from the point of view of the system as a whole, rather than of a single use value such as housing or a public service, i.e. in terms of the use values resulting from the organisation of these elements in space, the two types of intervention are inevitably linked in practice. Thus the elaboration of urban plans, which are the principal basis of land rights, also takes account of the technical tasks of defining the characteristics of public facilities, their size and location, and the planning of these facilities according to forecasts of the development of the needs of the various agents and of the form of urbanisation. Many urban plans are possible, which leads to the notion that many options must be studied. Doing this masks the different economic and social tendencies implied by a purely technical 'choice of alternative strategies'.

On the other hand, urban plans are also supports of other determinants. It has been indicated that one aspect of land rights is the transformation they cause in landed property and in the economic modalities in practice.

Land rights are a factor firstly in determing the maximum level of ground rent on a piece of land—which depends on the production for which this land is a means—and secondly the distribution between landowner and developer. Because the question of rent is very important in the public building and construction sector the relations of landownership and capital are of great significance in urban plans. Plans partly restrict the exercise of ownership, and rules of density and zoning increase the value of some plots of land and decrease that of others.

Within the limits of the agglomeration landowners are relatively secure in the possibility of using their monopoly situation to obtain rent for they know the most profitable land use permitted by the land rights. The weight of ownership can come into play more directly, as in the debate on the definition of alternative 'Coefficients of Land Occupation' (COS): 'technical' COS defining construction allowed in terms of existing or planned facilities; 'unquestionable rights' COS which ratified the existing practices and allowed construction accordingly; COS which was systematically low in order to boost receipts from the tax on excess density, etc.

It is the use which is made of plans which is important rather than their explicit content as such. The case of derogation is interesting because it dispels the distorted picture derived from a simplistic vision of urban planning. If undue attention is paid to the urban plan one neglects contradictory tendencies which can be invoked in the form of derogation, or negative planning. Derogation must be empirically studied to sort out this problem. As yet it has hardly been touched upon, but one can already indicate that there are many very different types of derogation, certain of which can be relevant to the practice of urban planning (such as the application of urban regulations to certain types of plot, or their strict application which can impede all amelioration of the urban tissue). Others are essentially relevant to the distribution of rent and the effects of these vary from the planning point of view, though in most cases they aggravate the saturation of public facilities.

In urban plans and derogations we can also see the determinations of politics and state intervention, sometimes going against the tendencies indicated earlier so as politically to maintain ownership. In the planning of public facilities one can see these links with the elaboration of urban plans. But the planning of programmes modernising the facilities of agglomerations, linked to the national plan, is itself much influenced by the character of the public finance programme, and to a certain extent the techniques of financial planning overwhelm the issue of use values. On the other hand, the planning and realisation of public facilities is strongly anchored in the sectoral logic of specialised sectors of the state apparatus, a logic appropriate to each individually and which can ignore, or make difficult, the necessary socialisaion of their products which implies a spatial and temporal coordination between the sectors financially, juridically and administratively. Moreover, through planning certain sectoral logics can influence urban plans themselves. Certain plans are no more than road schemes. So one finds political determinations equally at the level of the general orientation of state finance fitting into the Plan and the Budget, and at the level of the decision between central state and local collectives.

Notes

1. This article originally appeared as 'La Planification Urbaine: les contradictions de l'urbanisation capitaliste', in *Economie et Politique.* **236**, March 1974. Translation by Martin Boddy.
2. PADOG: Plan d'Aménagement et d'Organisation Générale de la Région Parisienne. The 1960 Paris regional plan.
   ZAC: Zones d'Aménagement Concert. Coordinated developments similar to British new towns. Author's footnote: 'Urban projects entrusted to a private developer can result in benefits to the developer resulting from the State's rights of intervention in landholding and control of construction, in exchange for provision by the developer of certain collective facilities or contribution to their finance.'
3. Valorisation is used throughout to stand for the French phrase meaning literally 'the process whereby value is given (or 'put into') capital'. Thus it indicates money which becomes active, circulating capital which is augmented in the course of the circuit, when it passes through the sphere of production. Devalorised capital, referred to later, is capital which is augmented at a zero, or below average, rate of profit.
4. The author provides an extended theoretical and methodological introduction to the subject of collective facilities in *Equipments collectifs, structures et consommation sociale,* Centre de Sociologie Urbaine, 118 rue La Tombe Issoire, Paris 14. 1975.

New Debates in Urban Planning: the Impact of Marxist Theory within the United States*

NORMAN I. FAINSTEIN and SUSAN S. FAINSTEIN§

The development of Marxist urban theory has raised new issues for scholars who believe that urban planning can be connected with social progress in the United States. Demysifiction of categories such as rationality and the public interest has been transcended by discussions of state autonomy, cooptation and the determinants of urban form. Critics of the present system have gone beyond demonstrating that traditional planning serves bourgeois interest and have begun to discuss strategies for structural change and the boundaries of action under capitalism. This paper briefly outlines the elements of the Marxist theory of urban planning in advanced capitalist societies, then examines in greater detail the terms of debate *within* this paradigm as it applies to the United States. Finally, it considers the relationship between theory and praxis in planning. For these purposes urban planning theory is defined as comprising two analytically separable but mutually dependent parts: a theory of planning process or activity and a theory of urban structure and development.

I. The Marxist Paradigm

Contemporary Marxist thought has focused on numerous phenomena ranging from war to conditions of labour. Its concern with spatial questions and the interrelationship between class structure and plan-

*An earlier version of this paper was presented at the Conference on Planning Theory, Division of Environmental and Urban Systems, Virginia Polytechnic Institute and State University, Blacksburg, Virginia, 4-5 May 1978.

§Originally published in the *International Journal of Urban and Regional Research*, Vol. 3, No. 3, September 1979.

ning have proved especially fruitful despite their novelty within the Marxist tradition. (The basis for this thrust in contemporary marxism can be found in Engels, edn. 1970). The modern metropolis, which freezes class relationships into the built environment and provides the setting for contemporary class antagonisms, has offered a key site in which to explore capitalist contradictions and the mediating role of the state. From this body of thought we have distilled a number of propositions about planning and urban development within which debates concerning explanation and strategies have arisen (see especially Castells, 1977; Havey, 1973; O'Connor, 1973; Miliband, 1977; Harloe, 1977; Lindberg *et al.*, 1975; Pickvance, 1976).

1. *Planning as activity*

1. Disparate interests within the bourgeoisie force it to organize itself through the state for the purpose of planning its common interest: 'The state is nothing more than the form of organization the bourgeois necessarily adopt both for internal and external purposes' (Marx and Engels, edn 1947, p.59). Its 'relative autonomy' results from the need to subordinate separate fractions of capital to the general good of the ruling class. The ideology of the ruling class, however, universalizes the state, thereby legitimizing state activities in the name of the whole society even while acting in the interests of the bourgeoisie.

2. Planning is necessary to the ruling class in order to facilitate accumulation and maintain social control in the face of class conflict. The modes by which urban planners assist accumulation include the development of physical infrastructure, land aggregation and development, containment of negative environmental externalities, and maintenance of land values. Social control is effected through a combination of containment tactics and the provision of social services.

3. Urban planners are predominantly agents of the state. Even those planners who are not employed by the state are forced to work within the agenda established by the state. For example, advocate planners representing citizens' groups usually respond to state initiative such as urban renewal or highway building. Only planners working at a very small scale on internal community projects can sometimes evade the omnipresent mould of state activities.

4. Urban planners specialize in managing the contradictions of capitalism manifested in urban form and spatial development. These include the inability of the private economy to produce sufficient low-cost housing for the low-income population; the strains on energy supplies produced by constant expansion of high technology industry; the increasing space consumed by structures and transportation facilities resulting in adverse environmental impacts; the obsolescence of central cities arising from expansion on the periphery. In confronting these problems planners simultaneously mitigate old contradictions and create new ones. For example, the problem of low-income housing is met by the provision of public housing. Limiting public housing to poor people results, however, in stigmatization, ugliness, and social pathology. Expanding residency to include middle-income groups overcomes this set of difficulties but clashes with the interests of property holders and developers.

5. Planners depoliticize, that is, cast in technical terms, the planning activities of the state. They further universalize the legitimating ideology by bolstering justification in the name of the public interest with arguments ostensibly based on scientific rationality. Thus, while the expanding role of the state deprivatizes all important issues, planners assist in limiting the arena of overt political conflict over benefit distribution.

> The permanent and over extending intervention of the state apparatus in the area of the processes and units of consumption makes it the real source of order in everyday life. This intervention of the state apparatus, which we call urban planning in the broad sense, involves an almost immediate politicization of the whole urban problematic, since the administrator and interlocutor of the social claims and demand tends to be, in the final analysis, the political apparatus of the dominant classes. However, the politicization thus established is not necessarily a source of conflict or change, for it may also be a mechanism of integration and participation (Castells, 1977, p. 463).

The activity of the planner, then, consists in applying conscious will to overcoming the contradictions of capitalism and in legitmizing state intervention as the product of a scientifically determined public interest. His or her role, however, while consciously conceived, is fundamentally based in the economic substructure which channels planning activity. The planner is limited first by class domination, itself rooted in the system of economic production and exchange. Second, he or she is restricted by the existing stage of urban development, analysis of which comprises the second component of planing theory and to which we now turn.

2. *Urban development*

1. Urban form reflects the mode of production and the mode by which the economic surplus is circulated. Modern production techniques, introduced for purposes of labour control as well as efficiency (see Braverman, 1974), result in land-consuming industrial development, regional shift, and urban expansion. The system of consumption and exchange produces suburbanization, high demand for consumer durables, real-estate speculation, enclaves of the rich and the poor, inadequate housing for low-income groups, and development according to the logic of finance capital.

2. Class domination expresses itself in space most obviously in the greater amenities enjoyed by the rich than the poor: 'The rich group can always enforce is preferences over a poor group because it has more resources to apply either to transport costs or to obtaining land in whatever location it chooses' (Harvey, 1973, p. 135). The consequence is that 'poor groups must, of necessity, live where they can least afford to live' (Harvey, 1973, p.137), either because rents in central places are high or access from peripheral locations to social services and jobs is poor.

The wealthy, through control of territory, do more than monopolize amenities, however. In the United States social and political boundaries coincide, allowing privileged groups to use their physical location to provide themselves with tax shelters, superior schools, élite social environments, and investment opportunities. Political defence of privilege through the enforcement of territorial boundaries increases the exchange value of land and structures with these boundaries, creating in effect a 'class monopoly rent' (Harvey, 1975).

3. The inevitable outcome of capitalist land use patterns is uneven development. Marxists reject the assumption of liberal economic planners that the pattern of 'take-off' and steady economic growth can be repeated by any country or region with entrepreneurial skill and an infusion of capital resources. Instead, capital flows rapidly and on unequal terms to places where new development ensures the highest profits, or labour can be best exploited; the proceeds from investment are

exported from those places providing the lowest production costs and returned to the centres of finance capital (see Bluestone, 1972).

4. The spatial isolation of income and racial groups simultaneously insulates the bourgeoisie from rebellion and sharpens and mobilizes class and racial conflict. The concentration of poor people and racial minorities threatens American central business district investments and fosters political unrest, albeit often without an available target. Urban planners in this situation find themselves mediating among spatially defined collectivities without being able to affect the social basis which gives rise to the unequal distribution of benefits.

II. Issues within the Marxist Paradigm

For American planners drawn to their profession by values which give priority to alleviating human misery, the Marxist paradigm raises a number of difficulties and alternative paths of action. The principal source of tension derives from the relationship between the planner and the state and the way in which state intentions are determined. Planners must inevitably confront the issue of whether their activities, even if conducted democratically and with the interests of the relatively deprived as a criterion of benefit, can avoid primarily serving capitalist objectives.

1. *Planners and the state*

The critiques of American city planning formulated in the 1960s sought to show the roots of planning, and more generally of progressivism, in upperclass protection of privilege (see Gans, 1968; Hays, 1964; Fainstein and Fainstein, 1974). A new series of prescriptions, aimed at making planning more redistributive and democratic, directed planners to offer alternatives (Davidoff and Reiner, 1962), be user-oriented (Gans, 1968), and advocate unrepresented interests (Davidoff, 1965; Fainstein and Fainstein, 1971). But these efforts were quickly attacked by radical thinkers, who claimed that planning necessarily benefited the upper class and involvement of poor people in planning activities was simply cooptive (Cloward and Piven, 1974). Thus, those planners seeking to advance the interests of deprived groups were either working contrary to their goals or were wholly ineffective (see Needleman and Needleman, 1974). The debate within America largely revolved around examinations of the practice of planners in model cities programmes or community planning boards to determine whether their behaviour did or did not produce desired outcomes.

The cooptation argument appears convincing in theory, yet has sufficient weakness to raise at least the possibility of effective action in opposition to bourgeois interests. If the state is the executive committee of the bourgeoisie and only the state sets the agenda for planning, then planning perforce serves the bourgeoisie regardless of the intentions of planners. But the capitalist state is not monolithic and has sufficient leeway to respond to non-élite interests if pressed, provided that the concessions granted are not so great as to threaten overall bourgeois hegemony. A less than deterministic conception of state actions views them as responsive to the character of state officials, on the one hand, and to the forces making demands, on the other.

The possibility of changing the character of the state through incorporation of new interests into its structure is, of course, the old question of revisionism. Within the United States the options for radical planners to participate in this process are restricted by the absence of socialist parties for which they could work directly. Even here, however, planners within the state apparatus can exploit the relative autonomy of the state and their insulation as technical experts to expose or resist policies harmful to lower and working class interests. An important, if somewhat unique, example is provided by planners in Cleveland, Ohio, a declining industrial city with a large minority population. The Cleveland City Planning Commission has committed itself to the explicit goal of 'promoting a wider range of choices for those Cleveland residents who have few, if any, choices' (Krumholz *et al.*, 1975, p. 299). Its executive director has defined an interventionist role for professional city planners:

> In Cleveland, experience indicates that planners can have considerable impact on public policy if they will do two things. First, they must become activists prepared for protracted participation and focal intervention in the decision-making process. . . . Second, . . . [they] must offer something that decision-makers want and can relate to. What the Cleveland City Planning Commission tries to offer is not rhetoric, but information, analysis, and policy recommendations that are relevant to political decision-making (Krumholz *et al.*, 1975).

The Planning Commission thus seeks to work on behalf of the lower classes without losing its main source of legitimacy and power, its professional expertise.[1]

In the absence of mass, left-oriented parties, deviants within the state bureaucracy lack social support and tend to succumb to role socialization. Nevertheless, for those state planners with links to universities or urban movements some opportunities exist, and they may enlarge during critical times. Lack of unity within the state élite can encourage crucial defections and a tendency to meet opposition movements with material concessions rather then symbolic gestures or repression.

There are many examples of local groups allied with sympathetic government planners effecting major changes in plans and policies. While concessions frequently extend no further than the withdrawal of an objectionable proposal, at times government officials are prepared to translate 'external' public pressure into positive agency programmes. Thus, citizens' organizations and urban planners opposed to a large-scale highway project in Cambridge, Massachusetts, eventually achieved a mass transit programme for the entire Boston region when a sympathetic new state secretary took office (Fellman and Brandt, 1973). Community forces likewise shifted planning emphasis from urban renewal to neighbourhood preservation and minimal residential displacement in the New York City Cooper Square Project when they linked up with allies in the City Planning Commission (Fainstein and Fainstein, 1974, pp. 43-6). North Side Forces, a community organization in the old mill town of Paterson, New Jersey, worked for ten years to construct low-income housing on a ghetto site originally declared 'too small'; success required a new national administration and change in officials within the area office of the US Department of Housing and Urban Development (Fainstein and Fainstein, 1974, pp. 130-47). If, as Piven and Cloward (1977) argue, protest works only when its takes the form of disruption, it still only achieves results when the governement chooses not to respond with overwhelming force or cold indifference. The character of the governmental response depends on the factual analysis and value orientations of those within it. The ideology of planners within government can be a crucial determinant of policy at critical moments.

The role of planners outside government is limited by their lack of resources and authority. The furore over advocacy planning has largely ebbed with the ending of financial support for community-based groups. But planners continue to assist urban political movements (see Perlman, 1976; Fainstein and Fainstein, 1974) in their efforts to block neighbourhood destruction on behalf of accumulation. Paul Davidoff (1965), who invented the term advocacy planning, has used planning expertise to strike down suburban exclusionary zoning in the courts with considerable success.

For the advocate planner, questions of cooption arise in different form from those confronting the state employee. The advocate planner often must decide when a group should drop its demands or what is the best deal obtainable. The formulation of 'realistic' alternative plans within the capitalist context seems still to imply playing according to rules laid down by the dominant power (see Hartman, 1974, chapter 8).

Nevertheless, the case is not, as Piven and Cloward suggest in a book widely read by United States leftists, that the development of operational objectives within an organizational context means giving up what gains can be obtained 'in the streets'.[2] They approach the question of tactics for insurgent groups in an oddly positivistic manner, correlating events with social policy—worker mobilization in the thirties with the Wagner Act; riots in the sixties with expansion of the welfare rolls—and assuming direct causality. They ignore simultaneous efforts at conciliation, and they tend to dismiss as inevitable subsequent repression. In fact, the attempt to find a universally valid tactical guide for social change in 'spontaneous' insurgent movements offers no greater assurance of success than did the quest for a universally rational model of planning. Protest without a programme is usually ephemeral and merely cathartic:

> Any historian of past social movements is familiar with episodes which conform exactly to the Piven-Cloward formula of escalated defiance winning concessions undisturbed by the desire to collect dues, draft constitutions, and organize congresses. But *only* historians are familiar with them, since in the absence of organization, they disappear rapidly, leaving nothing behind (Hobsbawm, 1978, p. 46).

A dialectical analysis should relate strategy to context; it begins by accepting Lenin's exhortation in *Left wing communism* (1940, p. 82) to flexibility in tactics, so as to take into account 'the *specific features'* (Lenin, 1940), p. 72, italics in original) which struggle assumes in different circumstances. For the planner working on behalf of an insurgent group, this means seeking to determine what is the interest of the group, what is attainable, and how much is lost through compromise. Switches in tactics may be valuable in themselves for their advantages in keeping the opposition off its guard (see Hirschman, 1970; Fainstein and Fainstein, 1974, chapter 7). At any rate, strategists for the weak must be constantly opportunistic, seeking leverage by whatever means can be found.

Withdrawal from the state system presents in some places another option for planners (see Morris and Hess, 1975; Institute for Self-reliance). Operating within the counter-economy of squatters, cooperatives, and subsistence production, planners cease acting as a separate cadre. They plan in the morning and fish in the afternoon. Here the problem of irrelevance arises. Are such groups being allowed to play games because of their harmlessness? Do they represent the development of alternative modes of social organization and new productive relations? Or are they simply utopians designed for internal disaffection and failure? The limitations of this mode are obvious, but again the use of energy in one direction does not preclude alternative thrusts.

The three options for planners within capitalism, of operating within the state to make its character more humane, working outside the state to affect governmental policy, and developing autonomous centres of production and distribution, are not mutually exclusive. Whether any of them can alter social conditions depends partly on general social forces. Activities which in one situation result in sell-out can in another produce gains. Diverse factors, ranging from the state of the economy, to the general level of mobilization, to which party is in power, act to expand or constrict the planner's impact. In addition the effectiveness of planners depends on the functions which planning fulfils within advanced capitalism and its importance to the maintenance of the economic systems. The question of the functions of planning for capitalism constitutes another principal issue of theoretical concern and disagreement.

2. *Planning and capitalist stability*

All observers of advanced capitalism, regardless of political view-point, have identified the expanding role of the state as a correlate of economic development. Marxists have particularly emphasized the importance of state planning for stabilizing the economy and averting system crisis:

> The [urban] planner's task is to contribute to the process of social reproduction . . . In so doing the planner is equipped with powers *vis-à-vis* the production, maintenance and management of the built environment which permit him or her to intervene in order to stabilize, to create the conditions for 'balanced growth', to contain civil strife and factional struggles by repression, cooptation or integration (Harvey, 1978, p. 223).

The development of what Hill (1978, 230-2) terms the state capitalist city, combined with various social welfare expenditures, becomes the means by which monopoly capital fends off urban catastrophe. Recognition of the management capacity of a state seemingly forever able to re-equilibrate the system, however, negates the revolutionary tendencies of capitalist contradictions unless new sources of tension are located.

Whithin the United States the force from monopoly capital pushing towards planning and rationalization is countered by conflict among governmental units and private corporations (see O'Connor, 1973, p. 89). The American government does not seek to discourage competition among regions, states and localities. Such rivalry takes the form of tax incentives and direct subsidies to developers and footloose industries, restrictions on labour unions, low-cost social services and public relations schemes. Every American locality tries to zone within its borders the most desirable uses and exclude those that are costly or noxious. The interests of fractions of capital become vested in the system of territorial mercantilism, which when reinforces intra-class disunity and limits planning capacity.

For the American left, the question becomes which tendency to applaud. The anarchy and consequent crisis of federalism and the market? Or planning in the interests of monopoly capital? All capitalist countries display the conflict between the rationalizing tendencies of large-scale production and competition among producers that Engels (edn. 1935, p. 74) termed 'the contradiction between socialized organization in the individual factory and social anarchy in production as a whole'. In the United States the aversion to rationalization through the state is extreme. The dilemma for American radical planners is whether planning which seeks to overcome this contradiction can also serve interests outside the bourgeoise. Baran and Sweezy (1966) argue that capitalist means necessarily serve capitalist ends; but do they *only* serve capitalist ends?

The specific example of housing indicates the dimensions of the dilemma. In Europe the public role in planning and supplying housing for the bottom half of the population is extensive as compared to the American system. American planners have frequently lauded the quality and scope of council housing and new town provision in Britian and Scandinavia or worker housing in Germany, seeing them as vastly superior to American public housing. Yet European social critics (Lamarche, 1976, p. 117) see these developments, which due to problems of land acquisition and policies of deconcentration are frequently located on the peripheries of metropolitan areas or in rural isolation, as devised to contain restless populations.

The contrasting cases of Europe and the United States indicate differing governmental responses to the conflicting pressures of accumulation and legitimation. In both places government sponsorship of construction contributes to accumulation. But legitimation in the United States is achieved through subsidizing homeownership for the middle class while doing little for the poor. European governments subsidize almost everyone's housing costs. The analytic problem is to determine whether such large-scale subsidy constitutes a social wage won by the working class through political action (see especially Gough, 1975) or simply a neat dovetailing of the accumulation process with cooptative efforts to provide the working class with minimally acceptable amenities.[3]

Even, however, if one accepts the possibility of a progressive state role, the institutional structure of American government inhibits its implementation. The United States presents an extremely segmented state and fragmented urban planning function. Segmentation may be seen first of all in the federal structure. Local governmental units are the primary agencies responsible for urban planning and development, while the national government provides most of the revenue for planning activities (e.g. housing, public facilities) which benefit the lower classes. As a result, local officials and professional planners who may be motivated by egalitarian concerns are nonetheless constrained by national budget decisions which reflect the interests of corporate capital and suburban voters. The social costs of insufficient urban investment remain for the most part encapsulated within urban political jurisdications.

Furthermore, at the local government level where 'community' pressure is most effectively mobilized, one finds a second kind of segmentation, this time in terms of functions. As Friedland *et al.* (1977) demonstrate, accumulation activities are usually carried out by insulated, often invisible, government departments and special authorities, while legitimation (social wage?) activities are effected by visible and relatively permeable agencies. The latter are susceptible to community pressure, but their economic resources are limited by local revenue raised principally through real estate taxation. To the extent that city governments expand redistributive programmes, they find themselves in fiscal strain; just the conditions under which capital argues for economy in 'unnecesary' expenditures, new 'economic' development projects and expanded business subsidies, in order to increase the city tax base (sometime in the unforeseeable future).

Segmentation in its various forms creates contradictory potentials for influencing the system. From one perspective the American state appears relatively pluralistic, with multiple points of political access and a good deal of local democracy. Yet from another perspective, major economic resources are bottled-up at the national level by well-organized moneyed interest groups, and in local 'accumulation' agencies such as the New York Port Authority and even the so-called economic develoment corporations for ghetto districts. When political activism confines itself to urban jurisdictions, fiscal strain may be the price of success; if it turns towards Washington, it becomes diluted without the unifying force of a working-class political party. Caught in these dilemmas, leftists are forced to guess which of their limited alternatives is more likely to be productive. Not surprisingly, given this context, local factors may make all the difference between mild success and total defeat—and variation from one city to the next in political situation itself contributes to the difficulty of creating a national programme.

Planners operating at the local level (where most work) must calculate the extent of this variability so as to devise specific strategies and educate their constituencies. Such a calculation involves both a political understanding of urban social movements and the state (see Castells, 1977) and an evaluation of the parameters set by urbanism within the framework of advanced capitalism. In other works, planners must analyse the political and economic determinants of their role and the dialectic between the two. Our discussion has so far concentrated on the political realm; the remainder of this paper examines the influence of contemporary capitalism on the American metropolis.

3. *Ruling-class actors and urbanism*

The Marxist paradigm provides not only a new set of categories through which to interpret planning activity, but also a theoretical reformulation of the character and structure of urban form and human settlement. Urban development is at once a crystallization of the forces and social relations of production, an object of production, and a determinant of economic and social life. 'Urbanism' embodies elements of substructure and superstructure, of production and consumption, of institutional patterns and group relations. Without claiming to go much beyond the level of outline, we have reduced the questions now confronting the Marxist theory of urbanism in the United States to the following central issues: (1) which substructural forces determine urban form and spatial patterning? (2) how narrowly determined is urban development by the mode of production?

While agreeing that urban form is the outcome of economic forces, Marxist urbanists disagree over which capitalists are directly responsible for urban development. The issue is whether urban form can be explained more or less directly by the interests and the activities of industrial capitalists, the ultimate producers of value for most Marxist theoreticians. David Gordon (1977), Larry Sawers (1975), and other Marxist economists (see Tabb and Sawers, 1978) have generally emphasized the primacy of industrial capital in determining urban form. David Harvey (1975), on the other hand, stresses the importance of finance capital, landlords and developers, especially in the most recent period:

Urbanism has consequently been transformed from an expression of the production needs of the industrialist to an expression of the controlled power of finance capital, *backed by the power of the state,* over the totality of the production process (Harvey, 1975, p. 165, emphasis added).

Even greater emphasis on the role of the state is found among 'structuralists' such as Castells (1977), Lojkine (1977) and Stone (1978). In their view the state penetrates deeply into the substructure, both 'backing' finance capital (Harvey, 1975) by socializing control activities and reproduction functions, and also influencing class formation and capitalist activities. Their analysis discards the equation of substructure with 'economic' activity, much less with industrial production, in favour of a complex model of multiple causality rooted in the mode of production, but also profoundly affected by the mode of distribution. The problems, as we see it, is that as one moves from Gordon, for example, through Harvey to Castells, Marxist urban theory fits better and better the empirical evidence of urban development, just as it increasingly loses its theoretical elegance and predictive power. An effort to identify the elements involved in the connection between substructure and urbanism substantiates this point.

There are, at a minimum, three elements within the substructure which interactively determine the character of urbanism. These are, first, *processes* of economic activity; second, *structures* by which economic processes are carried out and/or expressed; and, third, *active agents,* i.e. the individuals, élites, and whole fractions of capital whose behaviour in the aggregate creates and sustains processes and structures (see Fig. 1). In this scheme, the objective interests of active agents are rooted in the particular processes from which they profit as these are shaped (mediated) by political and economic institutions. The activities of these agents in turn affect processes and reinforce or alter the structural arrangements underlying urban form.

The Marxist approach identifies typical patterns of relationship among substructural elements. Thus, Gordon (1977) creates a diachronic typology showing correspondence between stages of development in the mode of production and urban type; commercial, industrial and corporate processes and structures of accumulation produce specific kinds of cities. His synchronic analyses then specify city types rooting them in the capitalist epoch during which they

PROCESSES	Production of value Extraction of value Circulation of value Reproduction of productive forces

Industrialists, Builders Landlords Bankers, Merchants Political parties and Movement organizations State officials	ACTIVE AGENTS

STRUCTURES	Spatial pattern of investment
	Spatial pattern of class and/or
	  racial occupancy
	State organization
	Physical character and organization
	  of built environment (urban form)
	Social relations of production

Fig. 1

underwent major development. Similarly, Hill (1978) equates his planned 'state capitalist city' with the advanced or monopoly capitalist mode of production and the needs of its corporate sector. Each author creates a single ideal type of urban form to root in an idealized mode of production.

Our reading of the Marxist literature suggests several tentative conclusions concerning the determinants of urban form in the United States. First, in this century, builders, mortgage lenders and land speculators have been the primary active agents in producing urbanism. Second, the industrial bourgeoisie has become decreasingly interested in the shape of specific urban environments as it has been able to free itself from the need for dense aggregations of labour power, and as capital markets have extended to regional, national, and finally, international scales. Third, the state has *always* been a direct active agent in creating urban form and socializing many of the expenses of production. (Inclusion of the state in the substructure, however, introduces a high degree of indeterminacy in the analysis.) Finally, in the present era capitalist development has been associated with a sharp spatial disaggregation of the bourgeoisie consequent to the separation of its production and consumption activities. Thus, a unified 'local' bourgeoisie is rarely the direct determinant of urban form, even in cities which start as company towns.

4. *Determination by the mode of production*

Urbanism is shaped by the capitalist mode of production; as Sawers (1975, p, 52) puts it, 'urban form flows out of and must remain consistent with the basic structure of the society of which it is a part'. Major problems surface, however, when we attempt to name those aspects of urbanism which arise directly out of the mode of production, those determined by the character of differing national and local sociopolitical systems under capitalism, and those which are constrained but not determined by either the mode of production or the typical dynamics of class conflict. Thus, interpretation of the degree of variation among advanced capitalist cities causes considerable difficulty.[4] Northern Europe does not produce South Bronxes, nor leave housing production and land use largely in private hands. The question is whether these differences are meaningful and can be explained through political analysis. In any case, the apparent variation of urban phenomena even within a single capitalist society raises troubling problems for the Marxist effort to explain urbanism within the single totality of *the* capitalist mode of production in its monopoly stage.

Whereas in the previous section we emphasized direct instigators of urban form such as mortgage bankers, now we approach the subject from a systematic perspective. State activity to control urban development must conform to the social relations of production. Moreover, it must operate within the technological capabilities of a specific historical period. The effectiveness of the bourgeois state in maintaining capitalism depends on the extent to which conscious activity can affect the social and physical environment. The potential of planning, even in the interests of monopoly capital, rests on this issue. We therefore need to know what aspects of urbanism *cannot* be controlled or negated within the capitalist mode of production, i.e. which aspects are necessarily determined by the system of capitalism and the logic (see Habermas, 1975) which confines *all* active agents within that system.

Table 1 presents three categories of factors which define the systemic quality of advanced capitalism: *structural forms* embodied within and organizing the social relations of production; *functions* which need to be performed for monopoly capital; and *technological constraints* which affect the ways in which functional needs are met, even while the development of technology is itself confined by the social relations of production. The lower right-hand cell of Table 1 summarizes certain new technological capabilities which are particularly significant in their impact on urbanism. The outline permits some general comments about the theoretical connection between the mode of production and urbanism and what seem to be general tendencies in urban development under advanced capitalism.

While system-maintaining functions can be performed in a variety of ways, historically specific forces limit the 'solutions' to capitalist functional requirements. The possibilities of capitalist praxis, including urban planning, are confined at any historical moment by four important factors. The first of these is technology. It is clear enough, for example, that corporate production requires the spatial juxtaposition of capital and labour. Under technological conditions of inefficient transportation and labour-intensive production (the big factory of 1900, say), labour *must* reside in high-density settlements within walking distance of production sites; hence, the working-class district or factory town. With new technological possibilities, the *same* functional needs can be met with suburban settlements, automobiles and super-highways.

Technological development may set more or less narrow limitations on how functions are performed, and thus on how directly determined is urbanism by capitalist social relations of production. But changes in urban form are not required by technology, except to the extent that technological capabilities have influenced the manner in which other capitalist needs have been met. Thus, corporate efficiency may depend upon a land-intensive organization or production processes which make central city locations too 'expensive' for corporate units free to externalize the social costs of their movement to the countryside.

TABLE 1. *Elements in the capitalist mode of production which constrain urban development*

Social relations of production (structures)	Functional requirements
Monopoly corporations as main units of production and institutional accumulation	*Corporate profitability* and autonomous control over corporate activities constrained only by narrowly bounded economic rationality
Families and households at main units of consumption and reproduction of labour power	Maintenance of adequate *aggregate demand* in the face of class inequality
Hierarchical division of labour in production units	Sufficient *growth* to permit continual reinvestment of surplus
Class inequality in consumption and bourgeois domination of production units	Mass *compliance* to the needs of structures arising from the social relations of production
Commoditization of labour power: mobility, standardization	*Reproduction* of social relations of production
	State coordination of corporate activities and socialization of certain expenses of reproduction, *direct state production* of goods with low profit potential

Technological constraints shaping urban form	Technological capabilities under conditions of advanced capitalism
1. *Productive power* of labour	1. With increasing development of the productive power of labour, the service sector becomes large, commodity production becomes freed from vertical systems of energy transmission (the 'high-rise' factory), and worktime is reduced and replaced with leisure, i.e. organized consumption to fulfil system-induced needs
2. *Communication technology* necessary to control within corportate units and over their markets	
3. *Transportation technology* sufficient to (a) amass labour, (b) produce agglomeration savings, and (c) connect corporations with their markets	2. Electronic communications permits spatial decentralization of corporate operations without loss in central control capabilities; computer technology simultaneously increases control capabilities without additional dependence on headquarters labour supply. Together these developments permit decentralization of productive facilities. Simultaneously, radio and television permit corporate production to an ever-larger consumption market, which does not require their proximate location.

Table 1 *(cont)*

Technological constraints shaping urban form	Technological capabilities under conditions of advanced capitalism
	3 . The advent first of railroads, and then of auto and air transportation has increasingly freed producers from topographical constraints (e.g. riverside locations). Labour forces are now highly mobile and may commute long distances to isolated production sites. Thus, even labour-intensive production is compatible with low density and dispersed urban settlement. Moreover, communication and transportation technologies reduce the connection between production location and agglomeration benefits. Finally, goods can be transported rapidly over long distances to reach spatially distant and low-density consumption markets.

Although new patterns of urbanization may be less constrained by technology than previous ones, 'older' settled areas also reflect the layering of past urban forms. A contemporary pattern of urbanism embodies previous 'solutions' to the needs of capital under diffferent conditions of technology, class structure, state organization, and so on. Present responses to functional needs are thereby limited in a second way, by the physical reification of urban forms created by the necessities and choices of prior stages. Thus, cities are composed by dense working class districts and housing patterns no longer required by monopoly capital; the location of old urban cores along natural transportation routes is a given. These layers of urbanization represent enormous sums of social capital which can no longer be created under the conditions of extreme exploitation of labour which characterized the urban past. They are simply too expensive to replace. What is done about sunk urban investment, however, is limited (mediated) by the the current mode of production. Use value may be allowed to deteriorate if profits lie in new urban development (the South Bronx versus the South-west) and if the state does not either force capitalists to recompense those hurt by their departure or regulate the movement of commerce and industry. But now we come almost full circle, introducing an historical and political specificity into the connection between urbanism and the extant mode of production, thereby raising new problems for the marxist theory of correspondence. How determined is determined?

There is a third way in which solutions to the functional needs of the capitalist mode of production are confined by the dynamics of the present capitalist system. Ruling classes develop vested interests in the institutional arrangements which maintain their privileges. Take the relationship between class hierarchies and geographical stratification. In the United States, with is particularly fragmented state structure, class relations are strongly expressed in a spatial form. The intergenerational transfer of economic position by the upper classes is tied up with local government control over school systems, for example. In northern Europe, the geographical element in dominant class reproduction is muted and replaced by an equivalent solution, in this case, class-based streaming within regional and national educational systems. New urban settlements, patterns of migration, and state planning are restricted by the particular arrangement through which class privileges are maintained. Both England and the United States are class societies, but in the latter suburban encapsulation performs the same functions as educational streaming. The implications for urbanism are thereby different. Only by recognizing nationally specific institutional facts can Marxist theory successfully explain divergent patterns of urbanization without giving way to a totally voluntaristic approach.

Fourth, alternatives to the accumulation and legitimation needs of monopoly capital are circumscribed by the goods and the bill of goods which have already been sold to the public. The case of the automobile is most interesting in this regard. As a mass consumption item with continuous obsolescence built in, automobile sales help maintain sufficient aggregate demand for corporate profitability, among the automobile producers themselves, and also among a whole panoply of other capitalists who are subcontractors, manufacturers of related products, or suppliers of fuel, road-repair services, and the like. Now that the United States has come so far with the automobile, a turnaround is extremely difficult. It is not only that roads have been built, and factories located along these roads, and low-density suburbs constructed which are only accessible by car. Equally important, the availability of the automobile serves to legitimize the system which has sold that auto as an indicator of economic well-being and quite literally, a source of freedom through consumption. The auto and its manufactured cultural imagery fit so well into the American identification of liberty with mobility as to preclude a change of direction now, energy shortages and pollution notwithstanding. Thus, while dependence on the auto is not itself a necessary outcome of the capitalist mode of production, those societies where the auto gained early hegemony in affecting both mass consumption patterns and urbanizaton have little choice but to drive on by car.[5]

Our analysis leaves unanswered the question of the direct impact of planning on the urban environment. From the previous discussion we would expect that the answer cannot be provided in general. On the one hand, specific paths of institutional development have produced stronger or weaker planning capabilities in capitalist states (Fainstein and Fainstein, 1978). On the other hand, the effectiveness of planning efforts is mediated by balances of class power, the severity of urban contradictions and, significantly, by the political effects of planning programmes themselves (Heidenheimer *et al.,* 1975, 278). Accordingly, a considerable amount of national variation will be found both in urban development and in the role of planning praxis in shaping urban form. To say more requires empirical studies, both historical and comparative.

III. Theory and Practice

Marxist theory and radical planning practice have lived uneasily with one another, in part because marxism cannot provide a completely satisfactory guide for what planners should do and still remain planners, and in part because seemingly radical planning activities have themselves been demystified by marxism. Thus, marxism points to the severe limitations of the most typical forms of left-oriented planning activity. Radical advocacy, from a Marxist perspective, suffers from its cooptative tendencies, its negation of the planning function and transformation of planners into political agitators (thereby raising questions about the special legitimacy of planners to lead the masses), and its inability to move beyond triumphs of veto and negation to orchestrated, positive, system-wide movement. Guerrillas in the bureaucracy are seen as weak and easily eliminated, or more likely, absorbed into seemingly progressive activities which further legitimize the system even if they do not directly facilitate capitalist accumulation. Utopian withdrawals, e.g. tenant management, rural communalism, are viewed as having little potential for benefiting the masses of the urban poor, or for creating an objectively based social force for institutional reform. That such activities continue even while leftist planners may read marxism on the side suggests both that planning practice (of any political orientation) has never depended much on planning theory, and that Marxist theory leaves little room for progressive action by planners, at least within the American context.

The disjunction between leftist planning roles and Marxist theory is itself a reflection of two theoretical tendencies within the Marxist analyses which have, until recently, been most popular in the United States. First, marxism has not only demystified many elements in the capitalist system by showing their functions for system maintenance; it has also shown that planners, cloaked in an ideology of professionalism, even of reform professionalism, are intellectually naked (Harvey, 1978). Yet, by being unable to describe what a Marxist professional planner in a capitalist society would think or do, Marxist theory seems to have undermined the main power resource monopolized by planners as they confront other officials and capitalists, that is, their professional expertise. Leftist planners who do not themselves believe in their professionalism must either be two-faced, be easily replaced by planners who do believe, or see the planning function narrowed and weakened. Second, Marxist theory seems to advance a fully determinist analysis of urban development which leaves little room for activity which is not either in the interests of bourgeois accumulation or system legitimation. The cumulative impact of the determinism of David Gordon and the radical populism of Piven and Cloward leads intellectually alive radical planners to conclude that system change lies in the mode of production of which they are *not* a part, or in spontaneous rebellion which they can only deflect and dissipate.

The version of the Marxist paradigm which we have emphasized in this paper cannot tell practising planners what to do. But it can show them both the determinist elements in capitalist societies and the areas in which 'progressive' planning can make a difference. Several roles have been suggested for leftist planners, though the possibilities are greater in western Europe than in the United States. Planners may be part of an emerging class of technical experts whose functions are needed by capitalists, but whose working conditions are becoming increasingly proletarianized. This 'new class' does not derive its income from ownership and is committed to a technical rationality which may help transform capitalism. The question, of course, is whether such a transformation will be progressive. In good part the answer must depend upon whether the technical strata ally themselves with a proletarian movement, an especially unlikely prospect in the United States. Whether or not there is a powerful proletarian party, however, planners can exacerbate capitalist crises by action as system-demystifiers, by using their expert knowledge to show the consequences for the lower classes of solutions proposed by monopoly capital. Planners can create alternative solutions which address systemic problems, but do so with minimal harm to the lower classes. Thus, practising planners can advance working class interests so long as these are not directly opposed to those of the ruling class, and so long as they are aided by a force from below. Improving life for the lower classes, from this Marxist perspective, is at least as likely to result in further contradictions of capitalism as to eliminate a revolutionary potential.

But what about the situation in the United States, where there is neither a proletarian party nor much working class consciousness? What propositions should guide leftist planners besides a correct understanding of the system and a self-reflective view of their role therein? We suggest three, each of which comes back to the central issues of Marxist theory and could be much debated.

1. The better the better, as opposed to 'the worse the better'. To the extent that planning furthers the material situation of the lower classes it is progressive, even it it legitimizes the system in the short run. The issue is then whether a particular programme such as Community

Development Block Grants actually provides poor communities with material benefits. Given a choice between social control being exercised through symbolic manipulation or coercion on the one hand, and bribery on the other, Marxist urbanists should support bribery.

2. The more planning the better. The lower classes are better served by planning in the collective interest of monopoly capital than by the unplanned outcomes of market forces. To the extent that liberal states must be responsible for urban outcomes because they have been planned within the political sphere, such outcomes are more likely to reflect at least partially the interests of the lower classes than will the results of 'the economy' left to its narrow, profit-oriented rationality.

3. The expansion of the planning and welfare state should be encouraged. State capitalism in liberal regimes represents a marked improvement over market capitalism from the perspective of the proletariat. The larger the public sector, the greater the possibilities of proletarian political forces directing benefits to the lower classes, and the smaller the sector of the population dependent upon maintaining capitalist institutions. The expansion of the state is more likely to mark a transition to socialism than its alternative.

These propositions are both general and assume that revolutionary crisis is remote in America. Marxist theory cannot do much more for the practice of left planners, however, until it begins to inform the activities of the rest of the population. And there are good 'Marxist reasons' why this is an unlikely development in the United States (Karabel, 1979).

IV References

Baran P. A. and Sweezy, P. M. (1966) *Monopoly Capital.* New York: Monthly Review Press.

Bluestone, B. (1972) 'Economic crisis and the law of uneven development', *Politics and Society* 3 (Fall), 65-82.

Braverman, H. (1974) *Labor and Monopoly Capital.* New York: Monthly Review Press.

Castells, M. (1977) *The Urban Question: a Marxist Approach.* Cambridge, Massachusetts: MIT Press; London; Edward Arnold.

Cloward, R. A. and Piven, F. F. (1974) *The Politics of Turmoil.* New York: Pantheon.

Davidoff, P. (1965) 'Advocacy and pluralism in planning', *Journal of the American Institute of Planners* 31 (December), 331-8.

Davidoff, P. and Reiner, T. (1962) 'A choice theory of planning', *Journal of the American Institute of Planners* 28 (May), 103-15.

Engels, F. (edn. 1935) *Socialism, Utopian and Scientific.* New York: International Publishers.

(edn. 1970) *The Housing Question.* Moscow: Progress Publishers.

Fainstein, S. S. and Fainstein, N. I. (1971) 'City planning and political values', *Urban Affairs Quarterly* **6** (March), 341-62.

(1974) *Urban Political Movements.* Englewood Cliffs, New Jersey: Prentice-Hall.

(1978) 'National policy and urban development', *Social Problems* **26** (December), 125-46.

Fellman, G. and Brandt, B. (1973) *The Deceived Majority.* New Brunswick, New Jersey: Transaction Books.

Friedland, R., Piven, F. F. and Alford, R. R. (1977) 'Political conflict, urban structure, and the fiscal crisis', *International Journal of Urban and Regional Research* **1,** 447-72.

Gans, H. (1968) *People and Plans.* New York: Basic Books.

Gordon, D. (1977) 'Capitalism and the roots of urban crisis'. In Alcaly, R.E. and Mermelstein, D., editors, *The Fiscal Crisis of American cities,* New York: Vintage.

Gough, I. (1975) 'State expenditures in advanced capitalism', *New Left Review* no. 92, 53-92.

Habermas, J. (1975) *Legitimation Crisis,* Boston: Beacon Press.

Harloe, M., editor (1977) *Captive Cities,* Chichester and New York: Wiley.

Hartman, C. (1974) *Yerba Buena: land grab and community resistance in San Francisco,* San Francisco, Glide Publications.

Harvey, D. (1973) *Social Justice and the City,* Baltimore: Johns Hopkins University Press; London: Edward Arnold.

(1975) 'Class monopoly rent, finance capital and the urban revolution'. In Gale, S. and Moore, E. G., editors, *The Manipulated City,* Chicago: Maaroufa Press.

(1978) 'On planning the ideology of planning'. In Burchell, R. W. and Sternlieb, G., editors, *Planning Theory in the 1980s,* New Brunswick, New Jersey: Rutgers University, Center for Urban Policy Research.

Hays, S. P. (1964), 'Politics of reform in municipal government in the progressive era, *Pacific Northern Quarterly* (October), 157-69.

Heidenheimer, A. J., Heclo, H. and Adams, C. T. (1975) *Comparative Public Policy,* New York: St Martin's Press.

Hill, R. C. (1978) 'Fiscal collapse and political struggle in decaying central cities in the United States'. In Tabb and Sawers, 1978.

Hirschman, A. O. (1970) *Exit, Voice and Loyalty,* Cambridge, Massachusetts: Harvard University Press.

Hobsbawm, E. J. (1978) 'Review of Piven and Cloward' *Poor People's Movements. New York Review of Books* **25** (March 23), 44-8.

Institute of Self-Reliance: *Self-Reliance.* Periodical, published bi-monthly.

Karabel, J. (1979) Review of W. Sombart, *Why is there no Socialism in the United States? New York Review of Books* **26** (February 8), 22-5.

Krumholz, N., Cogger, J. M. and Lenner, J. H. (1975) 'The Cleveland policy planning report', *Journal of the American Institute of Planners* **41** (September), 298-304.

(1978) 'Make no big plans . . . planning in Cleveland in the 1970s'. In Burchell, R. W. and Sternlieb, G., editors, *Planning Theory in the 1980s,* New Brunswick, New Jersey: Rutgers University, Center for Urban Policy Research.

Lamarche, F. (1976) 'Property development and the economic foundations of the urban question'. In Pickvance, 1976.

Lenin, V. I. (1940) *Left Wing Communism: an Infantile disorder,* New York: International Publishers.

Lindberg, L., Alford, R., Crouch, C. and Offe, C., editors (1975) *Stress and Contradiction in Modern Capitalism,* Lexington, Massachusetts: D.C. Heath.

Lojkine, J. (1977) 'Big firm's strategies, urban policy and urban social movements.' In Harloe, 1977.

Marx, K. and Engels, F. (edn. 1947) *The German Ideology,* New York: International Publishers.

Miliband, R. (1977) *Marxism and Politics,* New York: Oxford University Press.

Morris, D. J. and Hess, K. (1975) *Neighbourhood Power,* Boston: Beacon Press.

Needleman, M. and Needleman, C. E. (1974) *Guerrillas in the Bureaucracy,* New York: Wiley.

O'Connor, J. (1973) *The Fiscal Crisis of the State,* New York: St Martin's Press.

Perlman, J. E. (1976) 'Grassrooting the system', *Social Policy* **7** (September/ October), 4-20.

Pickvance, C. G., editor (1976) *Urban Sociology: Critical Essays,* New York: St Martin's Press: London: Tavistock.

Piven, F. F. (1975) 'Planning and class interests', *Journal of the American Institute of Planners* **41** (September), 308-10.

Piven, F. F. and Cloward, R. (1977) *Poor People's Movements,* New York: Pantheon.

Sawers, L. (1975) 'Urban form and the mode of production', *Review of Radical Political Economy* **7**, 52-68.

Sawyer M. (1976) 'Income distribution of OECD countries', *OECD Economic Outlook, Occasional studies,* July, 3-36.

Stone, M. E. (1978) 'Housing, mortgage lending, and the contradictions of capitalism'. In Tabb and Sawers, 1978.

Tabb, W. E. and Sawers, L., editors (1978) *Marxism and the Metropolis,* New York: Oxford University Press.

Notes

1. For a discussion of the accomplishments of the Commission, see Krumholz *et al,* 1978. Interestingly, one of the leading radical critics of city planning and reformism, Frances Fox Piven, describes the activities of the Cleveland planners as 'compelling, even stirring'. She contends: 'Their efforts suggest that the rest of us, eased by our murky professional doctrines, have not really tested the boundaries of what it is possible for us to do as city planners. We have not discovered whether our skills in analysis and data gathering can be put to the service of working-class and poor people just as they have been put to use against them. We have not discovered this because we have not tried' (1975, p.309).

2. '. . . Insurgency is always short-lived. Once it subsides and the people leave the streets, most of the organizations which it temporarily threw up and which élites helped to nurture simply fade away. As for the few organisations which survive, it is because they become more useful to those who control the resources on which they depend than to the lower class groups which the organizations claim to represent. Organizations endure, in short, by abandoning their oppositional politics' (Piven and Cloward, 1977, p.xi).

3. More generally the various routine provisions of the welfare state—health insurance, disability benefits, old-age pensions, family allowances, and shelter subsidies—seem clearly to represent gains for the working classes. But they are gains

largely financed by the same groups which receive them. The state acts in order to ensure coordination and predictability and to effect horizontal transfers (i.e. from young to old, from healthy to disabled). The working class thus depends on the interventionist state to rationalize its interests through providing socialized mechanisms for raising and distributing revenue in accordance with long-term needs. The state role in this respect in analogous to the one it plays for the upper class—to act as a relatively autonomous agent to respond to long-term class needs. It does not act on behalf of the proletariat against the bourgeoisie but rather mediates the interests of fractions of the working class. The welfare state is more redistributive in some countries than others, but even in Sweden and the Netherlands, which are the most egalitarian, the ratio of income shares received by the top and bottom deciles after taxation is seven to one; in the US this ratio is 15:1 (Sawyer, 1976).

4. This 'difficulty' is more often avoided than addressed head on. Sawers (1975), for example, discusses cases of socialist urbanization, but does not attempt to demonstrate what is uniquely capitalist (or even American) about US patterns. O'Connor (1973) largely ignores national variations among capitalist states and avoids dealing with the question of just how determined state activity is by the mode of production.

5. In northern Europe, where urban sprawl has been better contained that in the US and where mass-transit systems provide alternative modes of transportation, the automobile has finally arrived. In good part this may be so because of the role played by the US as the advertising leader of world capitalism. To the extent that American capitalists have shown the world the good life, they have conditioned mass expectations to the auto age. A chicken in every pot has become a car in every garage, even in societies where cultural conditions were initially less favourable to auto motion.

Local Government as Local State

CYNTHIA COCKBURN*

We need a view of local government that explains the connections thrown up in this story of corporate management, the working connections between central government and the local government, local councils and other state authorities at local level, connections between the world of government and the world of business. We need an analysis that sets local government in the context of the real economic situation of the period in which we live and asks: what is its job? Such an approach involves stepping outside the conventional frame of reference and seeing local government, our old red-brick town hall, for what it really also is: a key part of the state in capitalist society. Such a step doesn't come easily. We have been taught to think of local government as a kind of humane official charity, a service that looks after us 'from the cradle to the grave', protects us from the misfortunes of life, hardships such as poverty and homelessness that fall on us by fate—or are perhaps even our own fault. If the town hall doesn't seem to work in our interest we put it down to 'inefficiency' or 'red tape'. It is by no means obvious that a local council is part of a structure which *as a whole and in the long term* has other interests to serve than our own.

There is no ready-made theory of local government: It is necessary to piece together a number of concepts about the state as a whole and draw conclusions from them for local government. There are three fundamental ideas in the early writings of Marx on which later work has built. They are crucial for any real understanding of the role of local government. The first of these is that the state can only be understood by looking at the way wealth is produced in a particular society. It is specific to the mode of production.

*Originally published as Chapter 2 of *The Local State,* London, Pluto Press, 1977.

175

> The social structure and the state are continually evolving out of the life pro-
> cesses of definite individuals, but of individuals, not as they appear in their own
> or other peoples' imagination, but as they really are, i.e. as they operate, pro-
> duce materially and hence as they work under definite material limits, presup-
> positions and conditions, independent of their will.[1]

We cannot think of the state in the abstract—it is always specific to an historical time and place. In reaching an understanding of the local state in Britain today, therefore, we should be clear that this is to say little about the nature of the local state arising from different modes of production.[2]

The second basic idea is that the state in capitalism is an instrument of class domination, that in the modern state the bourgeoisie, the dominant class who won capital and employ workers, holds political sway.[3] As such, the state is at the heart of the perennial struggle between the bourgeoisie and those it exploits—the working class. Indeed it exists because of this struggle, because the society has become entangled in an insoluble contradiction with itself and is irreconcilably divided.[4] In looking at the state as we know it, then, even our own London borough local state, we cannot avoid considering local and national class interests.

The third theme in the original Marxist concept of the state is that its characteristic function is repression: its main role is to keep the working class in its place and to set things up, with forceful sanctions, in such a way that capital itself, business interests as a whole, normally survive and prosper. The state in this view is seen as above all being the armed forces, the police, the judges and courts of law.

We should look in more detail at these last two ideas, the relationship of the state to class, and the changing role of the state. They have been amplified by recent work, some of which can help the understanding of local government. This contemporary theory, though, in no way weakens the identification of the state with the economic base of society, nor as the agent of capital. What it does is to increase the scope of the services the state is seen as performing for capital and explain in more detail how it performs them. In looking at these two developments of Marxist theory we can see too how they make sense of changes in local government and its management system.

Class and State: the Hidden Links

To take the first question first: how do such relationships between class and state find expression in a pace like Lambeth? One way of describing the population of Lambeth is in terms of their type of occupation. This distribution is given in Table 1 which shows, clustering in the north and central ward of the borough, a population, mainly of

Table 1. *Lambeth's population described by the occupations of its male workers*[5]

	North Lambeth (%)	Central Lambeth (%)	South Lambeth (%)
Group A: employers and managers, professional workers, etc.	8.5	12.0	20.0
Group B: foremen and supervisors, etc.	33.0	31.0	30.0
Group C: non-manual, clerical, sales, etc.	20.5	25.0	29.0
Group D: unskilled manual workers, etc.	38.0	32.0	21.0
Total male workers	100.0	100.0	100.0

relatively poor people, semiskilled or unskilled workers or unemployed; and in the more salubrious southern wards a population that is relatively better-off, with more skilled manual, professional and managerial people. The territorial boundary is not as distinct, of course, as this summary implies. The popular view, and one which seems to be shared by the Conservative and Labour councillors in Lambeth, is that such statistical distributions demonstrate a borough divided into a middle class and a working class who are in competition with each other over the rate burden and for the resources of which the council disposes. Indeed the council seems sometimes to forment differences between different groups of residents for the purposes of control. False categories are played off against each other, the 'ratepayer' against 'the council tenant', 'council tenant' against 'homeless' or 'squatter'. This definition of relatively minor differences of interest obscures a much more fundamental class division that operates in Lambeth—one which the authorities are at pains *not* to invoke. This is the division between this urban population as a whole and the class that owns capital in Lambeth, controls its land and employs its workers, collects both rents from the tenants and interest on the mortgages taken out by owner-occupiers. Seen this way, it is laughable to suppose that the owner-occupiers of Norwood or Streatham in the south, taken as a category, are the class enemy of the council tenants of Vassall and Angell wards in the north. With their semi-detached properties and a couple of thousand pounds invested through a unit trust, many are as vulnerable to the bankers, brokers and building societies as tenants are to landlords. They may sometimes act competitively with the poorer working class, they may vote Tory. But the real dominant class of Lambeth are infinitely more powerful than this, and are in the main invisible.[6]

Lambeth is mainly a domitory area. Many manufacturing firms have moved away. We shall see why and with what effect in Chapter 3. Those that remain are on the whole the smaller and less competitive firms. This face of the local bourgeoisie seems relatively aged and feeble. The class forces that work more powerfully on Lambeth's population are the shareholders and directors of commercial firms in the City of Westminster that employ Lambeth's commuters, the finance companies in the City of London and abroad from whom the council borrows a fair proportion of its massive loan, and whose operations lie behind so many movements of capital in the borough. The property dealers and speculators that own and develop Lambeth's land: shareholders of building companies that find their business in its housing programmes; professionals in the big firms of estate agents, solicitors and quantity surveyors that make a livelihood out of these processes—few of these live in the borough, but they are its dominant class nonetheless.

If we have to dissolve the borough boundary to see the real class divisions that exist there, we have to do the same in order to see the real 'local' authorities. It is clearly not the council alone that represents the state at local level. The powerful business interests scarcely notice a local council. Deals that matter most to them, over taxation and employment policy, grants and controls, are deals done with Westminster and Whitehall. The council is only a small part of a large state structure.

The state nationally has its headquarters in London but it comprises nationwide and permanent institutions. The armed forces, the judiciary and the police are found in local barracks, courts of law and police stations. In the same way central government departments dealing with education, housing and health, while they may have large offices in London SW1, carry out their work in and through schools and education offices; housing estates and local housing departments; hospitals and local health authorities. These are often technically the responsibility of a local council or other local or regional authority. Their officials nonetheless are state employees. Certain services are administered locally direct by the central state—one such is social security, another is the post office. Together these local agencies make up the state at local level.

It is widely believed that local government is in some way constitutionally independent of central government. Herein lies the source of the confusion, for example, over the question of whether or not we are seeing a 'decline in local democracy'. Central government has more and more of a say in local government affairs. But if local councils' responsibilities and activities and expenditure are continually increasing, as they have done for many decades, how can it be that we are witnessing a decline in local government, which many officers and councillors in local government believe to be so? The misapprehension lies in the belief that local councils spring from some ancient right of grassroots self-government. This is not the case. They are, and under capitalism have always been, subject to central government. Lord Redcliffe-Maud, probably the most authoritative voice on local government in Britain and chairman of three major commissions, insists:

> Local government in modern England is the creation of Parliament . . . the organs of local government today take all their important characteristics from Acts of Parliament. Further, Parliament has not been content merely to give them powers and a set of bounds beyond which they may not pass: in some cases it has also positively prescribed what they must do. Local authorities are thus obliged to provide certain services and allowed to provide others. They can do practically nothing else which costs money.[6]

Thus local authorities, including local health, water and transport authorities as well as local education, housing and planning authorities, are aspects of the national state and share its work. When I refer to Lambeth Borough Council as 'local state' it is to say neither that it is something distinct from 'national state', nor that it alone represents the state locally. It is to indicate that it is part of a whole.

As to the relations between state and capital, it should not be surprising that it is difficult to see direct and immediate connections. The dominant class operating upon Lambeth, as anywhere, is divided into fractions with somewhat different interests. Although the prospects of all of them objectively depend in the long run on the health and growth of the capitalist system, big city finance may well have different short-run interests, when it comes to developments in Lambeth, to those, say, of local manufacturing industry. The state can hardly play to so many marginally different interests the simple role of 'secretariat'. The several 'fractions' of capital cannot alone overcome their economic differences. Besides, the militancy of the working class aggravates their problems. So the capitalist state looks after the bourgeoisie's interests as a whole and sets up and maintains the cultural and political domination of the working class that capitalism as a whole needs if it is to continue.[7]

In order to do its work of organising the dominant classes and politically disorganising the working class, the state keeps a certain distance from any one bourgeois fraction.[8] It does not directly or continuously represent, for instance, Times Furnishing of Brixton Road, Imperial Chemical Industries or the International Monetary Fund. It is not entirely in the pocket of the products of Malborough and Eton; or of the legal profession or the top military. It could not do its work for capital if it were. An example of this relative autonomy of the state was the transfer of corporate management from capitalist enterprise to local government—the world of business did not intervene directly; the routes taken by the new management principles were various and indirect.

In spite of its multiplicity, however, the state preserves a basic unity. All its parts work *fundamentally* as one. In the corporate management movement we saw how central government, local government, the universities and research institutes, the professional associations and the political parties worked together, achieving an effective change in a short time. In Lambeth the homeless are finding, likewise, that the police, the electricity board, the gas corporation, the social security and the local council reveal a practical unity in their efforts to put an end to squatting. This detached integrity is important at an ideological level too because it helps to perpetuate the idea that the state does not represent the particular interest of capital but the general interest, the general will, the political unity of 'the people and nation', bosses and workers alike.

Nominally in control of the permanent structure of the state is a changeable component: the elected bodies. They comprise both Parliament and the many elected local councils.

The conventional view of electoral representative government takes two forms. For those who believe that the nation is basically united in its interests, the democratic process exists to give form to this consensus. For those who take the liberal view that uncontrolled *laissez-faire* has detrimental effects on ordinary people, the democratic process exists to keep a check on capital's excesses, looking for fair solutions. But if the state is, as the materialist view supposes, an expression of dominant class interests in capitalism, existing specifically to perpetuate a class system, neither of these conventional views holds water. What part then do elections and a political party system play?

One of the contradictions of capitalism is the necessity of maintaining a class system while at the same time weaning the working class away from class identification that could lead to class militancy. Electoral democracy, with its set of political parties, helps in this situation in that it appears, to those who insist on thinking in class terms, to enable adequate representation of the working class. Yet it also contrives to appear classless in a classless society.

The engagement of a social-democratic party 'of the working class' in such a system is an important mechanism for legitimating state power, for securing the cooperation of working class leaders, channelling political action into an institutional mould. It ensures a cutting-off of the political activity of the working class from its economic power and organisation on the shop floor of industry. Ralph Miliband has documented the history of the young, idealist Labour Party of the first two decades of this century. The members of parliament that the labour movement had hoped would put working class interests on the agenda of the House of Commons were manipulated and co-opted into a 'national interest'.[10] Miliband chronicles many instances in which the Labour Party leadership was led to forfeit working class interests in their concern 'to reassure the dominant classes and the business elites as to their intentions, to stress that they conceived their task in 'national' and not in 'class' terms, to insist that their assumption of office held no threat to business.'[11] We should not be surprised, then, when a Labour group on a local council espouse the principles of corporate planning and urban management, as they did in Lambeth. We should be surprised if they did not. In their turn, as Miliband showed, the left-wing radicals of the Labour Party are transformed as they step into the Party's national leadership.[12] Likewise we should not expect the handful of militant leftwing backbenchers in the Lambeth Labour Group to attain high office, or having atained it, to keep it unless they modify their former political stance.

The process of parliament and of local councils serves to institutionalise class contest and to project a colourless version of the fundamental struggle that takes place elsewhere. The state has, besides, developed certain defences against the incursions of working class interests via parliament and councils.[13] As the working-class won the vote in the reform acts of the late nineteenth and early twentieth centuries and came to be in a position to send their representative to Westminster, the power of Parliament gradually receded into the civil service and to the cabinet, more amenable to the permanent interests of the state. Likewise, in Lambeth and other local authorities power long ago shifted from the Council Chamber to committee and thence, with the introduction of corporate management, to the top-level Policy Committee. Leftwing backbenchers are left with the trappings of power—the real thing lies with the leadership, those who are ready to adopt the proper behaviour of urban managers. And a Labour leadership showing any tendency to socialist zeal is quickly curbed by the decision-making power of senior permanent officials.

The story of Clay Cross provides a recent illustration of these mechanisms at work. The militant Labour councillors of Clay Cross, a small coal-mining town in Derbyshire, refused to implement the Conservative Housing Finance Act, 1971, which would have required them to raise the rents of their council tenants. At first they were only one among many Labour-controlled councils to stand out against the Act. One by one, however, the others capitulated until finally it was only Clay Cross councillors who stood firm against the threat of personal bankruptcy. (The state has the power to 'surcharge' elected members personally for council expenditure that is outside the bounds sanctioned by government.) The working class of Clay Cross were for a brief period fully represented by their 'representative' council—the class struggle had been extended from the coalfield to the council chamber. But the conditions for such an achievement in local electoral democracy are rare and, when they occur, short-lived. A Housing Commissioner was despatched to Clay Cross by central government to bring the Labour group to heel and to administer housing directly. The District Auditor was sent in to assess the cost of the councillors' revolt. The members were taken to court and the Labour Party nationally failed to stand by its local militants. By a neat, but not altogether fortuitous, turn of fate, the local government reorganisation following the 1972 Act, implemented some months later, wiped the local authority of Clay Cross from the map of government.[14]

This tendency in parliamentary democracies clearly does not lead to an absolute condition of working class impotence, nor is the struggle all sham for being institutionalised. In Clay Cross it was real enough. The play within the structure of the state, needed to enable the co-ordination of the interests of a divided dominant class, also affords opportunities for working-class militancy to win concessions. The stance of the state at any one time will depend in part on the pressures brought to bear by the working class. The situation is dynamic: the state is not tightly in control of circumstance but is continually coping with a changing balance of power. Though capital and the state *structure* the situation of struggle, they by no means always have the initiative. This gives meaning to the several stages of the introduction of the new management measures into local authorities, as we shall see.

Welfare State: Serving or Servicing?

To move now to the second question, that of the practical job of the state in modern capitalism. Recent history, the growth of a 'mixed economy' and of a welfare state, has made it clear beyond all doubt that the state has an economic as well as a purely repressive role in society. This is not to deny that the state uses force for political ends—Northern Ireland is a contemporary reminder. Nor that it is indifferent to property rights—witness the current proposals for tightening the law of conspiracy and trespass. These roles remain as crucial to capital as ever. But, because of changes in capitalism, it has been forced to intervene increasingly in the economic sphere.

The state's primary role is continually *to reproduce the conditions within which capitalist accumulation can take place.* In many of its economic interventions it does this more or less directly. It attempts to control the economy and its business cycles, deflating, reflating and so on. It provides cheap utilities (power, communications, etc.) that help national industry to compete with foreign capital. In response to a decline in manufacturing industry the state has recently taken on yet more direct intervention, investing capital in ailing firms, affording grant-aid and tax relief to more. 'Planning agreements' introduced by the Industry Act, 1975 are a further step: an attempt to integrate company development with state economic planning. What is sought (in the words of Lord Ryder, the ex-chairman of Reed International and current chairman of the government's National Enterprise Board) is a 'cooperative partnership with industry'.[15]

The term 'mixed economy' is often used to describe the situation that results from the state's direct intervention in economic matters, implying a half-socialist hybrid. This is misleading. Nationalised enterprises such as road, rail, electricity and gas undertakings are more significant to industry in assuring cheap basic utilities than they are to the worker—who finds himself in an unchanged wage relationship with them. They may be termed 'mixed economy' but 'whatever ingenious euphemism may be invented for them, these are still in all essentials and despite the transformations which they have undergone, authentically capitalist societies'.[16]

So the state intervenes directly and increasingly in productive aspects of the capitalist economy—it exhorts, regulates, controls, buys and invests. Typically this is the role of the central state, of Westminster and Whitehall. But local authorities too are increasingly involved directly in the affairs of capital. A number of recent studies have traced the connections between local councils and local business.[17] The Community Land Act, 1975, obliging councils to buy and manage redevelopment land, will involve an urban council such as Lambeth more deeply with property and finance capital; many have already tried out profit-sharing schemes, and councils are increasingly interested in investing share capital in local firms.[18]

Figure 1 shows the state role of 'contributing to capitalist production' and places it adjacent to another function, called 'contributing to capitalist REPRODUCTION'. This reproduction role we have to look at more closely, because it is in this that more of the activities of local councils, certainly those we think of as most typically town hall business, can be found. To understand management developments like corporate planning and community development in local authorities it is necessary to understand *what it is* that local government is trying to manage.

The capitalist system is based upon production, what goes on in the mines, factories, farms and building sites. But naturally, if production is to continue indefinitely, it also depends on renewing, extending and modernising all the time the 'general conditions' and means of production. Capitalist societies must therefore have mechanisms for REPRODUCING themselves.[19] Specifically, two things must be reproduced. First, the productive *forces*. Second, the existing *relations* of production.

Renewing productive forces means, at one level, that capital, machinery, raw materials, building and so on must be continually forthcoming. Even in this limited respect it is easy to see that one firm alone cannot provide for its future in this way. One company exists in a whole linked structure. The machinery it needs for its processes is the manufactured product of a second firm. The steel for that machinery originates in a third. A sure supply of raw materials and growing export markets depends on external relations between nations. Nothing less than a system is needed.

At another level, though, there is *labour power* to reproduce as well: the capacity of men and women to work is the most important productive force. This process of reproducing labour power goes on mainly outside the firm. It occurs on the whole by giving people wages

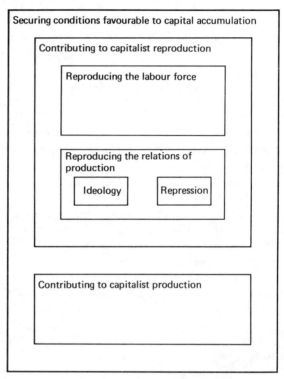

Fig. 1. Functions of the state in capitalism.

so that they can do it for themselves, buy their own food and housing and pay for their transport to work. But capital needs labour that is skilled and appropriate to the job, and the type and level of labour changes continually. It is no use reproducing the labour of the 1930s for the industry of the 1970s. The state therefore takes steps, on behalf of the capitalist class collectively, to do the job of *extended reproduction*: to plan for and provide education, housing, health and social services for the country as a whole.

The role of the state in reproducing the labour force existed from the earliest days of capitalism. The factory system called for state intervention in such matters as conditions and hours of child and female labour. The capitalist system could not go on indefinitely using up several generations of labour in the space of one.[20] The state also had to intervene quite early on in regulating the condition of housing and later in actually providing working-class dwellings. It was already in the nineteenth century involved in the provision of basic free education.

But it is in this century that the state's responsibility for the reproduction of the labour force has increased dramatically. National insurance was introduced before the First World War. The share of council building in all house building increased rapidly in the twenties and thirties. And after the Second World War the State's education system was rationalised and extended in the Education Act 1944; a National Health Service was set up; and the national insurance scheme was greatly extended. As the country recovered from the war a massive urban reconstruction and public housing programme was set in motion. Local councils were, in the main, the agencies made responsible for this extended task.

In looking at the local state management systems in this book we are at the heart of the contradictions intrinsic to the local state. There is no way therefore we can evade confronting these basic contradictions fully now, as they apply to capitalist reproduction. These services through which the state plays its part in reproducing the labour force are also services won by the working class. Years of militancy and negotiation lie behind council housing and the National Health Service. Though the capitalist mode of production may perpetuate the exploitation of the working class, workers nevertheless have to live within it. They can only build up the strength they need to challenge capitalism as a system by fighting for and and winning material concessions and democratic freedoms here and now. In this respect the welfare state was a *real* gain for the working class. Nonetheless these services are not *total* gains, because to the state and capital they are not *total* losses. As the working class has an interest in receiving services, so capital has an interest in seeing them serviced. Not only does capital need efficient and appropriate labour, it also needs to disarm working class discontent that might otherwise disrupt society. The level of public expenditure is, however, always a crucial question for the capitalist economy as a whole. The struggle thus takes place over levels of provision and over the amount of control over provision given to the consumer.

The point that it is important to establish is this. The fact that we need services in no way nullifies the fact that capitalism needs us reproduced, just as the fact that we need a job and a wage in no way invalidates the truth that capitalism needs to exploit our labour power. In the account that follows of new developments in the local state we should, in the same way, not expect to see clear-cut gains or losses for either class, but a jousting for initiative in an ever-developing situation of contradiction.

Returning to the second aspect of reproduction, if capitalism is to survive, each succeeding generation of workers must stay in an appropriate relationship to capital: the *relations* of production must be reproduced. Workers must not step outside the relation of the wage, the relation of property, the relation of authority. So 'reproducing capitalist relations' means reproducing the class system, ownership, above all reproducing a *frame of mind*.[21] Extended reproduction, in this context, calls to mind that as capital develops and its contradictions and crises develop too, so the relations of production have to shift dynamically also. This is a continual challenge and struggle for the dominant classes. Take one specially important relation, that of the local population to its local authority. In the recent official measures known as 'participation' and community development (discussed more fully in Chapters 4 and 5) (of *The Local State*) we are witnessing the extended reproduction of this particular capitalist relation.

The job of reproducing capitalist relations is done partly by actual repression and coercion. The political nature of the police in Britain is becoming more clearly recognised.[22] Nor should we underestimate the repressiveness of many agencies that appear to have only welfare functions. The benefits system is structured to induce labour discipline. Social security and the dole, with the weekly 'signing on' requirement, closely restrict the mobility and freedom of claimants. The 'cohabitation' rule ensures that a man living with a woman takes on the responsibility for maintaining her children. This rule promotes marriage, it polices the morality of women and imposes the officially-determined share-out between state and family of responsibility for the support of children. Among those on the local payroll, school attendance officers and, less overtly, teachers and social workers are asked to regulate and control behaviour. Much more typically, however, in Britain today, reproducing capitalist relations is carried out not by repression but by ideology—by inculcating a view of the world to bring about consent.

This idea makes sense to those of us who work in or struggle against or depend upon local government in Britain. It is clear to us that Lambeth council is not simply a repressive apparatus. Indeed in some ways it would be simpler (though less comfortable) if it were, because we would see more clearly what was happening to us. Instead, reproducing capitalist relations is more and more a cultural affair. It means school, social work, electoral politics. Where fascism uses force, liberal-democracy uses cultural persuasion. As Antonio Gramsci wrote fifty years ago from an Italian prison the formal apparatus of the state is only an advance trench. Behind it lies a robust chain of fortresses—which we think of very often as unofficial, private things.[23] Ideology is particularly effective in the way it permeates many apparently private and independent domains such as the family and the media. All can be enlisted this way in the defence of the capitalist mode of production and thereby the state is massively expanded.

Historically it was the church and the family that were the most important ideological extensions of the state. The church taught obedience, brotherly love, it blessed the meek and encouraged people to turn the other cheek—no recipe for militancy at work or in politics. And the family was the place where the child was inculcated with Christian virtues. Now we have many state and so-called 'private' institutions doing the original job of the church and sharing that of the family. We have a complex set of organisations embodying a single assumption: that the existing mode of production and the system of relations that goes with it are the best and only conceivable ones for us, facts of life and laws of nature. In them we create our 'common sense' and 'know' that unfairness, inequality, poverty, homelessness or failures of justice in Britain today are merely errors in the system, errors that good intentions and good management could put right. The totalitarian experiences of twentieth-century Russia and Eastern Europe 'prove' that the overthrow of capitalism must mean the end of freedom. Democracy is ranged alongside capitalism; oppression is paired with socialism: two sets of natural twins. The working class, through bourgeois culture, is offered bourgeois values without bourgeois powers. 'The bourgeoisie poses itself as an organism in continuous movement, capable of absorbing the entire society, assimilating it to its own cultural and economic level. The entire function of the state has been transformed; the state has become an 'educator'.[24]

Local State: Family Partnership

A local authority such as Lambeth Borough Council is deeply involved in reproducing the local labour force. Though it is not, itself, an all-purpose authority it nonetheless runs housing and social services, leisure and recreation facilities. It pays a higher authority (the Greater London Council) to educate its children; the Metropolitian Police to control them; and it collaborates with the Area Health Authority to keep them fit. The state at local level is, naturally enough, that aspect of the state as a whole that specialises in the relationship with the individual. 'Local government' is a face-to-face affair. The rent officer, the social worker, the school teacher—these represent the government to the man, woman and child in the 'client' population. Normally, however, and by preference, the state deals not with individuals but with *families*. More often than not it deals with the *woman* of the family. Who answers the door when the social worker calls? who talks to the head teacher about the truant child? who runs down to the rent office? the woman, wife and mother.

Why the family and why the woman? Because the primary responsibility for capitalist reproduction, regardless of the growing intervention of the state, remains that of the family. 'The costs of reproduction borne by the state would be infinitely greater, both if adequate socialised care were provided for all the dependants, both children and others, that have remained women's responsibility within the family and if women were to receive equal state benefits in their own right.'[25] The state is dominant in the enterprise, but it cannot do without the family.

Though the church may have lost nearly all its role to the state in this century and the last, the family still has important functions in reproducing capitalism. We should hardly be surprised by the strong contempory link between the local state and the family. Engels a century ago showed how the two developed over long historical periods side by side in continual interaction.[26] Recently, the women's movement has taken the analysis further by recognising and arguing for greater emphasis of the concept of 'capitalist reproduction' in Marxist economics. Mariarosa Dalla Costa in 1971 pointed out the inadequacy of the traditional Marxist definition of the housewife's role.[27] Marxist theory had always supposed that when women remained outside social production, that is outside the paid workforce, they were performing not labour but *work*. Domestic work created use-value, benefiting the individual and the family but having no relevance to capital. Dalla Costa argued that women do not have to go out to work to be working for the capitalist system—they may not be 'producing' tangible goods in a factory but they are 'reproducing' no less tangible workers. By maintaining the worker (and the child who is learning to be worker) the housewife, unpaid by the worker's boss, yet turns out the man each morning ready for the job, fed, clothes mended, sexually serviced, cocooned by the woman's caring against the most severe of the frustrations of wage work.

'Domestic work produces not merely use values but is essential to the production of surplus value. . . . What we wish to make clear is that by the non-payment of a wage when we are producing in a capitalistically organised world, the figure of the boss is concealed behind that of the husband.' Recognising that housewives contribute directly to capitalist reproduction and hence indirectly to capitalist production, need imply neither that housework is 'productive labour' in the Marxist sense nor that an appropriate demand is for a 'wage' for this work. The insight is more important for the possibilities it opens up for women's awareness of their own domestic situation, the relationship between their work at home and their own and their husband's work outside the home, and between themselves and the state through services addressed to the family, such as education, health, social work and housing. It reveals more clearly than before that 'the family' is a working part of the capitalist mode of production.

A consequence of this understanding of the economic role of the family is a recognition that if family relations are not to be capitalist relations, then a conscious struggle over the practice of family life has to take place. The traditional family performs an ideological service for capital. A conventional sociological view of the family expresses this clearly (and endorses it warmly): 'it impels the individual not only to identify with the family group and so uphold its standards, but it also exerts pressures on its members to conform to the norms, laws, mores and folkways of the wider community of which it forms a part.'[28] Within the family, often for reasons of fear, the very real anxieties of parents for their children in a bigger and more hostile world outside, the young are taught to live within the conventions, to be obedient to adult authority. Home and school combine to create acceptance of a way of life. Above all, the child is 'ascribed a social class' through the family into which it is born long before it acquires an objective relationship to capital through employment.[29] We saw the dialectical nature of the welfare state representing both gains and losses to each class simultaneously. The same is of course true of the family. We need it; and our need can be turned to our disadvantage. The state needs it—but this very need can be turned against the state. A child whose family life places her or him in the working class may not merely grow up to *work* as a worker but grow up to recognise and act upon her or his class interests. Much depends on the ideology and practice of those who live together and rear children.

Contemporary developments of capitalism and the welfare state, far from reducing the dependence of mother and wife within the family, have leaned on it.[30] In his report of 1942, the foundation stone of the welfare state, William Beveridge explicitly recognised capital's need of family and housewife.

> In any measure of social policy in which regard is had to facts, the great majority of married women must be regarded as occupied on work which is vital though unpaid, without which their husbands could not do their paid work and without which the nation could not continue. . . . Mothers have vital work to do in ensuring the adequate continuance of the British Race and of British Ideals in the world.[31]

Changes in the economy, notably the period of full employment following the Second World War, resulted in a huge increase in the number of married women in paid work outside the home. Meanwhile the welfare state raised working class living standards but did nothing to change the private nature of domestic work. So the combined result has been many more women than before working a double shift, one shift outside the home an another inside. The welfare services besides led to a more intrusive state supervision of the family.

> Already in the 1930s Eleanor Rathbone noted the increased state supervision of mothers in the home. She pointed out that at any time health visitors, school inspectors or rent collectors could drop in unannounced, putting pressure on the mother to improve the quality of labour power she produced and hold legal sanctions against her if she failed to meet the prevailing norms. Since the war the ideological pressure on women in the home has increased enormously and a veritable army of social workers has been trained in family case work.[32]

The family, then, is the unit to which state services choose to relate, which is reinforced and structured by local government. Housing is a case in point. Almost the only housing type that is available by direct council provision, or through council lending schemes, is the family flat or home, with just a few single-person possibilities for those who drop out of the family through age, sickness or the failure of marriage. The relationship of councils in the last few years to the homeless and to squatters has demonstrated laughable attempts to fit people into 'family' nomenclature: 'family squatters' are any household group that can rustle up a child between them; a person and child are not a person and child but a 'one-parent family'. Quite apart from cost, the state needs the family as a structure to match its own, to which to relate. One way of looking at 'family' is to see it as part of a management system. As I will suggest in due course, 'community' is best seen as part of this system too.

Financial Stress and Urban Crisis

One consequence of the great expansion of the kind of responsibilities the state undertakes in the social formation and the increased scale at which it is called on to fulfil them has been a continuous and massive growth in state expenditure. Local authority expenditure in particular makes panic headlines: it rose from £1528 million in 1954 to £12,778 million in 1974, approximatey doubling as a proportion of the Gross Domestic Product in twenty years.[33] More important perhaps in the eyes of central government is the fact that the local authorities are spending a greater part of the total government spending of the nation—which has itself been rising as a proportion of Gross Domestic Product. Local authorities expenditure, 23% of all public expenditure in 1954, was 31% by 1974. The number of people employed by local authorities rose from 1.5 million to 2.5 million between 1952 and 1974 so that by this latter date local government had on its payroll no less than 11% of the country's entire workforce.[34] No wonder the management of local councils has been subject to scrutiny.

Reasons for the growth in state expenditure appear to lie in two related trends: class struggle and the development of capital. First, the working class has its own interest in state spending. The welfare state, that 'post-war settlement between capital and labour', came into existence not least because of a shift in the balance of power in favour of the working class. Since its inception workers have gradually come to recognise that social welfare is part of their wage—the 'social wage'—and to press for increased provision. This pressure in particular forces the state to provide, even if only minimally, for the chronic sick and old, no longer part of the needed work force.

Second, as technology advances capital requires a more highly specialised and trained workforce: more spending is needed on education, for a start. The reproduction of the labour force is an extended job, each generation costs more to prepare for work and the state is more involved in its preparation. It is not surprising therefore to find that the fastest growing sector of state expenditure is the social services (health, housing, social welfare, social security and education) whose share of Gross National Product went up by 50% in the period 1951 to 1973.[35] The long-term shift from small competitive business to national and international monopolies noted in the previous chapter[36] meant that more and more people have become employees, either of business or of the state. No longer self-employed or of independent means they are at the whim of the job market and like others need state-provided social security and other services.

The processes of urbanisation have called for more spending on roads, water supplies, etc. The state has become increasingly involved in physical planning and the share of infrastructure in state spending grew in the fifties and sixties. It was a pattern reflected in other Western advanced capitalist societies. The growth and decline of modern cities is intricately connected with developments in capitalism. They are subject to inflows and outflows of capital of different kinds at different times as manufacturing, commercial, property and finance capital operate within their markets. Lambeth was a good example of this, experiencing the arrival and departure of manufacturing industry, the mushrooming and decline of property speculation, the activity in its housing programme of a local and national building industry, and so on. For capital to increase its productivity it must tend to socialise (that is to turn into a collective activity) the general conditions of capitalist accumulation. This is the role that maintains the city. The close packing of people and functions (shops, offices, banks, etc.) speeds up the movement of capital from the moment of production (at which moment alone wealth is produced) through the processes leading to consumption and thence back to investment where it can again make wealth. The city cuts down the unprofitable circulation time of capital.[37]

Many aspects of reproduction of the labour force also need to be carried on collectively.[38] Schools and universities demand a certain size of population. So do hospitals. Even housing is becoming a matter of collective use, because it is increasingly meaningless to separate 'house' from 'environment': water and power facilities, playspace, school, transport to work. The city is essentially a form of organisation whereby the collective activity of reproduction, that aspect of it in which the state is most involved, can be carried on. The city is as necessary to capitalist reproduction as the factory is to capitalist production. It is for this reason that the financial crisis of the state at local level has been experienced most acutely by the local authorities of the big cities, where the rate base was static or declining yet the nature of the physical environment and the condition of the population demanded above-average public spending.

Add to this the fact that state services are particularly vulnerable to inflation. Because of the nature of the work, productivity is relatively low, and difficult to raise without reducing the quality of output. Local authority trades unions have grown more militant in seeking wage increases. Besides, the national insurance scheme was designed for a period of full employment. With increasingly high levels of unemployment the delicate balance of contributions to benefits is tipped adversely. What is happening is that many of the costs of capitalist production are being socialised (paid by the state out of taxation) yet profits are private. The result is a structural gap in state finance alongside the tendency to growth.[39]

It is easy to recognise the alarm which the 'rediscovery' of poverty in the late 1960s caused to urban managers, civil servants and ministers alike. Britain had experienced the post-war boom, the hey-day of 'you never had it so good', every family seemed to be driving a Vauxhall Victor and watching a 20-inch TV. State expenditure on social services had been rising for years. Yet an apparently in-eradicable poverty continued—it seemed—to afflict millions of peo-ple, particularly those in the inner areas of large cities. It was revealed by reports of government-sponsored commissions and committees (Plowden's findings on primary school deprivation[40] were published in 1967); in the press statements of the poverty professionals (the Child Poverty Action Group exposed the Labour Party's failure to end poverty[41] in 1969 just before a general election). It showed up in homelessness ('Cathy Come Home' was screened on TV in 1966, SHELTER was formed soon after). And it began to find expression, as we shall see in the following chapter (of *The Local State*), in popular militancy and protest in cities.

Corporate management was thus a response to these two problems. On the one hand, the growing need to keep down costs, to manage scarce resources as fears grew about the level of public spending. On the other, the apparently undiminishing problem of deprivation, the shame of urban poverty in what was supposed to be a thriving and exemplary capitalist society.

The performance of local agencies of the state, particularly the authorities of big cities, gripped the attention of the central state in the sixties. The local councils and other authorities had to carry on their reproduction responsibilities but they had to do so at least cost—since the financing of growing state expenditure by running up debt was a dangerous long-term economic policy. Around the middle of the 1960s, what had been a nagging anxiety about levels of state spending began to turn into attempts to contain growth. Local authorities' resource problem (how to make the necessary rate increases politically palatable) was increasingly shared by central government which was supporting local councils to a growing extent through grants and subsidies. In 1954 rates represented 41% of local authorities' revenue.

By 1964 although rising massively in money terms they had fallen to 38% and by 1974 to 30% of a rapidly escalating expenditure.[42] The growing difference was made up by the centre. Curbed financially, local authorities nonetheless had to be spurred forward to deal more effectively with urban social and economic problems. The advantage to central state planners of local authorities' financial dependency was, of course, greater control over local council budgets which in turn gave them more of a say in the way they carried out their job.

If no more money was forthcoming, policies against poverty could hardly be radically developed. What could be changed, however, was the urban management system itself. The attraction of the corporate management reforms was that they might render local councils more directly responsive to the centre, more instrinsically geared to national economic and political priorities, and provide them with the skilled financial planning and resource management that could make centrally imposed cuts and incentives effective. Further—a long shot perhaps— it was hoped to make urban policy-making sufficiently informed, intelligent and analytical to find a solution (what solution was unclear) to the scandal of urban poverty. The promise of corporate management, however, in both respects far outreached its achievements.

References

1. K. Marx and F. Engels, *The German Ideology* (1846), Lawrence & Wishart, 1970
2. Cuba, for example, has introduced a system of local electoral democracy with mass participation which makes an interesting comparison. C. Cockburn, 'People's Power: the New Political and Administrative System in Cuba', Centre for Environmental Studies Working Note 435, 1976.
3. See K. Marx and F. Engels, *The Communist Manifesto* (first published 1848), and F. Engels, *The Origin of the Family, Private Property and the State* (1884), Lawrence & Wishart, 1972.
4. V. I. Lenin, *The State and Revolution* (1917), Peking: Foreign Languages Press, 1976.
5. From an analysis by Lambeth Borough Council, Directorate of Development Services, *Report* BPL/RD/ARP/42.05.471 of April 1975. The Socio-Economic Groups are as follows: A is SEGS 1,2,3,4,13; B is SEGS 8,9,12,14; C is SEGS 5,6; and D is SEGS 7,10,11, 15, 16 and 17.
   Note: A: includes employers and managers in central and local government, industrial and commercial establishments both large and small; professional workers whether employers or employees. B: foremen and supervisors of manual workers, skilled manual workers and own account workers (such as self-employed persons in trades, personal service or manual occupations). C: non-manual workers exercising

general planning or supervisory powers in non-manual occupations, and junior non-manual workers—those engaged in clerical, sales, non-manual communications and security operations. D: Unskilled manual workers, personal service workers, members of the armed forces (and occupations inadequately described).

6. A useful discussion of class occurs in a recent article by E. Olin Wright:
    'Some marxists have argued that only productive manual workers should be considered part of the proletariat. Others have argued that the working class includes low-level, routinized white-collar employees as well. Still others have argued that virtually all wage-labourers should be considered part of the working class. . . . It matters a great deal for our understanding of class struggle and social change exactly how classes are conceptualized and which categories of social positions are placed in which classes.'
    Wright argues that employees in 'unproductive' jobs, mental labour, supervisory labour and other doubtful categories must be seen as occupying objectively contradictory locations between classes. The more contradictory is a position within social relations of production, the more political and ideological relations can influence its objective position within class relations.
    In this study I adopt a similarly inclusive definition of working class. For instance I include local state workers, except for senior officers associated with policy-making. I would argue that if their subjective inclination and their political practice identifies them as workers there is no objective constraint to their inclusion. Likewise I hold it inappropriate to see owner-occupiers, as a category, as bourgeois. Successive governments have used owner-occupation purposefully as an inducement to workers to identify with bourgeois values. I reserve the term bourgeoisie for those who own substantial capital and who profit from the surplus value created by labour; plus those professionals, managers, etc., who identify with and further this process. See further discussion in Chapter 3. (E. Olin Wright, 'Class boundaries in advanced capitalist societies', *New Left Review*, no. 98, July-August 1976.)

7. Lord Redcliffe-Maud and B. Wood, *English Local Government Reformed*, Oxford University Press, 1974.

8. In this section I draw on N. Poulantzas, *Political Power and Social Classes* (Part IV), New Left Books 1973.

9. 'In order concretely to take on this relative autonomy which, inscribed in the play of its institutions, is what is precisely necessary for hegemonic class domination, the state is *supported* by certain dominated classes of the society, in that it presents itself, through a complex ideological process, as their representative: it encourages them in various ways, to work against the dominant class or classes, but to the political advantage of these latter.' N. Poulantzas, *op. cit.,* p. 282.

10. R. Miliband, *Parliamentary Socialism*, Merlin Press, 1972.

11. R. Miliband, *The State in Capitalist Society*, Quartet Books, 1969.

12. R. Miliband, as note 10 above.

13. 'It is often held that parliament presents itself to the dominant classes as a place of danger . . . it is, generally speaking, a myth.' N. Poulantzas, *op. cit.,* p. 313.

14. D. Skinner and J. Langdon. *The Story of Clay Cross*, Spokesman Books, 1974. R. Minns, 'The significance of Clay Cross: another look at district audit', *Policy and Poltics*, Vol. II, No. 4, June 1974.

15. *Labour Research*, 'State and Industry: a new partnership', January 1976.

16. R. Miliband, as note 10 above.

17. J. Benington, *Local Government Becomes Big Business,* CDP Information and Intelligence Unit, 1976.
Canning Town to North Woolwich, The Aims of Industry? Newham Community Development Project, 1975.
Jobs in Jeopardy, a Study of Job Prospects in Older Industrial Areas, CDP Information and Intelligence Unit 1974 (reprint).

18. Current research by J. Thornley and R. Minns at the Centre for Environmental Studies, sponsored by the Social Science Research Council, examines public authority/private enterprise shareholding schemes.

19. In this section I draw on L. Althusser, 'Ideology and ideological state apparatuses', in *Lenin and Philosophy and other Essays,* New Left Books, 1971.

20. A useful discussion of this theme is E. Wilson, 'Women and the Welfare State', Red Rag pamphlet No. 2, 1974.

21. As note 19 above.

22. T. Bunyan, *History and Practice of the Political Police in Britain,* Julian Friedmann, 1976.

23. A. Gramsci, *Sections from the Prison Notebooks,* Lawrence & Wishart, 1971 (written between 1929 and 1935).

24. *Ibid.*

25. Conference of Socialist Economists, 'Women, the State and reproduction since the 1930s', in *On the Political Economy of Women,* CSE Pamphlet No. 2, Stage One, 1976.

26. F. Engels, *The Origin of the Family, Private Property and the State* (1884), Lawrence & Wishart, 1972.

27. Mariarosa Dalla Costa, *Women and the Subversion of the Community,* Falling Wall Press, 1972.

28. Mary Farmer, *The Family,* Longman, 1970.

29. *Ibid.*

30. Conference on Socialist Economists, *op. cit.*; E. Wilson, as note 20 above.

31. W. Beveridge, *Report on Social Insurance and Allied Services,* Cmnd. 6404, HMSO, 1968.

32. Conference of Socialist Economists, *op. cit.*

33. Current and capital expenditure at current prices. Figures exclude debt interest to central government, and central government grants to public corporations.
The source for these and other figures given below is *National Income and Expenditure,* HMSO.

34. Department of Employment and Productivity, *Gazette.* Figures are for Great Britain and exclude traffic wardens and some other small groups of workers. In 1974, 55. 2% of the total and 86% of part-time workers in local government were women.

35. In the following paragraphs I draw on I. Gough, 'State expenditure in advanced capitalism', *New Left Review,* July-August 1975.

36. S. Aaronovitch and M. C. Sawyer, 'The concentration of British manufacturing', *Lloyds Bank Review,* October 1974, No. 114.

37. I draw in what follows on three essays in C. Pickvance, ed., *Urban Sociology,* Methuen, 1976. They are F. Lamarche, 'Property development and the economic foundations of the urban question'; J. Lojkine, 'Contribution to a Marxist theory of capitalist urbanisation'; and M. Castells, 'Theoretical propositions for an experimental study of urban social movements'.

38. The term collective is used to mean that the financial provision is no longer an individual and family responsibility. It does not mean that people necessarily undertake the activity together. Council housing is an example—it is state provision but families live in separate dwellings.
39. A useful discussion is J. O'Connor, *The Fiscal Crisis of the State*, St James Press, 1973.
40. Central Advisory Council for Education, *Children and their Primary Schools* (Plowden Report), HMSO, 1967.
41. F. Field, *Poverty and the Labour Government*, Child Poverty Action Group, 1969.
42. See *National Income and Expenditure*, Annual, HMSO.

PART FOUR

Alternatives and Contradictions

Introduction by the Editor

The three readings in this section reflect on 'alternative' approaches to planning that have received popular attention since the late 1960s.

Donald Mazziotti sets out to question the assumptions on which 'advocacy planning' was based. Advocacy planning had been proposed, particularly by Paul Davidoff (1965), as a way of opening up official planning to groups whose views and interests had not previously been served. It was an attractive idea and appeared to offer scope for a more egalitarian process of urban planning. It assumed, however, that society is open enough for the power of logical argument, from the mouths of advocate planners, to sway decisions on urban development. That assumption, as Mazziotti argues, is not tenable and radicals must look elsewhere.

This view of advocacy planning, as can be appreciated from the date of Mazziotti's article, was increasingly held by radicals on both sides of the Atlantic by the early 1970s. One response in the UK was the idea of 'community planning'. Developed mainly by radical planners, often young lecturers in schools of planning, the aim of community planning was to develop a style of political involvement bringing together planners and working class communities. It was very much linked to the growth of 'community action' and was seen partly as an attempt to counterweigh the growing bureaucracies of planning with their esoteric techniques and impenetrable jargon. But could a commitment to working class communities in itself ever be more than a *reaction* to institutional planning? Moverover, some commentators feared that the growth of community action was a potentially diversive development in that an emphasis on local issues could obscure the overall nature of causes:

> . . . poverty and the other kindred deprivations are not *separate problems: they are aspects of one central* problem whose roots are not at all local but are to be found in the total social system which creates inequality and constantly

> reinforces it. This system can never be effectively challenged from one peripheral
> point . . . (Coates and Silburn, 1972).

Cliff Hague's essay, specially written for this book, looks back on his own and other people's involvement in community planning during the 1970s, and by use of a case study highlights the severe constraints on community planning as a viable radical alternative to conventional planning.

The third contribution in this section is part of a report by the National Community Development Project (CDP), reflecting on the state poverty programme. The title of the report, *Gilding the Ghetto,* derives from the minutes of a conference in 1969 that had been called by Harold Wilson to discuss anti-poverty projects in the UK and the USA. An inspector from the children's department of the Home Office said:

> . . . there appeared to be an element of looking for a new method of social
> control—what one might call an anti-value, rather than a value. 'Gilding the
> ghetto' or buying time, was clearly a component in the planning of CDP and
> Model Cities (CDP 1977).

Gilding the Ghetto outlines the history of the state's poverty programme in the context of economic crisis during the 1960s. The CDP authors argue that the central problems for the state had become those of explaining away the existence of inequality and 'keeping the lid on' growing discontent. I have included part three of *Gilding the Ghetto* which discusses the approach taken by government to newly emerging urban crises, though some of the vibrancy of the original, unfortunately, has had to be lost because we could not include its photographs and illustrations. The sort of analysis used was subsequently disowned by the Home Office and local CDP projects were quickly run down. There can be no doubt, however, that the CDP reports, of which *Gilding the Ghetto* is only one, provide a wealth of information on, and criticism of, state urban policy which are of very considerable value. Ironically, we can see the CDP as an attempt by the state to learn 'at the grass roots' about disaffection in the working class—this rebounded as many CDP workers used their position to learn more about the capitalist state and its methods of seeking to resolve the contradictions of its own existence.

References

Coates, K. and Silburn, R. (1972) 'The scope and limits of community action', *Community Action*, No. 1, February 1972.

Community Development Project (1971) *Gilding the Ghetto: the State and the poverty experiments,* London: Community Development Project.

Davidoff, P. (1965) 'Advocacy and Pluralism in Planning', *Journal of the American Institute of Planners,* Vol. 31, November 1965 (reprinted in Faludi, 1973a).

The Underlying Assumptions of Advocacy Planning: Pluralism and Reform

DONALD F. MAZZIOTTI*

This article examines the underlying assumption of 'political pluralism' which has characterized the theory and practice of advocacy planning since its inception. In particular, political pluralism is cast as a prevailing social myth which has become the *modus operandi* of all planning activities in the United States. The growing concentration of economic and political power centres, the alienation of people from the decision making process, the effective lack of meaningful access into the political process by groups and individuals, and the failure of conventional, electoral politics are identified as the primary indicators by which the failure of political pluralism and advocacy planning can be measured. Finally, several general conclusions are drawn which suggest that planners consider the so-called 'radical' analysis of planning in the development of alternatives to the existing institutional setting.

The Pluralism Assumption

Follow the introduction of the concept of advocacy planning to the planning profession by Linda and Paul Davidoff, Lisa Peattie, and Marshall Kaplan, a persistent series of assumptions concerning community power structure have been asserted and, with some notable dissenting views (Funnye, 1970; Hartman, 1971; Kravitz, 1970; Piven, 1970), accepted by the vast majority of planners practicing advocacy planning. The assumption which is central to the concept of advocacy planning, as presently practiced, is that of pluralism:

---

*Originally published in the *Journal of the American Institute of Planners* Vol. 40, No. 1, 1974.

The prospect for future planning is that of a practice which openly invites political and social values to be examined and debated. Acceptance of this position means rejection of prescriptions for planning which would have the planner act solely as a technician.

Determinations of what serves the public interest, in a society containing many diverse interest groups, are almost always of a highly contentious nature. In performing its role of prescribing courses of action leading to future desired states, the planning profession must engage itself thoroughly and openly in the contention surrounding political determination. (Davidoff, 1965, pp. 331-322.)

Advocate planners take the view that plan is the embodiment of particular group interests, and therefore they see it as important that any group which has interests at stake in the planning process should have those interests articulated. In effect, they reject both the notion of a single 'best' solution and the notion of a general welfare which such a solution might serve. Planning in this view becomes pluralistic and partisan—in a word, overtly political. (Peattie, 1968; p. 81)

Although the nature of the 'pluralism' described is never carefully examined by the initiators of the advocate planning concept, the arenas within which advocate projects are to operate, i.e. the political parties, ad hoc protest groups, and chambers of commerce (Davidoff, 1968) suggest a rather protracted analysis of the 'overtly political' processes with which the advocate planners must deal. Given the political context described by the adherents of this pluralistic model, it seems reasonable to classify the Davidoffs' pluralism as only the broadest kind of generalization. A synthesis of data concerning our urban condition would result in a three-dimensional model of America's social structure, revealing a complex, dispersed network of competing interest groups at every scale. Below the social strata one would find an even more complex aggregation of natural and social resources which are, at once, the subject of competing claims and the measure of society's potential for exploitation and development. Thus, it is this array of conflicting public and private groups—a surface characteristic of virtually all modern, industrialized societies (Etzioni, 1964)—to which the term 'pluralism' is ascribed.

Used in this very broad way, the overt political strategies which are consistent with this kind of pluralism amount to little more than the process of advocacy restated by Paul Davidoff in 1971:

In trying to reshape the nature of America's urban communities, there is one area, one set of institutions, practices, within America, that allows you to contribute greatly to the work that you seek to do as a professional planner. This is work with political parties that are shaping policy for this urban community. (Davidoff, 1971; p. 331).

To suggest that advocacy planning responds to the condition of pluralism by participation in the traditional political process leaves unanswered the more fundamental question of whether the reality of pluralism is but a smoke-screen called democracy. It can be argued that the Davidoff definition of pluralism is the standard by which advocate planners plan, wherein the suboptimal planning which characterizes both public and private groups becomes the operational criteria for social change.

If, on the other hand, by pluralism we mean that the opportunities and resources necessary for the exercise of power are *inclusively* rather than exclusively distributed and that neither the enjoyment of dominance nor the suffering of deprivation is the constant condition of any one group (Parenti, 1968) then the issue of whether we exist within a pluralistic society is neither patently apparent nor easily resolved. The analysis proposed here is that, in point of fact, political pluralism is a well-constructed social myth which provides the rationale for instituting social programs designed to placate the politically and economically disenfranchised. The purpose and scope of this inquiry is to critically analyze the pluralist assumptions of advocacy, the constraints these assumptions impose, and to raise issues which will stimulate a discussion of alternative modes of advocacy given the existing political economy.

Assumptions Concerning Political Pluralism

From a purely technical perspective, the antithesis of pluralism is 'monism' which means that the state, or some institutional surrogate, is the supreme sovereign power, to which all its constituent parts are legally or ethically bound. As traditionally expressed, pluralism is a political philosophy which assumes the validity of a representative democracy as the decisionmaking vehicle and argues that private interest groups of all kinds should enjoy an active, legitimized, and influential role in the formulation of public policy. This political philosophy specifically rejects the Hegelian nation state as well as anarchism:

> The common life of society is lived by individuals in unions, institutions of all kinds. The religious, the scientific, the economic life of the community develop through these. Each has its own development. There is in them a sphere of

initiative, spontaneity, and liberty. That sphere cannot be occupied by the state with its instruments of compulsion. (Lindsay, 1943; p. 245.)

In essence, political pluralism conceptualizes the process of decision-making as a system of social relationships whereby the expression of power among and between competing group interests ultimately shapes the direction and structure of the social system. Legal scholars (von Gierke, 1950), sociologists (Durkheim, 1947), social critics (Dewey, 1954), political scientists (Hunter, 1953), and economists (Commons, 1959) have embraced the pluralist interpretation of the American social system since at least the beginning of this century. This widespread acceptance of the theory, despite radical structural and institutional changes in the social fabric of the United States, makes it possible to note the basic assumptions of pluralism and critically examine its mythological character.

A first assumption of pluralism is that the existence of diverse interest groups provides the broadest representation of private interests within the state. John R. Commons' economic pluralism provides the rationale for this assumption when discussing the free enterprise market mechanisms which, in his view, could not operate with fairness unless the existence of economic pressure groups were a reality:

> 'To get back to first principles of representative government (historically as well as logically), each of these diverse interests should be permitted to assemble itself and elect a spokesman. The negroes would then elect Booker T. Washington; the bankers would elect Lyman J. Gage and J. Pierpont Morgan; . . . the trade unions would elect Samuel Gompers and P. M. Arthur; the clergy would elect Archbishop Comigan and Dr. Parkhurst; the universities would elect Seth Low and President Eliot.' (Commons, n.d.)

The structural and institutional disparities for the pluralists are solved only when the control of vested interests over government bodies are wrested from them by the bargaining power of plural pressure groups; conflict among plural groups results in social progress and reform in an otherwise irrational market system. What Commons and others overlook is the fact that the collision of group interests may and frequently does result in policies which are at variance with the asserted and unasserted claims of a broader, unorganized public, usually composed of individuals in their role as consumers (Presthus, 1964). The pluralism assumption fails to account for the inherent inequality of bargaining power as between groups; in this sense, the first assumption of pluralism ignores the realities of disequilibrium in the relative distribution of power among interest groups, the inequitable nature of access routes into the political structure, and the unorganized majority of citizens who are unrepresented by a particular group or set of pressure groups. Using the group interest representatives listed by Commons, it becomes apparent that while J. Pierpont Morgan and President Eliot may have represented differing interest groups, both were from the same economic elite or class and both wielded effective power over the system which had little or nothing to do with their relationships with the railroads or universities, per se. This same class-power condition exists in present-day society. Thus, the mere representation or advocacy of a group's interests in no way significantly disturbs the existing pattern of status and power distribution in society.

A second critical assumption of political pluralism is that spirited competition and participation between organized *groups*—and not individuals—occur over time within the existing social structure. As has been discussed by Mancur Olson and others, effective group influence can occur only where the group *organization* is given access and the opportunity to participate in the decisionmaking process (Olson, 1968). Because the reality of organizational behaviour is one which places the definition of group interests in the hands of a few, it cannot be logically argued that the representative organization exhibits the interests of the group while enjoying an existence which is apart from its members. The group advocates, who may be synonomous with group leaders, operate under an assumption that the group will act in a way which in fact advances group interests without examining individual group member interests. An impressive body of empirical data exists which make the second assumption of pluralism little more than a contentious, illogical distortion of social reality (Burns and Peltson, 1960; Key, 1958; McKean, 1949, Roberts, 1956); interest groups tend to develop goals and objectives which become increasingly at variance with the interests of the members of that group. Advocates or leaders of the organization's goals and objectives increasingly depart from representation of the individual interests of group members. Although this development can be explained in a number of ways, Olson argues that it is primarily a function of group size and the behaviour which is associated with size:

> One obstacle, it would seem, to any argument that large and small groups operate according to fundamentally different principles, is the fact, emphasized earlier, that any group or organization, large or small, works for some collective benefit that by its very nature will benefit all of the members of the group in question. Though all of the members of the group therefore have a common interest in obtaining this collective benefit, they have no common interest in paying the cost of providing that collective good. Each would prefer that the others pay the entire cost, and ordinarily would get any benefit provided whether he had borne part of the cost or not. (Olson, 1968; p. 21.)

The tendency of individual members to take this anticollectivistic attitude, however, depends upon the size of the group and the opportunities for members to become intimately familiar with the goals of the group and the decisionmaking process. The larger the group, the further it will fall short of providing an optimal amount of a collective good; like the American trade unions, the organizational interests become primary to the interest of the worker and the individual worker shows less interest in the organization, ultimately becoming manipulated by the organization's decisions.

A third assumption concerning pluralism has recently emerged as a modification of the first two and a shifting of the pluralist theory to accommodate changed social conditions. Because voluntary associations and interest groups have become oligarchically governed bureaux (Kariel, 1961), pluralists have accepted a redefinition of the concept of pluralism to mean a condition which exists only if no single elite dominates decisionmaking in every substantive area; thus, competition among elite interest groups becomes the criteria by which we are asked to judge the condition of pluralism. The pluralists fail to examine or explain how this redefinition affects the central notion of individual representation through interest groups or how a theory centering on the operation and influence of elite pressure groups can pretend to remain consistent with notions of representative democracy—both of which were essential components of the pluralistic argument.

It would appear reasonable, given the inconsistencies of the pluralist position, to assert a set of preconditions for the existence of pluralism which can be evaluated. Robert Presthus has suggested five conditions upon which pluralism must rise or fall (demurring on the logical inconsistencies and accepting—for purposes of analysis—the redefinition of pluralism):

1. That competing centers and bases of power and influence exist within a political community;
2. The opportunity for individual and organizational access into the political system;
3. That individuals actively participate in organizations of many kinds;
4. That elections are a viable instrument of mass participation in political decisions, including those on specific issues; and
5. that a consensus exists on what may be called the 'democratic creed.' (Presthus, 1970, pp. 109-110)

The extent to which five prerequisites of pluralism exist in American society gives a fair evaluation of the concept as the basis upon which advocates of social change may rely upon it in formulating strategies or mechanisms to accomplish change. That so-called competing centres and bases of power and influence exist within a political community is a social reality in America. The pluralist criteria discussed before, however, requires that the competition must be among a number of groups and that the bases of power associated with groups are variable (e.g. economic power conflicting with technical power, communications power, etc.). This competition is critical to the validity of pluralism and the corollary concept of countervailing power, i.e. the assertion that there exist social stabilizers wherein the movement toward dominance by one power base will inspire or mobilize another power base which will bring the social system into a relative balance.

A test of this first condition for pluralism can be constructed around the resource allocation system—the corporate economy. The central fact about the American economy is that it is a highly concentrated, nonatomistic system of centralized industrial firms. In virtually every important manufacturing industry, a handful of firms produce a major share of output, employ a significant portion of the work force, and make the decisive investment-production decisions (Nossiter, 1970). The concentration of the American economic system is vividly illustrated by examining Census Bureau statitics:

(a) second look at the very biggest giants offers a strong hint that more and more of manufacturing is being drawn into fewer and fewer hands. Between 1947 and 1958, the top 50 firms enlarged their share of the industrial pie from 17 percent to 23 percent; the biggest 200 from 30 to 38 percent. In other words, the 200 greatest corporations increased their slice of a much bigger pie by more than one-quarter.

'In the eleven years from 1950 through 1961, the 500 biggest industrial firms picked up 3,404 other companies, an average of seven apiece. The top 200 acquired 1,943 or an average of nearly ten each. (Nossiter, 1970; p. 10).

Because the 'new' pluralism finds the growth of competing elite groups consistent with the pluralist faith, the mere concentration of economic wealth is a tolerable, even a healthy, social condition. If concentration of economic power does not interfere with other power bases, the pluralist notion remains tenable; the fact is, however, the other power bases are not left intact. Hegemony of corporate captilism over the economy, despite decades of progressive taxation, unionization, Social Security, Medicare, and antitrust legislation, has not resulted in a significant redistribution of income of power to other groups. The social power of capital is a great as it was at the time of the trust-monopolists; expanded social welfare benefits and government programs have served to rationalize the system, not change it (Greer, 1970).

The condition of economic concentration does not end with the trend toward corporate merger. Beyond this trend lies the existence of 'finance capitalists' which represent an even more centralized, concentrated power group—a fact ignored or unknown to the political pluralism theorists. During the period of competitive capitalism, industrial corporations in the United States became increasingly dependent upon a small group of banks that were alone capable of financing capital growth or rescuing failing enterprises. Financial control of industry or 'finance capitalism' characterized the end of the era of competitive capitalism in the United States at the close of the nineteenth century.

Most political economists, including leftist theorists, believed that the finance capitalism which continued through the first quarter of the twentieth century would disappear as the split between the banks or finance capitalists and the corporate managers widened. Such a belief was based upon the reasonable assumption that the speculation interests of the finance capitalists and the growth and development interests of the corporate managers would result in the end of finance capitalism. A recent assessment of this condition reveals that, in fact, the condition of finance capitalism continues to exist and is growing:

> As the corporation grows, owners must delegate power to the managers and carry out public financing. In the case of stock offerings, their ownership is diluted; in the case of long-term financing, both owner and management are subjected to conditions demanded by finance capital. Either type of public financing makes outside directors *mandatory,* with a resulting formalization of the board. The trend toward outsider, i.e. finance capital, domination appears in corporations with sales between $50 million and $500 million. At this level of enterprise the issue of control is most sharply fought. Generally speaking, however, managers are not the principal figures in the struggle, although they are frequently the spokesmen for the competing stockholder and financial interests. As the corporation reaches sales of a billion dollars or more, the domination of the corporation by outsiders is generally complete. (Fitch and Oppenheimer, 1970, p. 85.)

Studies based upon evidence of the Patman Committee, reports of the United States Internal Revenue Service, and the Securities and Exchange Commission indicate that the sheer size of finance capitalists' assets has grown to 46.3 percent of all assets held by U.S. financial institutions. Between 1950 and 1955, there were 376 consecutive bank mergers without a single disapproval by the United States Comptroller; between 1953 and 1962, there were 1,669 mergers and absorptions, the largest of which occurred at the very top of the commercial banking empire. As a result of this series of mergers, the top five New York City banks by 1962 held 15 per cent of all deposits in New York City. This is more than double the concentration ratio of 1922, the height of unrestrained financial power.

The significant point, in terms of this analysis, is that the condition of finance capitalism goes beyond even the vision of huge corporate giants, controlling different parts of the economy. The fact is that major US financial institutions control the 500 largest corporations in America through a series of interlocking devices which place the control of aircraft, mining, paper production, electronics, automobiles, resources exploitation, and so forth, in the hands of a very few financial institutions.

Even if the dominance of wealth and production is overlooked, however, the pluralists neglect to face what two scholars have called the power of 'nondecisions' (Bachrach and Baratz, 1962). This means that there exists an institutionalized bias in a society dominated by concentrations of economic and political power which makes the theory of pluralism nothing more than an euphemism for corporate capitalism. When the pluralists ignore the implications of corporate dominance and a nationwide institutional bias which favours such blatant singularity, they perform the questionable service of perpetuating a myth which prompts individuals to view society as one based on diffused power, where every person may have a significant impact on the decisionmaking process.

In a system dominated by interlocking corporate giants, individual and organizational access into the political system (a second, essential condition of pluralism) is conditioned by the extent to which such access will not disturb existing centers of power. A crucial point to note, which links the concentration of economic and political power to the exercise of power by individuals and organizations, is the fact that the social demands made by a group outside of the prevailing structure are predetermined by the capitalistic structure. For the urban and regional planner, this linkage should be immediately apparent: the private automobile becomes a social necessity, urban space is organized in terms of private transportation; public transportation becomes a secondary infrastructural consideration, land-use decisions are made in conformance with industrial demands and development markets, the social costs generated by industry, i.e. use of air, light, space, water, land, animals, etc., are absorbed by consumers, and the beat goes on. The *de facto* dictatorship of concentrated interests displaces less organized groups. As suggested by Gorz (1970, p. 44). 'it passes through a certain number of intermediate steps, it asserts itself essentially through the priorities it controls, by the subordination and conditioning of the range of human need according to the inert exigencies of capital'.

In the environment where capital equals political power, the opportunity for meaningful impact by the competing interest groups envisioned by the pluralists becomes a pathetic tribute to the conditions of access, participation, and democracy in the American decisionmaking process. The pluralist fails to recognize that the economic power base extends to affect control and access over a political power base; the myth of pluralism may mask the institutional bias of a corporate-controlled state, but an analysis of the political process negates the validity of the pluralist view:

> Politics is not an arena in which free and independent organizations truly connect the lower and middle levels of society with the top levels of decision. Such organizations are not an effective and major part of American life today. As more people are drawn into the political arena, their associations become mass in scale, and the power of the individual becomes dependent upon them: to the extent that they are effective, they have become larger, and to that extent they have become less accessible to the influence of the individual. (Mills, 1963; p. 28.)

The third criterion or condition of pluralism, i.e. that individuals actively participate in and make their will felt through organizations of many kinds, is subject to the same analysis which has been set out above and is inextricably related to the fourth condition of pluralism—that elections are a viable instrument of mass participation in political decisions. The new pluralist theory produces a political theory which is at variance with classical liberal democratic thought; the dangerous populist notions of the classical model are eliminated to accommodate the elitist character of modern corporate statism, the passive nature of the electorate is especially vulnerable to modern pluralism, and mass politics are encouraged to transmit a feeling of participation while operating in accordance with power centers which are unrelated to individual or small group interests within society (Blackburn, 1970). As discussed at length by Michael Parenti, widespread and effective mass participation in the decisionmaking process, at any level, is atypical of our contemporary 'pluralist' society. As discussed by Parenti (1968, p. 16). 'politicians are inclined to respond positively not to group *needs* but to group *demands,* and in 'political life as in economic life, *needs* do not become *marketable demands* until they are backed by 'buying power' . . . for only then is it in the 'producer's' interest to respond.' Parenti's exhaustive analysis of community power in Newark confirms this view:

> Furthermore, in places like Newark, the one institution theoretically designed to mobilize and respond to the demands of the unorganized lower strata, the local political party, fails to do so. One of the hallowed teachings of American political science is that the political party is the citizen's means of exercising collective power; the stronger the party system the abler will it effect the polyarchic will. But the party organization in Newark is less a vehicle for democratic dialogue and polyarchic power and more a pressure group with a rather narrowly defined interest in the pursuit of office, favor and patronage.

Political elections in this context do not provide a meaningful method of generalized mass influence over political leaders. The electoral instrument appears less accessible as a means of influence than as a means of expressing issue-oriented disturbances. The most potent mechanism in the pluralist theory is a facade for the reality of corporate concentration, elitist decisionmaking formed around that concentration, institutional bias, nondecision, and the patent lack of competing power bases.

The fifth condition of pluralism, that a consensus exists on what may be called the 'democratic creed', requires that the value system of the society support the normative propositions underlying the social system, and that voting, organizational membership, and other political activity (Presthus, 1970) are made operational by a system of decisionmaking that conforms to principles of representative democracy. The crucial, analytical distinction to note regarding this condition of pluralism is that it must be *operational*—not a social myth.

The growing feelings of political alienation—notwithstanding the mythmaking and supporting effects of the mass media, market conditioning, and the psychology of mass politics—have been empirically recorded and studied. These studies have shown that large numbers of people, while subscribing to democratic principles, feel that they are not part of the political process, that their role makes no difference (Levin, 1962). Feelings of alienation grow out of the perception that political decisions are made by a group of political insiders who are not responsive to the average citizens which, as has been discussed, are valid perceptions of the operational characteristics of the political economy. Applying the pluralist theory in the context of social reality produces an inherent challenge to democratic theory; it becomes a system of proportional representation at best and an elitist state at worst. Joseph A. Schumpeter described the nature of such a system, calling itself one thing and operating as another: 'it merely means that the reins of government should (are) be handed to those who command more support than do any of the competing individuals or teams' (1950, p. 273).

The central assumptions made by leading writers and practitioners of advocacy planning has been the uncritical acceptance of a social myth called 'pluralism.' Because the assumption is incorrect, the strategies associated with advocacy planning are developed in a way which responds to a myth and not a social reality. If acceptance of the pluralist theory merely meant recognition that the forces of influence and power in the public decisionmaking process got through cycles of influence, changing from one group to another, one might argue that advocacy planning is a relatively new and realistic method of accomplishing social change. The fact is, however, that pluralism is *not* an operational feature of American society, even if all of the modifications of the new pluralists are considered. Basing strategies on a faulty assumption about the decisionmaking process renders those techniques ineffective, illusory, and in many cases, counterproductive in light of the gross inequity which is an inherent part of corporate capitalism in the urban-industrial state.

A radical interpretation of the political economy takes the basic position that structural change and reform within an inherently defective and corrupt system is not possible. The pluralist theorists fail to recognize the fact that social, cultural, and regional underdevelopment on the one hand and rapid development of 'affluent' consumer goods and services industries on the other are simply two sides of the same reality. If collective needs of people are not being satisfied in social and public services, education, urban and rural development, and the entire spectrum of conditions which have been identified as 'social problems', while at the same time the oligopolies, monopolies, and conglomerates which produce articles for individual consumption enjoy a spectular prosperity and control over the political economy, the reason is not that the collective needs are public in nature and the individual consumptive needs are private in nature. On the contrary, the reason for the scandalous disparities between social need and social satisfaction of those needs is explained by the phenomenon of contemporary corporate capitalism—supported and advanced by the state—which has secured the position of the driving role in economic development and political control of present-day society.

The Advocate Analogy: A Liberal Metaphor

Since the inception of the concept of advocacy planning in 1965, the *modus operandi* of this new planning technique was based upon an analogy drawn between the role and function of the legal advocate and the role and function of the advocate planner (Piven, 1979). The planner-advocate would plead for his or her client's point of view: furthermore, the planner would provide more than information, analysis, and simulations—specific substantive solutions would be argued. Davidoff's analogy between lawyer and planner was stated specifically in his classic article, 'Advocacy and Pluralism in Planning':

> Thus, the advocate's plan might have some characteristics of a legal brief. It would be a document presenting the facts and reasons for supporting one set of proposals, and facts and reasons indicating the inferiority of counter-proposals. (1965; p. 333.)

While the analogy was constructed around the adversary dimension of the legal advocate, and makes no pretense that both lawyer and planner would or should possess the same technical skills, the generalized analog even raises some crucial issues concerning the appropriateness of the comparison.[1]

The argument made here with respect to the analogy between the advocate lawyer and planner is that the uncritical acceptance of such a comparison assumes that the adoption of the legal-advocate model will somehow establish an effective urban democracy, one in which citizens may be able to play an active role in the process of deciding public policy. The analogy is an extension of the pluralist faith that, given the opportunity to be heard, the demands of competing groups will go through an adversary process through which the best decisions concerning planned community change will result.

There is substantial danger in using analogy carelessly, i.e. using only logical rationalizations and never resorting to testing or making a discovered induction without proving the degrees of similarity. In this case, the danger of drawing an analogy between the legal-advocate and the planner-advocate has materialized into another unrealistic guidepost. A fair test of the analogy is to examine the nature of legal advocacy and whether that model, in fact, maximizes citizen participation or access into the realm of decisionmaking, results in the best or most justified decision, or arrives at a truth which is the synthesis of groups competing equally before public tribunals (given the opportunity to be heard).

As the socioeconomic organization of American society is based upon property rights and the balancing of public and private relations, so the law serves the most powerful property interests; as argued in the section dealing with the myth of pluralism, the masses of people and interest groups who have no direct connection to the bases of power are governed by rules intended to maintain and fortify existing power relationships (Lefcourt, 1971). To the assertion that the adversary process establishes equality before the law, a radical critique of such a sweeping statement can be placed with a well-constructed and documented syllogism: law serves power, the law is made by those holding power, it perpetuates those in power, it decides what the tolerable limits of justice are—law is made by the power elite to protect and enshrine its own interests.

The good liberal, particularly the good liberal lawyer will respond to the radical critique by pointing to the host of legal decisions which have expanded the civil rights of men and women, the extensive social welfare systems which has been constructed to help, not control, the economically disadvantaged. They may well allude to, as do the pluralist-advocate planners, the 'guarantees of fair notice and hearings, production of supporting evidence, cross examination, reasoned decision(s)', (Davidoff, 1965; p. 332.)

The ostensible goal of the advocate planner is, through the use of advocacy, to meet the 'just demand for political and social equality on the part of the Negro and the impoverished' (Davidoff, 1965; 331) to provide social change which will benefit 'those who are, through lack of education and of technical sophistication, particularly ill-prepared to deal with the presentation of issues in a technical framework' (Peattie, 1968; 81) and 'defend or prosecute the interests of his clients' (Kaplan, 1969; 97). The critical issue is whether the superimposition of the legal-advocate model upon the planner will work to achieve these goals. Clearly, recent court decisions, based upon an expanded theory of equal protection, used very broad egalitarian rhetoric in the criminal law area, encouraging attorneys for the poor to apply this same argument to other social problems, e.g. inequality in education and the unequal provision of state and municipal services (Goodpaster, 1970). Again, the problem of myth versus reality rolls into operation; the general public, including naive planners, assume that headline cases mark 'high impact' social decisions which serve to ameliorate the position of the poor and disenfranchised. The analysis of the impact of a visible social decision, however, falls short of examining anything but the outcome, without asking whether the process of decisionmaking has been materially affected.

A critical view of the process would reveal that legal advocacy, like planning, has severe institutional restraints imposed upon it. A cursory examination of the criminal courts in America would reveal that enforcement and conviction is almost always directed at the working person, the poor, and the political activist. A corporate official who conspires to fix prices, utilize deceptive advertising, and proffer limited guarantees on products sold at inflated prices, rarely suffers the demise of the poor, the working, or the activist. The poor are arrested more often, convicted more frequently, sentenced more harshly, rehabilitated less successfully than the rest of society. Just as economic inequality within the United States has remained virtually constant throughout this century, inequality before the law, despite rigorous substantive and procedural safeguards, has remained relatively unchanged.

Conclusion

That persons occupying positions of control over capital are among the key wielders of local influence and control has long been one of the most commonplace assumptions of American sociologists and, more recently, planners. While it is clear that to ignore particularly local configurations of economic and political power in developing strategies for advocacy planning efforts would be innapropriate, this analysis has attempted to suggest that there are clear and growing indicators of power concentrations which are apart from the local community. Furthermore, the development of capital concentration within a growing corporate structure imposes rather substantial external controls over local decisionmaking. There is increasing evidence which suggests that local planning decisions are becoming the function of private market decisions and that this characteristic is an inherent component of the way corporate capitalism has developed in the United States.

This analysis does not suggest that elitism and concentration of power is an inherent element of capitalism—anymore than to suggest, for example, that a socialized economy would be inherently free of such control. What is specifically suggested is that the evolution of capitalism in the United States has developed into a system with inherent defects which can be modified only by changes in the nature of that system per se. The analysis raises significant implications for both planning education and planning practice.

From a conceptual and theoretical standpoint, the great majority of commentators on advocacy planning either explicitly or implicity make inaccurate, misleading, and incongruent assumptions regarding the political economy within which advocacy must be made operational. Acceptance of the assumptions discussed here requires an endorsement of the political myth of pluralism, a posture which must ultimately embrace the status quo or the liberal-reformist approach to solving complex social problems, and the adoption of a set of tactical strategies which emulate existing professions so as to preserve centers of power and frustrate the notion of participatory democracy.

Given this radical critique of the theoretical foundations of the Davidoff-Peattie-Kaplan model of advocacy planning, the classroom disaffection with planning strategies which embrace a pluralist framework, and the spread of advocacy-like positions in the planning job market, it would appear that the profession of urban and regional planning is faced with a series of criticisms which deserve something more than casual discussion. The bulk of planning literature concerned with advocacy fails to suggest new strategies to confront persistent social problems, continues to assume the necessity for gradualist or reform-oriented solutions, and implies that the prime criteria for effectiveness must be the existing institutional setting.

The final and fundamental point to be made in this brief discussion is to suggest the infirmities of existing advocacy planning theory and to stimulate renewed debate and contention over alternative strategies of advocacy planning—especially with respect to the so-called 'radical' techniques of advocacy which have received scant attention in the literature.

Notes

1. Roger Starr (1968) 'Advocates and adversaries' *Planning 1968* (Chicago: American Society of Planning Officials), pp. 33-8. This article records the author's distaste for advocacy planning, viewing advocacy efforts as frustrating urban renewal efforts. Starr also, for the wrong reasons, challenges the notion of equating the role of an urban planner to that of the 'noble profession of law'.

References

Bachrach, P. and Baratz, M. (1962) 'Two faces of power'. *American Political Science Review* **56** (Dec.), 947-952.

Blackburn, R. (1970) 'Defending the myths: The ideology of bourgeois social science, pp. 154-69, in T. Christoffel *et al., Up Against the American Myth,* New York: Holt, Rinehart and Winston.

Burns, J. M. and Peltson, J. W. (1960) *Government by the People,* Englewood Cliffs, NJ: Prentice-Hall.

Commons, J. R. (1959) *Institutional Economics.* Madison: University of Wisconsin Press.

Commons, J. R. (n.d.) *Representative Democracy,* New York: Bureau of Economic Research.

Davidoff, P. (1965) 'Advocacy and pluralism in planning' *Journal of the American Institute of Planners* **31** (Nov.), 331-7.

Davidoff, P. (1971) 'Community planning and the advocate in the suburbs' *Planning Comment* **7** (Winter), 2-13.

Dewey, J. W. (1954) *The Public and Its Problems,* Denver: Allan Swallow Publishers.

Durkheim, E. (1947) *the Division of Labor in Society,* trans. George Simpson, Glenco. Ill.: Free Press.

Etzioni, A. (1964) *Modern Organizations,* Englewood Cliffs, N.J.: Prentice-Hall.

Fitch, R. and Oppenheimer, M. (1970) 'Who rules the corporations?' *Socialist Revolution* **1** (Sept.-Oct.), 85-6.

Fitch, R. and Oppenheimer, M. (1970) 'Who rules the corporations?' *Socialist Revolution* **1** (July-Aug.), 97-9.

Funnye, C. (1970) 'The advocate planner as urban hustler', *Social Policy* **1** (July-August): 35-37.

Goodpaster, G. (1970) 'The integration of equal protection, due process standard and the indigent's right of free access to the courts', *Iowa Law Review* **56**, 223-66.

Gorz, A. (1970) 'Private profit versus public need', pp. 32-47 in T. Christoffel *et al., Up Against the American Myth,* New York: Holt, Rinehart and Winston.

Greer, E. (1970) 'The Public Interest University', pp. 338-343 in T. Christoffel *et al., Up Against the American Myth,* New York: Holt, Rinehart and Winston.

Hartman, C. (1971) 'Community planning and the advocate in the city', *Planning Comment* **7** (Winter), 16-22.

Hunter, F. (1953) *Community Power Structure,* Chapel Hill, NC: University of North Carolina Press.

Kaplan, M. (1969) 'Advocacy and the urban poor', *Journal of the American Institute of Planners* **35** (March), 96-101.

Kariel, H. (1961) *The Decline of American Pluralism,* Stanford Cal.: Stanford University Press.

Key, V. O. (1958) *Politics, Parties, and Pressure Groups,* New York: Crowell.

Kolko, G. (1962) *Wealth and Power in America,* New York: Praeger.

Kravitz, A. S. (1970) 'Mandarinism: Planning as handmaiden to conservative politics', pp. 240-67 in T. L. Beryle and G. T. Lathrop, eds., *Planning and Politics,* New York: The Odyssey Press.

Lefcourt, R. (1971) *Law Against the People,* New York: Random House.

Levin, M. (1962) 'Political alienation', pp. 227-39 in E. and M. Josephson, eds., *Man Alone: Alienation in Modern Society,* New York: Dell Publishing Company.

Lindsay, A. D. (1943) *The Modern Democratic State,* London: Oxford University Press.

McKean, D. D. (1949) *Party and Pressure Politics,* Boston: Houghton Mifflin.

Mills, C. W. (1963) 'The structure of power in American society', in I. L. Horowitz, ed., *Power, Politics and People: The Collected Essays of C. Wright Mills,* New York: Oxford University Press.

Nossiter, B. D. (1970) 'Corporate power in the economy', pp. 19-32 in T. Christoffel *et al., Up Against the American Myth,* New York: Holt, Rinehart and Winston.

Olson, M., Jr. (1968) The Logic of Collective Action, New York: Schocken Books.

Parenti, M. (1968) 'Power and pluralism: A view from the bottom'. Unpublished revision of a paper sponsored by the Caucus for a New Political Science. Washington, DC: Annual Convention of the American Political Science Association.

Peattie, L. R. (1968) 'Reflections on advocacy planning', *Journal of the American Institute of Planners* **34**, no. 2 (March): 80-88.

Piven, F. F. (1970) 'Whom does the advocate planner serve?, *Social Policy* **1** (May-June): 34-41.

Presthus, R. (1970) Community power structure: theoretical framework', pp. 103-11 in in F. M. Cox, *et al., Strategies of Community Organization,* Itasca, Ill.: F. E. Peacock.

Presthus, R. (1964) *Men at the Top: A Study in Community Power,* Oxford, Eng.: Oxford University Press.

Roberts, B. C. (1956) *Trade Union Government in Great Britain,* Cambridge, Mass.: Harvard University Press.

Schumpeter, J. A. (1950) *Capitalism, Socialism and Democracy,* New York: Harper & Row.

von Gierke, O. (1950) *Natural Law and the Theory of Society: 1500-1800,* trans., Ernest Barker, Cambridge, Eng.: Cambridge University Press.

Reflections on Community Planning

CLIFF HAGUE

The British land use planning system was projected as a vital cog in the drive for national reconstruction in the years after the Second World War. The 'right' use of land and the 'balanced' distribution of industry, in the 'interests of all sections of the community' were the state's proclaimed intentions in the 1944 White Paper on *The Control of Land Use*.[1] By the time the statutory development plans were being churned out, such notions already looked threadbare. The tide of affluence, stirred by the shift in terms of trade against the under developed countries after the Korean War, rippled through even the British economy, and washed away the sand castle of a strong central planning role for the state. The current brought with it the driftwood of suburbia, and the husks of speculative office blocks, but it could not shift the well-worn pebbles of those cities and regions dependent on contracting industries.

In places such as Glasgow, Liverpool and Newcastle, town planning was embraced *faut de mieux* as a means of forced modernization. New houses were built by the conscious application of modern technology; roads were laid out to attract growth industries, and to carry their products, raw materials and labour force on their interminably proliferating trips; city centres were refashioned, fit for the offices of multi-national corporations, with shopping precincts where consumer sovereignty could be exercised in air-conditioned comfort. The development plans catalogued the legacy of obsolescence to be conjured into citadels for the 'post-industrial age'.

That same transformation that had to be engineered in the regions and in the hearts of the big cities threatened to disfigure the fair face of the English landscape in the south-east and the rural fringe. There country planning remained the sieve to resist the development pattern of advanced capitalism in an age of cheap energy. Green belts, conservation villages and simulated 'local' building materials cherished and embodied the idyll of a natural and changeless liaison between community and land, packaged and sold to those who could meet the asking price. As the contradictions of the modernization process became manifest in the cities, this other face of planning appeared there also. Familiar symbols that had unified past and present, people and place, were replaced by monuments to functional efficiency (albeit with high energy requirements) and land speculation. The promise of a decent house in a pleasant environment for many people materialized as the damp, multi-story flat on the peripheral estate bereft of essential facilities. Disillusion and then antipathy towards planned development became rife.

Jurgen Habermas' analysis of crisis tendencies in advanced capitalism provides an interesting framework for describing this process and the emergence of the notion of community planning.[2] The extended involvement of the state in the process of urban and regional development itself represents a very characteristic example of the class compromise within the British state, geared towards crisis avoidance.[3] Through town and country planning the state provided infrastructure directly related to production (factories and industrial estates, roads, etc.) and the indirect factors of production, such as housing and transport for a labour force. The same planning system was used to mitigate the externalized costs and environmental damage resulting from private production. This limited planning capacity has been exercised in relation to three discernible contradictory interests: the collective-capitalist interest in system maintenance, the interests of individual capital groupings, and the generalizable interests, oriented to use values, of various population groups.

These contradictory interests in urban and regional development were administered through the town and country planning system, where they generated new problems. The inability to reconcile the expectations of the consumers with the imperatives of the producers of the new environment led to a loss of public confidence in the technical capability and democratic accountability of the planning system in particular, and government in general. In the face of these problems of rationality and legitimation, local government was reorganized, the planning system restructured, and 'conservation' and 'community' became the vital catchwords, soft planning, bottom-up the proclaimed fashion.

Community Planning

Eric Reade has argued that though 'community planning' is a slogan rather than an analytical concept, it usually entails one or more of four prescriptive ideas:

(i) that the problems found in given localities could be effectively tackled if only the inhabitants would see themselves as a 'community' and generate 'community spirit',

(ii) that plans should be formulated not by the local authority alone, but also involving voluntary associations and other unofficial, informal and even private-sector organisations;

(iii) that the community as a whole (i.e. the population at large) should be involved in the making of plans;

(iv) that physical plans should not be made in isolation, but in conjunction with economic and social plans.[4]

In other words, community planning entails a loose assemblage of ideas that could be labelled community development, urban governance, participation and corporate planning. The meanings imputed to these encompass and attempt to suppress the contradictions which created them, blunting crises into steering problems susceptible to technical, managerial manipulation. 'Community' and 'participation' are concepts moulded by struggles: their ambiguities precisely reflect a distortion of language by the cleavages of interest and inequalities of power within the society. To discuss them is to engage in that same communication process, so as to discover through reflection the practical questions that have been obscured.

'Community' has been used by sociologists to describe a particular social entity, where social relations are primary, not purely contractual; social control is informally enforced from within the group; and association is obligatory. The destruction of community is a chronic feature of the uneven development dynamic of capitalism, with its shifting scale and location of labour requirements. In part this has been a progressive movement; the loosening of the shackles of traditional norms created new possibilities for both material and personal advancement. Yet the process remains deeply divisive: a superior external force overrides the community's deep belief in self-survival, devaluing pre-existing expectations, challenging the code by which community life is conducted. Within liberal capitalism this process appeared at the natural workings of anonymous economic forces. Advanced capitalism has seen the shifting of the boundaries of the political system into the economic system and into the socio-cultural system, exacerbating the difficulties of retaining the public realm in a depoliticized form. Thus when a set of bureaucrats in the local town hall pronounce that a community will be destroyed in a phased ten-year programme so that the city can be rebuilt to modern standards, the threat is comprehensible, and the enemy, while being characterized as 'faceless', seems clear and within range.

The class antagonisms inherent in the process of capitalist urban change have been fragmented and obscured by the intervention of the self-proclaimed expert and democratic system of planning. The secondary conflicts fought in the name of community against urban renewal should not, therefore, be depicted as systemic crises. However, they have directly provoked questions about the legitimation of state activity—technical argument and representative democracy were neither sufficient to fully realize the demands of the protestors, nor to wholly negate and depoliticize those demands. 'Community planning' can thus be seen as an attempt to refashion the class compromise, in response to the erosion of civic privatism on matters concerning urban development.

In this process the meaning of the word 'community' has been destroyed as systematically as the entity itself. As Reade observed. 'community' becomes

> . . . an incantation, or invocation, a kind of verbal sorcery. It is a 'good word'. By placing it before some other word, in order to describe an idea or activity, these ideas or activities are magically put beyond the reach of all criticism.[5]

Whilst the word 'community' has acquired a new elasticity, the meaning of 'participation' has been shrunk, so that it implies no more than publicity and public relations, with occasional forays into consultation.[6] The intentions have been two-fold: to improve public acceptance of administrative decisions, and to improve the information base on which decisions are taken. Reduced public opposition to plans has not been solely a political imperative; delays in the processing of plans as a result of public antagonisms have created difficulties within the administrative system itself, and created dislocations with the economic imperatives of the modernization process. Likewise better awareness of the values of those affected by plans helps the decision-makers to anticipate conflict and manage it more effectively. Yet as Habermas observed, participation is an extreme and risky way of meeting legitimation deficits.[7] Instead of speeding executive decision, participation has compounded delays, and given protest a new legitimacy, so that there are signs of disillusionment with the idea both within the planning profession and in government.[8]

The idea of 'community planning' therefore embodies the contradictions that spawned it. Hence it is both a false prospectus and an alternative to conventional planning that appeals to radical activists. Its practice can be illustrated by reference to an example.

The Craigmillar Festival Society

Craigmillar is a large council housing estate on the eastern periphery of Edinburgh, which has been identified by Lothian Regional Council as the most deprived area in the region. In the 1920s the area contained a scatter of small villages associated with coal-mining and local brickworks. Council housing began under the 1923 Housing Act, and continued in phases until the 1960s, so that in 1971 Craigmillar housed some 25,000 people, with 84% of the houses being council owned.

The early tenancies were let to families relocated through slum clearance from the St. Leonards and Leith areas. The development at Craigmillar was planned to accommodate 8000, but by 1936 the population had reached 10,000. The housing scheme soon drew criticisms. School provision fell behind targets[9]; the kirk fretted that in 1934, 8000 souls lived there without a church or community facilities[10]; and there was criticism of the housing and general environment that had resulted from attempts to economize on the construction.[11] The Edinburgh Council of Social Service (ECSS) reported in 1936 that health facilities were totally inadequate; shops too few, too expensive, and carrying a limited range of goods; and dampness was a problem in the houses. In addition two classrooms detailed on plans for

St. Francis RC Primary School had been cut as an economy measure, so the school was instantly overcrowded, and children had to travel out of the area for their schooling. The same ECSS report noted that male unemployment in the area had reached 40%.

More houses were built in the post-war housing drive, and in the 1960s multi-storey blocks were added. By 1962 Craigmillar still had no library, sixth-year school or community centre. A local mother, stung by the fact that there was no opportunity for her son to learn the violin at school, proposed that Craigmillar should put on its own 'festival' to demonstrate the talents latent within the children of the area, and to combat the area's poor image.[12] The festival prospered and became an annual event, and the Craigmillar Festival Society (CFS) was established, with the mother, Helen Crummy, at the helm. The Society ran on a voluntary basis for seven years, then obtained funds under the Urban Aid programme for a neighbourhood workers' scheme. This enabled local people to carry out a form of social work, and also gave CFS a community project fund of £1000. The strength of the scheme was that CFS could claim that local knowlege enabled them to provide caring and counselling services at least on a par with what could be achieved by outside professionals.

The society began to build links with professional 'advisors' who were sympathetic to their aspirations. Two issues in particular drew them to seek links with architects and planners. These were the threatened redevelopment of one of the old mining villages in the area, and a controversy over the siting of a secondary school to serve the area. In the early 1970s one of the local councillors became the first ever Labour Lord Provost of Edinburgh, and in 1972 the Lord Provost's Committee Pilot Project was initiated. It stemmed from a motion proposed by Councillor George Foulkes (Labour):

> That the Corporation set up a Joint Committee to examine the needs of a selected area of the city in need of rehabilitation, with a view to instituting a pilot scheme in that area to improve amenities, restore community life, and encourage self-help projects.[13]

The language pays homage to the bourgeois view of the people's problems; the matrons of Morningside could agree that the reluctance of the tenants to help themselves and to show the proper 'community spirit' were the real reasons why Craigmillar was a burden on the ratepayers.

The administrators saw the idea of an experimental inter-departmental project as a useful testbed for community planning just before local government reorganisation. Edinburgh Corporation's Director of Planning attended the Planning Workshop Conference organized by CFS in June 1973, and declared that the problems of the area stemmed from the fact that it was a one-class community. He expressed the hope that the pilot project would lead to more community initiative in caring for the environment.

For CFS the project meant extra funding to take on more full-time staff and to launch new projects. Holiday schemes and summer play schemes, and pensioners' lunch clubs proliferated. Planners from the corporation attended CFS Planning Workshop meetings, though the Housing Department, landlord to the area, showed scant inclination for such involvement. There were annual whole-day conferences, working parties galore, and close links with local councillors and the local Labour MP. The CFS coined the term 'liaison government' to express the sentiments of the project, in which a more effective treat-ment of the problems would be achieved by bringing government closer to the proverbial man in the street (see Fig. 1).

Soon after reorganization CFS pulled off an even bigger coup, win-ning major funding from the EEC's anti-poverty programme, with matching contributions from Lothian Region and central government. The award was the only one made directly to a community group. The money was given for action-research to answer the question,

> Can some new government/community partnership make real inroads into the problem? Or are there structural economic constraints that determine the fate of these areas? The project is the poor looking at the poor, the remedies and changes needed.[14]

The local state and the social relationships which it constitutes has played a crucial role in planning and developing Craigmillar. The in-dices of deprivation, empty, damp and difficult-to-let houses, and the perennial problems of vandalism, all express the failure of the ad-ministrative system to fulfil its declared intentions. That failure spawned the flourishing community group, who pressed for change, using the political resource afforded by local councillors and the MP, and the technical arguments fashioned by their professional advisors. The outcome has been an extensive and internationally acclaimed

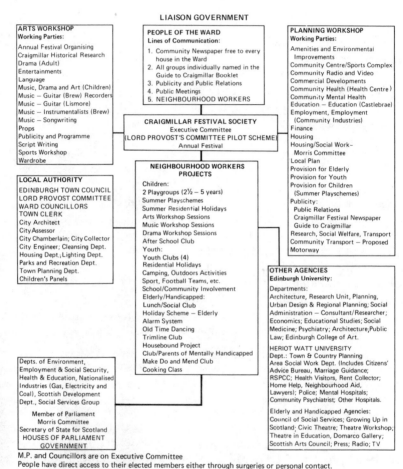

LIAISON GOVERNMENT

ARTS WORKSHOP
Working Parties:

Annual Festival Organising
Craigmillar Historical Research
Drama (Adult)
Entertainments
Language
Music, Drama and Art (Children)
Music — Guitar (Brew) Recorders
Music — Guitar (Lismore)
Music — Instrumentalists (Brew)
Music — Songwriting
Props
Publicity and Programme
Script Writing
Sports Workshop
Wardrobe

PEOPLE OF THE WARD
Lines of Communication:

1. Community Newspaper free to every house in the Ward
2. All groups individually named in the Guide to Craigmillar Booklet
3. Publicity and Public Relations
4. Public Meetings
5. NEIGHBOURHOOD WORKERS

CRAIGMILLAR FESTIVAL SOCIETY
Executive Committee
(LORD PROVOST'S COMMITTEE PILOT SCHEME)
Annual Festival

PLANNING WORKSHOP
Working Parties:

Amenities and Environmental Improvements
Community Centre/Sports Complex
Community Radio and Video
Commercial Developments
Community Health (Health Centre)
Community Mental Health
Education — Education (Castlebrae)
Employment, Employment (Community Industries)
Finance
Housing
Housing/Social Work—
Morris Committee
Local Plan
Provision for Elderly
Provision for Youth
Provision for Children (Summer Playschemes)
Publicity:
Public Relations
Craigmillar Festival Newspaper
Guide to Craigmillar
Research, Social Welfare, Transport
Community Transport — Proposed Motorway

LOCAL AUTHORITY

EDINBURGH TOWN COUNCIL
LORD PROVOST COMMITTEE
WARD COUNCILLORS
TOWN CLERK
City Architect
City Assessor
City Chamberlain; City Collector
City Engineer; Cleansing Dept.
Housing Dept.; Lighting Dept.
Parks and Recreation Dept.
Town Planning Dept.
Children's Panels

NEIGHBOURHOOD WORKERS PROJECTS
Children:
2 Playgroups (2½ — 5 years)
Summer Playschemes
Summer Residential Holidays
Arts Workshop Sessions
Music Workshop Sessions
Drama Workshop Sessions
After School Club
Youth:
Youth Clubs (4)
Residential Holidays
Camping, Outdoors Activities
Sport, Football Teams, etc.
School/Community Involvement
Elderly/Handicapped:
Lunch/Social Club
Holiday Scheme — Elderly
Alarm System
Old Time Dancing
Trimline Club
Housebound Project
Club/Parents of Mentally Handicapped
Make Do and Mend Club
Cooking Class

OTHER AGENCIES
Edinburgh University:

Departments:
Architecture, Research Unit, Planning, Urban Design & Regional Planning; Social Administration — Consultant/Researcher; Economics; Educational Studies; Social Medicine; Psychiatry; Architecture;Public Law; Edinburgh College of Art.

HERIOT WATT UNIVERSITY
Dept.: Town & Country Planning
Area Social Work Dept. (Includes Citizens' Advice Bureau, Marriage Guidance; RSPCC; Health Visitors, Rent Collector; Home Help, Neighbourhood Aid, Lawyers); Police; Mental Hospitals; Community Psychiatrist; Other Hospitals.

Elderly and Handicapped Agencies:
Council of Social Services; Growing Up in Scotland; Civic Theatre; Theatre Workshop; Theatre in Education, Domarco Gallery; Scottish Arts Council; Press; Radio; TV

Depts. of Environment, Employment & Social Security, Health & Education, Nationalised Industries (Gas, Electricity and Coal), Scottish Development Dept., Social Services Group

Member of Parliament
Morris Committee
Secretary of State for Scotland
HOUSES OF PARLIAMENT
GOVERNMENT

M.P. and Councillors are on Executive Committee
People have direct access to their elected members either through surgeries or personal contact.

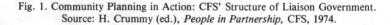

Fig. 1. Community Planning in Action: CFS' Structure of Liaison Government.
Source: H. Crummy (ed.), *People in Partnership,* CFS, 1974.

experiment in community planning. A full and systematic review of that experiment is beyond the scope of this essay. Suffice to say that CFS can justly claim some successes. The area now has community centres and even a sports centre (though the level of charges are beyond the pockets of many residents). There is a sixth-year school (though not on the sites CFS wanted). Some of the older houses have been improved (though it has been a protracted process, and much of the rehabilitation has been put back as part of the cuts). Industrial estates have been developed (though unemployment is well above the national average). Some of the contradictions integral to the community planning idea can be focused by one illustration.

The Royal Nurseries

The Royal Nurseries is an 89-acre green belt site adjacent to Craigmillar on the west. It forms part of a green wedge that is a distinctive landscape feature of the south of Edinburgh. The nurseries are a heavily planted ridge, providing a landscaped setting for the historic Craigmillar Castle. Sir Patrick Abercrombie in his 1949 Civil Survey and Plan considered this sloping foreground to be 'an essential feature of the composition of the landscape'. The land is classified Grade A and A+ by the Department of Agriculture for Scotland, and was zoned 'agricultural land within the green belt' in the Development Plan that was approved in 1957. In 1961 the site was purchased by James Miller and Partners, one of the building firms who dominated the residential land market of Edinburgh since the 1930s. Miller's objected to the 1965 Quinquennial Review zoning of agricultural land within the green belt, and within an area of Special Landscape Value'. The city planning officer responded with a report which argued that:

> A stong case can be made for setting the limits of development of this site at zero. This rests on the spatial and visual relationships of the area to other areas of special landscape value, the character of the site itself, and its function as a setting for Craigmillar Castle.[15]

A pair of consultants hired by the corporation to assess the possibility of residential development on the site, wholeheartedly concurred:

... it is *not* a question of how best to use existing open space of particular land-scape value for housing but rather a question of how best to use this open space as open space, and how to develop its full open space potential to the maximum extent in the best interests of both the present and the future recreational and amenity requirements of the city. Among other things these could include new school and university playing fields required by increasing standards of provision.[16]

The Secretary of State rejected Miller's objections. Instead he agreed that priority for any new development of the site should go to meeting Edinburgh University's playing-field requirements, affording them an extension of their adjacent site at Peffermill. He therefore invited the Edinburgh Corporation to consider a Development Plan Amendment which would allow zoning for a more definite purpose than just for green belt.[17]

The decision reflected the commitment of the professional planners to the preservation of amenity, and the priority placed on retaining the landscape character of the city as an integral part of its historical image, an image which both draws the tourists and perpetuates visions of the city as a national physical and social monument, enduring above the pettiness of divisons attributed to class. The entreaties of a former Lord Provost's building company were therefore snubbed, to facilitate the retention of the character of the land, and its use by another bastion of the Edinburgh establishment, the University.

The University is the pinnacle of the city's vaunted educational system. A finely tuned hierarchy of schools stretches from Fettes College through the other private schools and those run by the Merchants' Company, into the corporation-owned fee-paying schools (now fee-paying no longer), down to the poor relations, the local authority schools, each with their own nuances of esteem or stigma. On 27 May 1971 Edinburgh Corporation Planning Committee passed a resolution from Councillor Foulkes that the Town Planning Officer should consider what could be done to expedite corporation acquisition of land at Canal Field, in the south-west of the city, as a site for a new secondary school, needed to relieve pressure on existing inner area schools. Canal Field, owned by Edinburgh University, and used for playing fields, was zoned as private recreational open space. The University indicated that this land could be made available to the corporation, provided Miller's would let the University have part of the land at Royal Nurseries for playing fields.

That is the beginning of the story, for, as the Town Planning Officer reported,

The Royal Nurseries . . . is the key to a series of negotiations involving a number of interested parties.[18]

Not only would the acquistion of the Royal Nurseries allow the corporation school to go ahead, it would also facilitate the exchange of another university playing field at Craiglockhart Terrace to the Merchants' Company to build a replacement for the George Watson's Ladies College. Then the Merchants' Company could sell the existing Ladies College in George Square to the University who wanted to expand there. Furthermore, the Merchants' Company also hoped to dispose of former school playing-field land at Kirkbrae/Double Hedges Road, part of which was zoned for local authority housing in the 1965 Development Plan Review, the rest being allocated to public open space. Miller's were only prepared to release part of their land at the Royal Nurseries if the Mechants' Company would in turn sell them a suitable piece of land at Kirkbrae/Double Hedges for private housing development.

Thus while the fanfares of participation were blaring for Craigmillar, the Edinburgh establishment were the only ones participating fully in the formative stages of plans for use of land at Craigmillar. They owned land and hence could exert economic power as well as political influence. What must have appeared to the planning officers as a pragmatic attempt to optimize the use of various sites so as to meet functional needs and preserve amenity, can equally be interpreted as the local state whose actions reflect the dominant class interests within the city. The institutions involved are primarily involved in reproducing a labour force (training and housing) and in sustaining ideas such as the virtues of owner-occupation or the maintenance of educational standards, rather than being directly engaged in production (though Miller's produce houses). This does not undermine the value of a class analysis, but rather it emphasizes the particular nature of the class structure within Edinburgh.

It would be facile and misleading to conjure these various land deals into a 'plot'. Each part acted independently in their own interest, and indeed the inconsistency of their interests resulted in Miller's being squeezed out of the deal by 1975. The local authority had acquired land at Kirbrae for council housing, and so Miller's stood firm against releasing land at the Royal Nurseries unless they could build on part of the site. In effect Miller's were holding the others to ransom. As the Town Planning Officer had observed in 1971:

> If the present owner refused to sell land to the University new and important development would be frustrated not only at Royal Nurseries, but also, Canal Field, Craiglockhart Terrace, and George Square. In these circumstances the onus would be on the Corporation to exercise its special powers of compulsory purchase in line with the Secretary of state's decision.[19]

The Planning Committee of 17 April 1975 therefore agreed a Development Plan Amendment, rezoning 81.8 acres at the Nurseries to Private Recreational Open Sapce (University Playing Field). In addition the Castleworks part of the site (7.3 acres), comprising a quarry and woodlands occupied by a disused fireworks factory, and owned by a Mrs. Thomson, would be rezoned from private amenity open space to public amenity open space, and acquired by the Corporation, a possibility that had been floated in 1971, the acquisition being in compensation for costs incurred in protecing public safety.[20]

Despite the community planning experiment, with its emphasis on liaison government CFS found out about the proposed Amendment almost by accident. None of the local councillors sat on the Planning Committee, but one of them picked up the reference to the Nurseries when the Planning Committee minutes came before the full council. The councillor wrote to the Director of Administration requesting that a decision be deferred to allow time for local consideration of the proposed Amendment. The Amendment was submitted shortly afterwards.

The author became involved at this stage, as planning advisor to the CFS. The Society put in an objection on the grounds that the proposed Amendment would

> . . . serve to deprive a crammed housing scheme of some 25,000 people of the option to plan for the future growth of recreation/leisure space, sites and pursuits necessary for an area with a higher proportion of young people (32.5%) under 15 years old than the total city average.[21]

CFS also expressed dissatisfaction with the lack of community participation in the planning of the Royal Nurseries. Miller's also objected on the grounds that the Amendment made no provision for housing development.

CFS began to lobby. A delegation to the new District Council won an agreement to remit the matter back to the Planning Committee to consider the community's views. The Development Plan Sub-Committee of the Planning Committee visited the site in July 1975, and heard CFS' alternative proposals. These were that the site should rezoned for public open space, and developed as a park, linked to the castle. If that was not acceptable the society would favour retaining the existing zoning and agricultural use, thus keeping open the option of a park at a later date. If both these were rejected, then the University should be given no more of the site than they required to meet their short-term needs, with the rest being zoned for public open space.

The full Planning Committee were next to receive a delegation, but they still approved the sub-committee decision to go ahead with the Amendment. By now community planning had become community action, and CFS was campaigning locally and through the city's newspapers. Paul Nolan, vice-chairman of the Society, accused the Planning Committee of 'acting as property agents for Edinburgh University', and added,

> The local authority, elected by the people, should look after the public interest, rather than the private interest.[22]

The Labour Group on the District Council had been lobbied and persuaded to oppose the Amendment, and the support of the Edinburgh University student body and the Edinburgh Council for Social Service had been secured.

The climax of the campaign came on 28 August 1975 when CFS picketed the City Chambers as the full council met to hear yet another delegation. As the protestors watched from the public gallery the council voted 28-37 in favour of the Amendment. The vote was along straight party lines, with three Liberals voting with the Conservatives.

CFS was more successful with the Labour-controlled Lothian Region, where the Planning and Development Committee were persuaded to reject the advice of their Director of Planning that they should support the District's Amendment. Labour councillors were quoted as saying, 'Our whole attitude should be changing so far as land use is concerned . . . the time has come when we should stop this nonsense in terms of planning in giving large acreages to minority groups', and that it was wrong for groups like golf clubs to have exclusive use of Green Belt in densely populated areas of the city.[23] A deputation to the full regional council saw the Labour group carry a resolution to oppose the Amendment. The Region decided to negotiate with the University to obtain public access to the proposed playing field, and to secure more of the site for public open space.

Just before Christmas 1975, CFS met representatives of Edinburgh University. The University offered to continue their existing policy of renting out their facilities to organized groups of the general public, at times when they were not in use by members of the University. They would also be happy to lease part of the site for use as public open space, until their projected growth in student numbers came to fruition. However, a commercial rate would be charged for the lease, and in the circumstances it was scarcely likely that the District would opt to take up the offer.

CFS also met Miller's to explore scope for collaboration at the anticipated Inquiry, and began to prepare its own technical case, based on open-space deficiency locally, and the possible impact of playing fields on the amenity of the sloping site.[24]

But the Inquiry did not materialize. The deteriorating financial climate resulted in the Canal Field school being sidelined, and the complex of land deals was put into cold storage. The issue was not selected for discussion at the Lothian Structure Plan Examination in Public, though CFS had submitted written representations. Then in 1979 Miller's submitted an application for outline planning permission for 660 houses on the site, together with 35 acres left to be divided between university playing fields and public open space. CFS were invited to the architects' office to view the plans before the application was submitted, and the builder's propose that the land nearest the Craigmillar estate should be used for 160 housing association homes, which would be separated from the 500 private houses by the open space. CFS have lodged an objection against the application, which has not been determined at the time of writing.[25]

The Merchants' Company now have the site at Craiglockhard Terrace, and the Univeristy are developing the Ladies College site in George Square. Edinburgh District have decided to sell 12.7 acres at Kirkbrae/Double Hedges Road to private builders retaining just 2 acres for sheltered housing. This is despite an acute shortage of land for local authority housing in the city and a growing house waiting list.[26]

Some Comments

There are obvious problems in generalizing from this single illustration. The reputation of the CFS is exceptional rather than typical, and it can be argued that the Royal Nurseries issue is not an example of community planning anyway. However, the reflections in this essay are prompted precisely because CFS has been so widely acknowledged as a successful illustration of community planning. It is against this backdrop that form of the issues and community involvement in the Royal Nurseries is interesting.

The planning of the Royal Nurseries shows the nature of the local state as a set of social relationships, a form of class practice. It shows how this practice fashioned the meaning of community planning, insulating the rights of property owners from any question of 'community participation', and allowing the planning of the use of land to proceed in a 'normal' way in response to the institutions and interests that are dominant in the local state. The logic of this same practice is that the privilege of community planning status will be accorded on condition that the activists pose their negotiations in terms of the needs of the 'area' and 'community', rather than as systematic inequalities to be overcome through class struggle. For all that, community planning, by acknowledging 'deprivation' and inviting 'participation' carries the seeds of destabilization, inviting the shift into community action that occurred over the Royal Nurseries.

Community planning already looks passé, a hangover from the heady days of the late 1960s. A more evidently repressive state practice is being fashioned, with increased spending on policing and cutbacks on social welfare; enterprise zones, urban development corporations and dismantling of planning controls are the new prescription for area regeneration. The dilemmas these shifts pose have already been rehearsed in Craigmillar, when in the winter of 1976-7 the conservatives and their allies on Lothian Region voted to withdraw funding to CFS as part of a package of spending cuts. CFS responded by mobilizing extensive support both within and outwith the area, but ultimately had to appeal to the interests of right-wing politicians to survive in its existing form.[27]

In the climate that is developing radicals may well find themselves having to defend community planning against pressures to reassert a more orthodox form of planning practice. Such defence will be justified, provided it is done without illusions; the needs for legitimation fermented by the extension of the administrative system into the process of reproduction, the accompanying fragmentation of class structures, and the consequences of the restructuring within the state itself, all suggest that 'community' based demands and organization are a convenient and logical focus for political struggles. Furthermore, such campaigns have contributed experiences conspicuously absent in much of conventional left-wing politics—imagination in forms of opposition, service provision and even aspects of production controlled by those engaged in the activity, rather than by a public institution operating an impeccable capitalist morality. The struggle is to transcend the definitions and practices imposed by the state, to convert community demands into class demands, and to link community organization into the Labour Movement. Otherwise the plurality of area-based groups will be left competing for the charitable largesse of diminishing welfare programmes, with devil take the hindmost. The task is not an easy one, but we have no theoretical or empirical grounds for expecting it to be so.

Notes

1. *The Control of Land Use,* Cmd. 6537, 1944.
2. J. Habermas, *Legitimation Crisis,* Heinemann, 1976.
3. See J. Blackwell and P. Dickens, 'Town Planning, Mass Loyalty and the structuring of Capital: the origins of the 1947 planning legislation revisited', Urban and Regional Studies Working Paper 11, University of Sussex, no date.
   Also C. Hague, 'Land, the Community and Planning', paper to Urban Sociology Group, British Sociological Association, Warwick University, 1979.
4. E. Reade, 'Some Doubts about the Notion of "Community Planning" ', Zoo 11,

Dept. of Town & Country Planning, Edinburgh College of Art/Heriot-Watt University, 1976, p. 16.

5. E. Reade, *op. cit.,* p. 16. The Community Land Act is just one obvious, albeit unsuccessful, example in support of Reade's point.

6. See, for example, the Skeffington Report, *People and Planning,* HMSO, 1969. The statutory requirements are laid down in S(6) and S(10) of the Town & Country Planning (Scotland) Act, 1972, and amplified in the Structure Plan and Local Plan Regulations, 1976. Further guidance was given in SDD circular 28/1976, and Planning Advice Note 19. 'Publicity and Consultation in Structure & Local Plans', SDD, 1979, incidates the effectiveness of various techniques.

7. J. Habermas, *op. cit.,* p. 73.

8. See J. Ash, 'Public participation - time to bury Skeffington?', *The Planner,* **65** (5)(1979), 136-9. Also the 'Issues Report' of the RTPI Working Party on Public Participation, 1980. The Scottish Office have indicated that they will drop the requirement for councils to satisfy the Secretary of State as to the adequacy of their participation procedures.

9. Annual Report of the City of Edinburgh Education Committee, 1933.

10. '8,000 people: no church', *Scotsman,* 11 April 1934.

11. 'Drab houses - Niddrie, a scheme without beauty', *Edinburgh Evening News,* 18 January 1934. Also the Annual Report of the Cockburn Association, 1933.

12. The word 'festival' cocks a snoop at the Edinburgh International Festival, not an event in which Craigmillar residents would be expected to play much of a role.

13. Quoted in H. Crummy (ed.), *Festival of Change,* Craigmillar Festival Society, 1972, p. 40.

14. Quoted in Craigmillar Festival Society, *The Gentle Giant who Shares and Cares . . . Craigmillar's Comprehensive Plan for Action,* CFS, 1978, p. ii.

15. *Royal Nurseries,* report prepared by the Town Planning Officer, Edinburgh Corporation, 1966.

16. Letter from D. S. Wishart and M. Sargent to the Town Planning Officer, dated 17 October 1966.

17. The Secretary of State's Letter of Intent to Edinburgh Corporation, concerning the Development Plan Review, dated 9 May 1968.

18. Paragraph 2 of report entitled 'Royal Nurseries' attached to Departmental Memo from the Town Planning Officer to the Town Clerk, dated 2 July 1971. The University wished to centralize their recreational facilities at Peffermill and reckoned they needed 25 acres of the Royal Nurseries to meet their short-term needs, with the possibility for expansion thereafter.

19. Page 3 of the 2 July 1971 report.

20. Page 2 of the 2 July 1971 report.

21. Letter signed by Alice Henderson on behalf of CFS to the Chairman of the Planning Committee, Edinburgh and District Council (*sic*), dated 22 May 1975.

22. 'A fight for 82 acres of "vital land" - university site plan is attacked', *Edinburgh Evening News,* 15 August 1975.

23. 'Councils clash on use of 81 green acres', *Edinburgh Evening News,* 26 September 1975.

24. This is worked out and presended in N. A. Lewis, 'Local Planning and Community Need: A Case Study in Craigmillar, Edinburgh', B.Sc. Research Essay, Dept. of Town & Country Planning, Edinburgh College of Art/Heriot-Watt University, 1976. Lewis provides a fuller description of the case than is possible here.

25. This latest stage in the saga is covered more fully in D. A. West, 'Planning Aid', B.Sc. Research Essay, Dept. of Town & Country Planning, Edinburgh College of Art/Heriot-Watt Univ., 1980.

26. 'Council land sales anger Shelter', *Edinburgh Evening News*, 9 November 1979.

27. After visiting the area and talking to CFS workers, Councillor Valentine (Conservative) confessed that he had made the wrong decision in voting to withdraw funds from the Society. He wrote that through 'its own community involvement Craigmillar has pulled itself up by the bootlaces . . . and co-ordinated its needs in the most effective manner'. (Letter printed in *Edinburgh Evening News*, 20 January 1977.) See also 'Great stuff! says Tory Chairman', *Craigmillar Festival News*, January 1979. this describes a visit from the Chairman of the Lothian Region Conservative Group, who was quoted as being 'very impressed'.

A Task of Government
(Part Three of *Gilding the Ghetto*)

WORKERS FROM THE COMMUNITY DEVELOPMENT PROJECT*

PART ONE: LAW AND ORDER

> The urban problem is fundamental to the problems of our society and the level of crime in our society. . . . The level of crime is only the visible tip of the iceberg of social ferment lying beneath. (*Hansard,* Robert Carr (Home Secretary), 1.11.73.)

The most obvious of the State's instruments are probably the forces of control: the army, police, prisons and courts. Like the reflection of Robert Carr's image of crime they are the visible tip of the state iceberg. Facing them in the sixties was the old and central problem of government: if capital was to operate smoothly and profitably, a stable society and an orderly and well-disciplined workforce was essential, yet the process of capital development itself was constantly throwing up friction, conflict and violence with which the state had to deal.

The need to adapt to new conditions was recognised. During that decade expenditure on law and order almost doubled as a proportion of total public expenditure. In addition the police force was reorganised and a whole series of official reports gave their attention to one of the more serious issues of the time, the growing level of crime and in particular juvenile crime.

Expenditure on law and order as a proportion of total public expenditure

1910	1937	1951	1961	1971	1973
0.6	0.7	0.6	0.8	1.3	1.4

*Originally published as part of *Gilding the Ghetto,* a Community Development Project Inter-Project Report, 1977.

It was surprising perhaps that it was the Home Office, the government department responsible for the law enforcement agencies, that initiated most of the early poverty programmes. As well as having the task of coordinating the state's activity in relation to immigrants and, up to 1969, controlling the Children's Department which dealt with children in care and policy on the treatment and prevention of juvenile crime, it was now this department that produced first the Community Relations Commission and Urban Aid in 1968 and then CDP (1969); Neighbourhood Schemes (1971) and the Comprehensive Community Programme (1974). It was also a civil servant from the Home Office who chaired the government's high-level cabinet advisory committee on urban deprivation up to mid-1975, when the Department of the Environment took over. While all these programmes were avowedly designed to combat various aspects of poverty such as bad housing and dependence on the social services, the Home Office was a department with no responsibility for or control over any of these services. Why then the interest of the Home Office in urban poverty?

The origins of the community Development Project suggests that its concern was not in poverty itself, but in the consequence of poverty—specifically the rising crime rate and in particular the rapidly increasing rate of juvenile crime in the declining older areas.

At the same time as the Urban Aid Programme was being prepared in the Community Relations Department of the Home Office, the Children's Department was formulating a new approach to preventing juvenile delinquency at source. The resources of the community were to be mobilised both to support the family and to develop a wider sense of responsibility for keeping children under control. The Report expressed concern about the rapid increase in juvenile delinquency during the 1950s which could no longer be explained by a war situation and therefore could not be expected to die down of its own accord. New ways of coping with the problem had to be devised and the family had to be helped to do its job of bringing up children properly:

> The primary responsibility for bringing up children is parental and it is essentially a positive responsibility. It is the parents' duty to help their children to become effective and law-abiding citizens by example and training and by providing a stable and secure family background in which they can develop satisfactorily. (The Ingleby Report, 1960.)

Women and Children First

The idea was an old one and was firmly based on capital's continuing need for a healthy, well ordered workforce. The Beveridge Report of 1942 had made it clear:

> In the next thirty years housewives and mothers have vital work to do in ensuring the adequate continuance of the British race and of British ideals in the world. (The Beveridge Report.)

Clearly by the 1960s the state judged women to be failing in their onerous, unpaid task and decided to take action. The Ingleby Report was followed between 1960-65 by the Morrison Committee on the Probation Service, the Royal commission on the Police, reports by the Home Office Advisory Council on the Treatment of Offenders, the Longford Committee Report, *Crime; A Challenge to us all,* which recommended the setting up of Family service Units, and the Royal Commission on the Penal System, all of which dealt with aspects of juvenile as well as adult crime. The Home Office report on *The Child, the Family and the Young Offenders* (1965) took up some of the points relating to the family made by the Ingleby Report:

> The causes of delinquency are complex, and too little is known about them with certainty. It is at least clear that much delinquency—and indeed many other social problems—can be traced back to inadequacy or breakdown in the family. *The right place to begin, therefore, is with the family* [our emphasis]. (The Ingleby Report.)

The Seebohm Report on Local Authority and Allied Personal Services, which had been given the brief 'to review . . . what changes are desirable to secure an effective family service', was published in 1968 and recommended the reorganistion of social service departments in order to provide more integrated and co-ordinated services, as well as an increase in Community Development programmes.

Community Control

It is clear that, within Home Office thinking, the family and crime were inextricably linked. The rising rate of delinquency was an indication that the family was failing in its task of rearing law-abiding citizens. In addition to improving the methods of dealing with offenders themselves through the police and the courts, new ways had to be found to tackle the problem at source. The Community Development Project was to put this thinking into action. Established as an experiment in new ways of helping the family it was to use the 'community' as a focus for mobilising informal social control mechanisms, rather than the individual or the family in isolation. The police were involved in the planning stages of the Project and were prepared to work closely with it when established. Many CDPs were approached by the local constabulary with offers of assistance and cooperation in their early days. The North Shields CDP, for example, in addition to receiving frequent informal visits from local police officers during its first year, also received specially compiled monthly lists of indictable and non-indictable offences reported in the project area. It was some time before the police realised the project was not using the information and stopped compiling and sending it.

The social control element behind the programme was in fact recognised and acknowledged from the start. At the 1969 Ditchley Park Conference, called to discuss CDP and the Inner Area Studies in the light of the American Poverty Programme's experience, there was the following exchange:

> *Miss Cooper* (Chief Inspector, Children's Department, Home Office) said that in both the British and American plans there appeared to be an element of looking for a new method of social control—what one might call an anti-value, rather than a value. 'Gilding the ghetto' or buying time, was clearly a component in the planning of both CDP and Model Cities [the US Poverty Programme].
>
> *Miss Stevenson* (Department of Social and Administrative Studies, Oxford University) went along with this, pointing out that disordered behaviour in communities represented a nuisance to authority as well as presenting an idealistic challenge to administrators. She suggested that social workers were also interested in control, as much as the administrators. But the essence of CDP, as an example of hopefully progressive treatment, was the belief that people would respond to care, if they were not too frightened to do so. In other words, *one of its aims was to prove that there was an alternative to imposed control as a solution to social problems* [our emphasis]. *(Minutes of the Ditchley Park Conference, 1968)*

The Home Office played this prominent role in the Poverty Programme precisely because family and community had been identified as important starting points in the fight against crime. Small amounts of money spent on family and community support might prevent much larger sums being wasted later on extra police and new prisons. As Seebohm put it:

It makes no sense to us, either on humanitarian grounds or in terms of sheer economics, to allow young children to be neglected physically, emotionally or intellectually. By doing so, we not only mortgage the happiness of thousands of children, and the children they will in turn have, *but also pile up future problems and expense for society into the bargain* [our emphasis]. (The Seebohm Report.)

The idea of 'seed money' which would then have a multiplier effect' has been the favourite notion of Urban Aid and throughout, it has been heavily involved in financing projects relating to juveniles. In the very first phase of the programme, children's homes were one of three specified projects which would be financed and in subsequent phases a wide variety of projects geared towards the actual or potential young offenders were supported. These ranged from adventure playgrounds and playschemes to, in later years, intermediate treatment projects and other alternatives to residential treatment for young offenders.

The theme of family and community support was closely intertwined with another: race, racial tension, and race relations were a constant refrain in the Home Office poverty projects, and for similar reasons. Racial tension can lead to violence and disorder while unemployed black teenagers might seek to take out their frustrations on white society in general.

It was not just the plight of the immigrants themselves which was the cause of the state's concern, but the effect of their presence upon the already aggrieved white population as a potential spark for violence. Alex Lyon, speaking to Parliament as Minister for State at the Home Office about the deprivation initiatives, made the position clear:

The problem [of urban deprivation] is complicated by the fact that a great many of those who suffer in these areas of deprivation are black and immigrant *and, therefore, add to the deprivation felt by the indigenous population in these areas.* They add newness, inadequacy of language and the cultural differences which go to make up racial discrimination within our inner cities. (*Hansard,* 29.7.74 [our emphasis].)

Successive governments throughout the 1960s had taken the point. No longer short of cheap labour as the industrial shake-out proceeded, the policy they adopted to deal with this threat was to cut down on coloured immigration. With it went limited anti-discrimination legislation and attempts to dispel and pre-empt radical political organisation amongst the black population already here by setting up the Community Relations Commission and its network of community relations councils. Several of the poverty initiatives, especially Urban Aid, reflected a similar low-key policy of directing limited resources into a variety of programmes aimed at making immigrant integration easier through such projects as language centres, hostels for West Indians, and generally improving facilities for both black and white in these urban areas through the provision of playschemes, nursery facilities and similar schemes. While the main emphasis went on keeping more blacks out of the country the home situation was being kept in hand.

Urban Warfare

> . . . If there were to be in one of our big cities a situation such as that which obtained in Watts in Los Angeles at one time in recent American history, and if a similar pattern were to spread throughout our major cities, we would not have a President's commission to consider it; we would have Select Committees and questions in the House, and we would probably debate the subject ad nauseam (*Hansard,* Alex Lyon, 29.7.74.)

Alex Lyon and others too may have used the image of American race riots to emphasise the need for improvement of conditions in the cities, but there were examples much nearer home of what could happen in declining areas when a particular section of the population is consistently exploited and disciminated against. Northern Ireland, simmering in the late sixties, has finally exploded into uncontrolled violence. Clearly a situation of far greater mass and organised 'civil disorder' than anything occurring in Britain in recent history, it couldn't be forgotten that the latest 'troubles' were sparked off by Catholic civil rights demonstrations about discrimination in housing allocation and similar issues.

At first attempts were made in Northern Ireland to use both the Community Relations programme and Urban Aid to dispel the mounting tension between Catholics and Protestants in the early 1979s. The Northern Ireland Community Relations Commission, established in 1970, developed a programme of community development which in some areas managed to get Catholics and Protestants to work together over common issues like bad housing. But the Stormont Government had no interest in encouraging such work and within two and a half years both the chairman and the director of the Commission had resigned and the Commission was closed down in 1974.

With its low-profile approach discredited, the state was obliged to rely even more on the army to quell disorder, restore control and maintain some sort of calm in which the economic *status quo* could be shored up and a political solution explored. **But despite six years of immense cost and effort the army has been no more successful than the soft arm of the state in 'solving' the Northern Ireland 'problem'. Today the situation there is worse than in 1970. The obvious lesson is that quite apart from making the state's interests less conspicuous and costing far less, prevention is better than repression because it is more** *successful.*

It is clear that the Home Office involvement in the Urban Deprivation Programme reflects much more than concern for the welfare of the poor in this country. For the state, urban poverty means crime, juvenile delinquency, and in cities with large immigrant communities, potential race riots. The Home Office programmes represented to a large extent an attempt to breathe new life into the crumbling institutions of the family and the community in order to mobilise cheap, informal social control mechanisms. If the development of 'community identity', 'self-respect', 'parental authority' and 'self-help' could not stem the tide of vandalism and racism, the traditional law-enforcement agencies, the police and the courts, would have to solve the problem. But it would be at much greater cost and would also represent a setback for the governing idea that Britain can remain an orderly, self-disciplined society, free of violence, discrimination and crime without fundamental changes to the existing economic structure. Above all there was no guarantee, as the Northern Ireland situation had shown, that these more overt methods of control would be successful.

PART TWO: RULING IDEAS

Robert Car made it clear that the urban problem was more than just crime at the tip of the iceberg; there was *social ferment lying beneath.* In revitalising informal community and family methods of social control to fight crime the Home Office would of course be dealing with that social ferment as well, but not necessarily. Crime is an essentially disorganised method of hitting back at a social structure. It is troublesome, destructive and expensive to the state, but it is not revolutionary. For the state, the greater danger by far is the possibility of systematically *organised* political revolt. In Northern Ireland the civil disorder which the British Army had been brought in to control was a reflection of organised political opposition to the Ulster State. It could happen in this country too.

Carr's theme was the old, old fear—one of the driving forces behind the welfare state and the source of many concessions to the working class. It had been expressed many times before, among others by Sir John Gorst, a Tory MP of the 1880s and an advocate of the Settlement Movement, a nineteenth-century precursor of CDP

> Modern Civilisation has crowded the destitute classes together in the cities making their existence thereby more conspicuous and more dangerous. These already form a substantial part of the population, and possess even now, though they are still ignorant of their full power, . . . great political importance, . . . Almost every winter in London there is a panic lest the condition of the poor should become intolerable. The richer classes awake for a moment from the apathy, and salve their consciences by a subscription of money. . . . The annual alarm may some day prove a reality, and the destitute classes may swell to such a proportion as to render continuance of our existent social order impossible.

His contemporary, Charles Booth, made a subtler point

> . . . The impression of horror that the condition of this class makes upon the public mind today is out of all proportion to that made when its actual condition was far worse, and consequently the need to deal with the evils involved becomes more pressing. (*Life of the People in London, Vol. 2,* Charles Booth, 1891.)

One of the problems for the state in the context of the 1960s, as opposed to the 1880s, was just this: that the new manifestations of urban poverty would focus attention upon the continuing class nature of a society that was supposed to have left such problems far behind. The community approach might be useful in reducing crime, but because it would also bring people together to discuss problems, it might also result in them taking collective action—possibly radical action. Indeed, the experience of CDP workers in areas of industrial decline very quickly led them to raise fundamental issues about the distribution of wealth and resources within society and encourage the tenants with whom they worked to do the same.

To some extent it was recognised that this polarisation into THEM and US with all its political implications had already taken place and was continuing to perpetuate itself. A Home Office paper commented

> People living in deprived areas are often much more successful in communicating grievances amongst themselves, building them up into *symbols of their own social isolation,* than in communicating with the services who could help them. (*CDP Objectives and Strategy,* 1970.)

The problem was, as Derek Morrell, architect of CDP, put it at the meeting to discuss setting up the Coventry Project, how 'to help the people of Hillfields to frame realistic aspirations and enable them to attain the means to realise them'.

But what were those 'realistic aspirations' and how were the people of Hillfields—and others living in similarly rundown industrial areas—to be encouraged to direct their energies towards these rather than other, possibly more radical objectives?

Open repression through police and army could be used as a last resort in times of crisis, but for a supposedly democratic state the issue was not simply one of maintaining control by whatever means possible. Equally important was the need to maintain *consent,* to win public agreement to the official version of events. Not only was there the huge task of convincing all those outside the affected areas that all was well or going to be well, but the working class people within those areas had also to be convinced, against all their own experience, that their poverty was the consequence, not of their class situation in relation to the development and needs of capital, but of other factors which appear to have no connection with that relationship. The definition of what the problem really was, and thus how it could be solved—through the framing of 'realistic aspirations'—was a task of major importance.

The 1960s saw the state turn to the thriving academic industry of the social science for a new framework to explain urban poverty. With education expanding and the social sciences going from strength to strength there was no shortage of respected academics who could run the commissions of inquiry and produce the reports that would set the tone for state policy. Nor was there any shortage of social science graduates to staff the new poverty programmes. But their task was not an easy one. In 1969 at the personal request of Harold Wilson an Anglo-American conference was called at Ditchley Park, to compare CDP and EPA with their enormous American counterpart the US Poverty Program. High on the agenda at the conference was the idea that social science had so far failed to deliver a reliable 'macro-theory' that could be used to provide the public with explanations about the urban problem and that this failure might be a basis for the public 'withholding consent'. The social scientists were unfavourably compared with the economist—this was 1969 remember—

> . . . the success of the economist in being absorbed into the political system lay not in his capacity to predict effects, but in his capacity to generate a consensus about which results were worth achieving. (*Minutes of the Ditchley Park Conference*, J. Rothenburg.)

The economist had been able to build up a framework of theory that commanded widespread support and acceptance, irrespective of its accuracy. The restructuring of British capitalism to ensure profitability was meeting with little opposition, although it was quite clearly not in the interests of people in the older industrial areas who saw their jobs being lost and their neighbourhoods declining. Why shouldn't the social sciences do the same and provide the state and particularly local government—which was having to pick up the pieces on the ground—with a rational objective and scientific research framework in which to develop solutions to the urban problem?

So the poverty initiatives emphasised survey techniques, statistical analysis and computer models. With touching faith the social scientist, with his finely calibrated measuring instruments, was expected to provide the precise answers to the problem.

> [Evaluation] will continue throughout all subsequent phases, the object being to describe as accurately as possible what was done, when and by whom, with what expected results, and with what actual results, and hence when and how maximum return can be obtained for a given effort! (*CDP: Objectives and Strategy*, September 1970.)

The theories current at the time centred on the notion of the 'culture of poverty', the idea that people inherited poverty, not because they were victim of the process of industrial decline but because there was something about them, their lifestyle, their values, that made them unable to take advantage of the opportunities available to them. It was this idea that the social scientists were to pass on through the poverty programme. Nor was it any new departure for the state. The Charles Booths and other social reformers of the ninteenth century, though self-motivated rather than state-paid inquirers, had served exactly the same purpose for the state then in furnishing explanations of what was happening to people in general and the working class in particular. What was different about this period was that because of the development of social science as a pseudo-scientific discipline in the post-war period the sophistication and complexity of the explanations available had taken on a new lease of life.

Social scientists no longer needed to speak of the 'wretched, defrauded, oppressed, crushed human nature lying in bleeding fragments all over the face of society . . .' (Colman, 1845) nor did the media have to operate with the crude explanations used by the Church in the nineteenth century—

> The rich man in his castle,
> The poor man at his gate,
> God made them high and lowly
> and ordered their estate.
> *All Things Bright and Beautiful.*

Instead they had the 'objective' scientific language of multiple deprivation and stratification systems to draw on and had developed complicated methods of proving that the class division between labour and capital no longer exists.

It was this ideology or system of ideas which the state mobilised in the form of the Poverty Programme to counter the day-to-day experience of working class people in the inner cities. The initiation of the different poverty initiatives was itself part of the process. The existence of special projects, government departments, etc., to deal with the 'cycle of deprivation', 'social pathology' and their like clearly proved that these things must exist. The institutions were the definition made concrete.

'A Minority'

> CDP is based on the recognition that although the Social Services cater reasonably well for the majority, they are less effective for a minority who are caught up in a chain reaction of related social problems. (*Home Office Press Release,* 16.7.69.)

Thus, the CDP brief carried home the idea that there's nothing wrong with the social services, but there is a minority who fall outside its efficiency. Built into the National Project's very existence, its twelve small area teams, was proof that the unlucky minority live in isolated pockets dotted around the country in what are in affect very special circumstances. These were the 'areas of special social need' constantly referred to by the Home Office and the Department of the Environment. This idea of poverty affecting only small groups in marginal areas is a powerful one for it immediately reduces the scale of the problem. It also carries the implication that those who live outside these areas share no common interests or problems with the deprived within. The working class are effectively split into two and the scene is set for convincing those within that their problems have nothing to do with wider economic and political processes.

Drawing fixed boundaries around an area demonstrates the smallness of the problem. This is particularly misleading in inner city areas, but it is a good example of how the problem can be defined concretely for the local population. The boundary immediately sets them aside from the rest of the inner city, as small yet special. It turns them inwards and discourages them from seeking unity with neighbouring coummunities with identical problems.

Although the government has always stated that its projects were experimental, the small area focus has certainly diverted attention away from the scale of the issues.

Liverpool Inner Area Study estimate that the inner cities of the large conurbations alone house 3,800,000 deprived people, or 7% of the entire population. Plowden wanted to see 10% of the country's children in EPAs by 1971—an estimate that has been made redundant by Department of Education's insistence that it was for local education authorities to decide their own EPA boundaries. Yet when Birmingham, for example, wanted to designate 191 schools for 'educational priority' it was forced to cut this total drastically as it represented almost half the total number *allowed* for the whole country!

Once poverty and exploitation have been defined as marginal it follows logically that only minor adjustments are needed to make it go away. The assumption that the politics of government and the exercise of economic power are determined by the interplay of separate interest

The CDP areas: tiny areas deflecting attention from a
national map of inequality.

groups in society is supported without question. If marginal groups are excluded through imbalances in the democratic and bureaucratic system this just has to be remedied by the proper representation of all groups in the political process. So we get 'positive discrimination'. A central notion in both EPA and CDP, the basic idea is familiar: by making special efforts in particular areas or with particular groups of people a basis for 'equal opportunity' will be laid, and the normal paths open for achievement will be established. But this idea was very quickly challenged. 'Positive discrimination' touched the state's Achilles heel in implying provision of greater resources, a concession it was unable to make in the late sixties because of the economic situation. So the later Poverty Programme changed its tune and sang of the need to 'prioritise needs' instead.

Technical Solutions

But whatever the particular conception of the problem, the state's failure to deal with poverty is always presented as primarily a technical or administrative one. There is a continuing emphasis on management techniques—'area management', 'community development', 'co-ordinted social plan' and most recently 'an urban deprivation plan'. The implication is that the problems can be dealt with easily enough, once the right method or combination of methods have been found. Real solutions are seen to lie, not in the realm of politics, nor in the provision of extra resources, but in improving administrative practice with modern techniques, like programme budgeting, corporate management, computers and cost-benefit analysis. In this scenario there is no room for questions of conflicts, or debate about the fundamental issues involved. The ineffectual policies of the state are obscured by the apparent rationality of the way problems are to be dealt with.

In Comprehensive Community Programme schemes, for instance, CCP staff will draw up a plan for the area, prioritising needs and suggesting ways in which resources can be re-allocated within the local authority. The basic political question of much-needed *extra* resources is excluded by this approach. Even within the illusion of political response created by methods such as area management and CCPs, technical solutions involving no basic structural changes, are simply providing a diversion from the real issues.

Social Pathology

Although the major cause of poverty during the sixties was the decline of the industrial base of the older areas, few of the early poverty initiatives mention this fact. Instead poverty was called 'deprivation'. It was a problem of people, not of industrial change, and in case anyone was still in doubt a typical example would be thrown in.

> ... ill-health - financial difficulties - children suffering from deprivation - consequent delinquency - inability of the children to adjust to adult life - unstable marriages - emotional problems - ill-health and the cycle begins again. (*Home Office Press Release*, 16.7.69.)

In sociology literature this kind of description is known as a 'social pathology' model and at times the whole purpose of the poverty projects takes on a clinical connotation. The metaphor of the scientific experiment is implied in instructions about how to set up action projects:

> There are extremely intricate problems of measuring cause and effect in social action programmes, and the planning of project activities in each area will, therefore, need to be under-pinned by a research design which makes the social action amenable to evaluation by research methods. (*CDP Objectives and Strategy*, September 1970.)

and eventually it surfaces in the Neighbourhood Schemes where one of the aims is to 'act as a laboratory for CDP ideas as they develop'.

In the laboratory scientific rules must be obeyed. Dependence on the social services, for example, is viewed as some independent variable quite separate from any other factors affecting the people. The welfare state could solve people's individual problems, but when a significant number of these same people were concentrated in geographical areas—the old, the unskilled, the disabled, the unemployed left behind by the tide of industrial change—they become 'multiply deprived'. Whole families became caught in a 'cycle of deprivation' that was not only 'transmitted from generation to generation' like some hereditary disease but was also immune to the widely canvassed cure of 'equal opportunity'. Whole areas become affected, suffering from the 'social malais' of urban deprivation'. The Lambeth Inner Area Study, for instance, talks of 'the environmental problems that arise in areas of poor and deprived people' and, like Booth, suggests that the problems can only be ultimately solved by 'dispersing the concentrations'.

That such areas can be identified by physical overcrowding, high unemployment rates, dereliction and decay is not disputed, the distortion comes as the focus is turned on the people not the environment or the wider structural causes. The implicit metaphor of illness is ever-present: people are 'suffering' from 'chronic' deprivation.

The Continuing Task

If this description seems to be a caricature, it is worth looking again at the criteria by which CDP research teams were meant to assess the effectiveness of their projects. There were indicators of improved family functioning, community functioning, personal care, childrearing practices, education and support for young children and physical conditions. Nowhere is there any mention of increased incomes or resources. The kind of change envisaged is mainly in anti-social *attitudes*: for example, reduced damage to houses, increased marriage and cohabitation stability, reduced delinquency and crime rates, reductions in dissatisfaction with employment and reduction in abuse of social services through fraud and voluntary unemployment.

While it is true to say that over the last two or three years, academics and others have mounted some challenge to these explanations of poverty and pointed to the wider social processes which determine low wages, bad housing and unemployment, the pathological metaphors have become increasingly popular in local government circles. One interesting example is a recent document produced by Newcastle Council entitled *Top Priority — Newcastle's Approach to Poverty Areas*. Designed to put limited resoures into twelve of the city's twenty-six wards (most of which had suffered cuts in the expenditure review of September 1975) the programme is described as an attack on 'stress'. Whilst admitting that the project would not eliminate the root causes of 'stress', the leader of the Council described it as a 'declaration of Newcastle's war on poverty', and many other cities have already made direct approaches asking for ideas and advice on similar approaches. The Department of Environment too has agreed to sponsor research into its value and contribute £10,000 annually.

The task of ensuring that definitions of the problem are generally accepted and internalised by those who come into contact with the urban poor as well as the poor themselves is not an easy one. It is clear that the social pathology model is far from being universally agreed as a recent report from the Home Office's Urban Deprivation Unit and the Institute of Local Government Studies (INLOGOV) points out. Based on interviews with local authority officers in Birmingham and Nottingham it makes these wistful remarks:

> Our study has shown, not surprisingly, that there is no generally accepted definition of urban deprivation amongst those concerned with administering the local urban system. Many officers had not really considered the question previously. . . . Most had some intuitive notion about 'urban deprivation' although they may have been uncertain about its validity. . . .

Gilding the Ghetto

These attempts to draw run-down working-class communities into a debate with local councillors and officials about their needs illustrates one of the starkest contradictions of the state's position. Here are areas where there has been a steady rundown of the traditional manufacturing industries—a process that has been deliberately encouraged by state policies. Although some new capital investment has been attracted for activities like warehousing and distribution, the general economic base and the supporting social infrastructure of the areas remains depleted. Yet, if let to rot even further, they begin to pose a direct political threat—both by their very existence and by their potential for social ferment.

So area management, on the one hand, and devices like information centres and community councils, on the other, have been wheeled in to provide the illusion of political response. To quote Miss Cooper of the Home Office they were 'gilding the ghetto or buying time'.

> In the past the tendency has been to see urban deprivation in physical terms. It is not surprising, therefore, that the politics developed to tackle the problems have been basically physical policies. The emphasis given to housing characteristics in particular leads to the emphasis on housing programmes as the means to combat urban deprivation. This physical bias is still strong. *Our analysis raises the important issue of whether more weight should be given to other factors, for*

example, family problems, lack of community spirit, lack of access and lack of power. This would require major changes in the perspectives of many local authority and other agency officers [our emphasis]. (*Local Government: approaches to Urban Deprivation.*)

Still, in 1976, the Home Office and the Department of the Environment-supported INLOGOV are concerned that too few local government officials see deprivation as a product of family and community deficiency.

The usefulness of the state of defining the urban problem to the residents of the older industrial areas as a sickness to be 'treated' hardly needs stressing. It fits neatly alongside the idea that it is a marginal problem to be solved by increased discussion—with the Neighbourhood Council acting as a surgery and the Area Management Team as medical consultant. The emphasis on 'tackling social needs' in isolation inevitably distracts attention from the root causes of the problem, by focusing attention upon personal deficiencies. The people themselves are to blame for the problems caused by capital. It was doubtless disagreement around this point which caused the instant resignation of the first director of the Glyncorrwg CDP—a child psychologist. Glwncorrwg is a small South Wales mining town with remarkable community spirit but unemployment of about 30% caused by the closure of all the pits in the valley. The Town Clerk and the psychologist had clearly different opinions about the nature of the problems in the area. After a stormy discussion, the psychologist caught the first train home and was never seen in the area again! Elsewhere, however, in inner Liverpool or Birmingham, for example, the absurdity of the pathology model does not show up so clearly, although it has been implicitly or explicitly rejected by the staffs of all the EPA, CDPs and Inner Area Studies.

At the Ditchley Park Conference Derek Morrell, the civil servant who devised CDP gave this clear statement about the problem to which CDP and other poverty initiatives were to provide a solution.

The Chairman (Mr Derek Morrell) said the general context [of the discussion] was in his view the liberal-democratic process. It would be possible to discuss programmes and policy on the assumption that we had lost faith in this process, but he himself believed it had a highly creative future potential.

Looking, then, at the assumption about the role of government, or political process, it appeared to him that there were two principle ones to be considered. First, that the prime object of government was to maximise the total supply of welfare (in its British sense, not American) and, second, to produce a more equitable distribution of welfare. Inevitably, there was conflict between these two aims. . . . Some might take the view that only a socialist solution could reconcile the two, but this basis was not open to the conference, whose task was to consider how progress could best be made, piecemeal, along both paths simultaneously. Legitimacy for a policy of reconcilation could be sought in the process of obtaining consent, and the painstaking accumulation of evidence . . . the role of the social scientist was to produce evidence, while the role of the politician or administrator was to generate consent. . . . There was no doubt that this was very difficult. The whole process was wide open to manipulation, and involved practical problems of the transfer of power, from the 'haves' to the 'have-nots'—power, in the sense of the ability to effect or resist change. Even success, in this process, might be dangerous, and could destroy consent. But today's problem was not success, rather that consent might be withheld, because of accumulating evidence of failure. (Ditchley Park conference, 1969.)

Providing the definition of the problem alone was not enough. If people were to believe in these explanations there had also to be a solution. Here the answer was ready to hand: social democracy could be made to work. In fact it was of vital importance to the state that social democracy should be seen as able to provide a solution because in these areas of urban and industrial decline people already appeared to have lost faith in it. The turnout of electors at the local Council elections, low in the best of areas, was typically very low indeed in these areas. Yet as the Redcliffe-Maud Report warned:

If local self-government withers, the roots of democracy grow dry. If it is genuinely alive, it nourishes the reality of democratic freedom.

Participation and making local councillors more efficient were the ways in which belief in the political system—and thus the economic structure underlying it—could be restored. The need for *responsive* local government and for people to *participate* more was a constant theme of many of the official reports of the sixties, picking up and turning to their advantage the contemporary demand coming from students and the trade union movement for more participation in education and industry, in the sense of more control. Public participation was embodied in the planning legislation of 1968 and the 1969 Housing Act which gave local authorities the power to declare General Improvement Areas. It was also a theme running through the early Poverty Programme—the Urban Aid and the Community Development Projects were explicitly aimed at developing self-help and a new generation of local leadership which could then be involved in participating in local government decision-making.

The role of councillors was also a subject for discussion and experimentation in reports and programmes. The Bains Report (1972) suggested that councillors should become more involved with policy and less with the parish-pump. The brief of the Area Manager Trials of 1974 included the provision of a framework in which elected members can relate council policies to local case-work and vice-versa. They were also to explore whether 'elected members find their role in area management a satisfying one providing a perspective against which they can better judge the local impact of council policies in each subject area' *(DoE Press Release,* 6.9.74).

In 1974 in another circular (LG4/743/43) the Department of the Environment encouraged the setting up of Neighbourhood Councils. Their functions were to include familiar ideas: they were to stimulate self-help, foster a sense of community responsibility and most important, 'to represent to operational organisations (central and local government, firms with factories in the area, etc.) the needs and wishes of the local community'.

The Department of the Environment's own poverty initiatives, however, showed a lot more interest in the new idea of area management. Liverpool's Inner Area Study described this as 'an attempt to bring parts of the City's administration closer to the people it is designed to serve, through the actions of elected members and officials working with a formal area management structure'. Local government would be brought to the people. Having got it there the people would be expected to join in its deliberations through Neighbourhood Councils and Community Forums. The Area Management Trials (1974) are expected to answer such questions as 'Does it help the council to relate more immediately and sensitively to the view of neighbourhood councils and other groups, and to help them to participate effectively, for example, in the planning process?'

Behind that illusion though the projects did have their uses—but for the state, not the people living in the older urban areas. For the state has a continuing need to keep its fingers on the working-class pulse to know what is going on particularly in those difficult unorganised sections of the working class where there are no established channels, unions, or leadership to deal through. It needed to know what to expect from the ghettoes and to have accurate information with which to update the diagnosis of the problems and so produce the next set of policies.

Despite the similarity of the different initiatives, the feedback process can be seen at work even within the space of the poverty programme of the last decade: the 'action research' emphasis gives way to area management, 'positive discrimination' and to 'prioritising needs'. Even more clearly, the critical findings of CDP and some of the Inner Area Study reports with their insistence on the economic system as the root-cause of continuing poverty, can be seen today being fed back in mutilated form to the media via the 'structural' rhetoric of Peter Shore, for example,

> The causes [of inner area decline] lie primarily in their relative economic decline, in a major migration of people, often the most skilled, and in a massive reduction in the number of jobs which are left. . . . Many facilities in our inner urban areas need qualitative improvement, and some need total and often expensive replacement. (Peter Shore, 17.9.76.)

while the old, now unpopular 'personal pathology' approach is faded into the background.

Keeping the initiative is essential to the state's success. It has to update its ideas and change definitions to keep abreast with critical comment, working-class pressure and the inevitable failure of its piecemeal measures, if it is to maintain its own credibility and public consent.

The wide range of opinions and ideas represented by the professionals working for the state (never wider perhaps than at the height of the poverty programme) all go to help this process of ideological renewal on its way. While they seek new state 'solutions' to the 'problems' in good faith and genuine concern the state has within itself a valuable reserve of alternatives to turn to. To the outside world they create the illusion that government is really trying to do something to alleviate the problems and that given the *right* ideas social democracy does work. As the needs of the poorer sections of the working class are defined as 'realistic aspirations' and the blame is diverted away from the real source and onto those who suffer the consequences of decline, the institutions of the state reorganise and revitalise themselves.

PART THREE: MANAGING

Nowadays we hear a great deal about the need to save money and cut back public expenditure on the 'unproductive services'. In many ways this seems a far cry from the atmosphere of the sixties when the growth of public spending was at its peak. Yet by the time CDP and the Urban Programme were being set up there was already a growing concern in some parts of government that public spending was getting out of hand. How to cope with the 'bottomless pit' was already a central theme of the early poverty initiatives. And it has become the keynote of the recent schemes, with their concentration on saving money co-odination of services, cost-effectiveness and prioritising needs.

Today with the economic crisis considerably worsened the approach is out in the open. 'Explanations' of the economy are served up in the newspapers, on radio and television almost every day now. We know there is a 'crisis', we must all 'tighten our belts', we know about 'lack of investment', 'low productivity', unemployment. We are convinced that the 'national interest' is indeed our interest, even if it means unemployment and declining living standards for us and increased profits for the national and international corporations.

We know there is no money, and that what there is or can be found by cutting public-services must go to restore industrial profitability. So it comes as no surprise that no resources can be found to increase jobs or improve facilities. Nor does it seem wrong to hear other government statements that resources are limited and the experiments are actually aimed at better use of existing resources, including the 'untapped resources of the community' rather than tackling the issues for those who experience poverty.

The later poverty initiatives with their open emphasis on management and re-allocation of resources and conspicuous silence about the issues of urban exploitation are in tune with the times. In the sixties, though, the basic concern about finding ways of saving money was being introduced into a very different ideological climate.

The state's main concern was the enormous increase in local authority spending. Central government, hardpressed by huge borrowing to maintain public spending, became concerned about the increase and took steps to integrate and control it within the total pattern of state spending, recommending a vast range of new management and technical devices to improve the local authorities' budgeting. But at the same time public expectations were high and had been encouraged to rise by the optimistic rhetoric of the fifties and sixties. People were expecting more from the Welfare State, especially in high costs services like housing and education. White-collar workers were becoming tougher about pay increases; militancy worked, as traditionally respectable groups like the hospital workers found. More women going out to work meant increased demands for nursery care; the unpaid work they had done before—looking after the elderly and their sick relatives, as well as their children—put additional demands on local government services.

The government's own advisors, often echoing the wisdom of liberal academics, were also recommending increased spending. The official reports described earlier were designed to update the services organised by the state to maintain a healthy labour force, which also had the necessary manual and intellectual skill. They called, in effect, for extra spending. Milner Holland wanted more local authority housing in London; Plowden, more and better primary schools; Robbins, big increases in higher education; Seebohm, extra resources for the personal social services. The list was endless.

Alongside these reports, the government sponsored others to look at ways of updating local authority techniques of handling their burgeoning budgets. Maud, Mallaby and Bains, but particularly the last, recommended improved techniques that were already in operation in some local authority areas. There was clearly a need to extend and expand these services.

The poverty initiatives were primarily experiments with and on the residents of the older industrial areas. But they were also experiments with and on the local authorities themselves. Above all they were experiments *on behalf of* the central and local state. In this respect they were most important in providing a laboratory for both civil servants and local government officials to test our current and developing ideas not only about how to cut up the cake and distribute it, but how to get the best value for money. As ever the issue was presented as a problem of administration. The government, however, was quite clear about the political nature of resource allocation issues.

It would also be an essential part of the experiment to assess how far, and on what criteria of need, policies involving positive discrimination in the use of resources could be pursued without loss of financial control, and without provoking 'backlash' effects from other communities or areas of need. The latter consideration would be particularly important where the CDA [later CDP] contained a high proportion of immigrants: we should wish to include two or three such areas within the experiment. (*Report of an Inter-Departmental Working Party,* chaired by Derek Morrell, 21.5.68.)

Taken at face value it might seem that the state ignored the findings of its programmes, but with economic context and the real concerns of the state understood, it becomes clear that they were far from ignored. In fact the state has taken up the poverty programme suggestions in a systematic and highly selective way that reveals precisely its own interests. Recommendations to do with increased resource provision have been carefully ignored—the priority was not to improve the material conditions of the working class in the 'affected areas' in this way. But suggestions which have helped in the better management of urban problems without involving extra resources have been taken on board—the management of the poor is to be streamlined.

Coordination

The official wisdom of the sixties and to some extent today, is that there is a high risk of duplicating effort and cost in central and local state activity, unless there is strong coordination. Money might be wasted if, for example, social workers from two different sections went to the same family about different problems. The family and the local authority would benefit if all help and advice was organised through one social worker.

From this sort of simple and obvious example it was inferred that coordination was needed at all levels—between local authorities and voluntary agencies and groups, between local and central government and even between central government departments. Within the context of local government as a whole this idea was enshrined in 'corporate management'. The poverty initiatives focused principally on the coordination of service delivery aspects of the local authority.

CDP, for example, following the tradition of Seebohm, assumed that:

. . . the quality of co-operation that is needed, especially in poor communities, requires the coordination of inter-service teams concerned with neighbourhood areas. (*CDP: Objectives and Strategy,* September 1970.)

while the Department of the Environment considered that:

In the past the attitude has been a series of fragmented decisions not properly co-ordinated and not bringing about the improvement of urban areas which is necessary. (Peter Walker, Secretary of State for the Environment, 1973.)

A 'total approach' was needed—an idea later redefined as area management—'extending corporate management down to an area level'. Briefly, in 1973, the Home Secretary, Robert Carr, recognised that government urban deprivation policies themselves needed more 'comprehensive coordination'. This was what produced the Urban Deprivation Unit and in due course the CCPs too—the last word in co-ordination. Even Regional Planning Boards and central government departments were to be included.

Community Productivity Deal

But good coordination, at best, only provides an efficient baseline; and in most situations, as many local authorities have discovered, good coordination actually costs more. Much bigger savings can be effected by increasing productivity. In local government language this is called 'cost effectiveness'.

The focus of the poverty initiatives, however, was not on workstudy for social workers, teachers or planners, but on getting more out of the *community itself* and out of short one-off, professionally-run schemes which would initiate voluntary work on a longer-term basis. This 'multiplier effect' was the main principle behind Urban Aid and the EPA projects.

The theory is that an adventure playground, for example, employing one or two playleaders, will organise activities for the children which are useful because they keep the kids off the street. Meanwhile the parents of the children will get together initially as a playground committee but later to use it as a focus for other neighbourhood activities—Christmas parties, summer coach trips, visiting old people, fundraising for a community centre and so on. The Quality of Life Project was almost entirely about this kind of activity and there was an emphasis on *not* using local authority funds.

EPA, especially in Liverpool, was very involved in pre-school playgroups (which are usually run by local parents) and with the concept of the community school. This embraces Plowden's idea of teacher aides (teachers on the cheap) but also seeks to link up the community and the school curriculum. The spin-off for the state would be improved education standards—a continual concern as recent uproar about the 3Rs has shown. Indeed the overt philosophy of EPA was how 'to find the most economical way of getting the best results' *(Educational Priority Vol. 1)* and the project concluded that 'pre-schooling is an outstanding economic and effective device for raising education standards'.

CDP again echoes Seebohm with its aim of creating community spirit in order to

> . . . take some of the load off the statutory services by generating a fund of voluntary social welfare activity and mutual help amongst the individuals, families and social groups in the neighourhood, supported by the voluntary agencies. *(CDP: Objectives and Strategy,* 1970.)

Urban Aid was to have a similar role

> . . . the cooperation of parents in the running of the project can be of considerable importance in helping to foster the community spirit. The potential here is as yet largely untapped, and its value should not be underestimated. *(Urban Programme Circular No. 6,* December 1971.)

Though none of the projects are explicit, it is clear that parents usually means mothers, and voluntary social welfare workers are always women. Although there were growing numbers of women going out to work there were still plenty at home who could be roped in as an alternative the employing full-time, paid nursery teachers or social workers.

The idea of self-help and participation, too, had a potential pay-off for local government. Re-creation of community identity and feeling could perhaps lead to informal pressures on tenants to maintain their houses in better condition. Community activity around children would perhaps encourage adults to keep a tighter rein on the young people and discourage them from vandalising public property. A conference called by the Northumbria Police in 1975 on vandalism specifically recommended that local councils should encourage the establishment of local community organisation for these reasons.

And although local government may not now be responding to central government initiatives on the Poverty Programme with as much enthusiasm as before, certain ideas have rubbed off and been incorporated into their structures. The number of community workers employed by the local state has increased considerably over the years since the beginning of the Poverty Programme. Their role, as with the Poverty Programme in general, has been and remains to help the local state to solve its problems of maintaining credibility in the eyes of the poorer section of the working class and to manage them and its services more efficiently.

Redirecting Priorities

Whether these voluntary activities ever made or ever will make any substantial differences to state spending is impossible to assess. What is clear is that during the seventies local authority management has become the prime focus of the poverty initiatives. This goes hand in hand with increased government control of local authority spending. This year all expenditure has a fixed cash ceiling and local authority overspending is to be punished by deductions from next year's Rate Support Grants.

This trend has been accompanied by the new official recognition that only extra resources will solve the problems of the older industrial areas. As there are none, however, attempts are now being made to rob Peter to pay Paul—hoping of course that Peter will not notice until Paul can in turn be robbed. This is known as 'redirection of priorities' and has been the particular interest of projects concerned with area management and CCPs. The Home Office project is quite explicit:

> In the present economic climate when new resources are unlikely to be available, such redirection will involve difficult decisions about priorities and it is these which the CCP is intended to inform. (*Comprehensive Community Programmes: Home Office Note*, September 1975.)

It is perhaps for this reason that local authorities seem reluctant to cooperate in setting up CCPs.

Area management, as discussed earlier, is concerned with participation and legitimating technical solutions for political problems. But the exercise is also about the 'allocation of resources'—both within the

the local authority and within the area. With the present cutback in public expenditure it seems likely that in almost every area the allocation will be downwards and that area management will be exploring instead what working class communities are prepared to put up with—derelict schools OR unimproved housing OR minimal social services. Since it is not prepared to allow substantial expenditure on all three any more, it is important for the state to know which can be dropped with minimum opposition.

It would be a mistake, though, to think that the cuts in public spending represent a withdrawal on the part of the state after its heyday of expansion in the 1960s. It may represent a cutback in *spending,* there may be fewer and less adequate services for people who are poor, ill, in need of education or a home, but the tentacles of the state are not being retracted. This precisely is the usefulness of recent management developments.

Take, for example, the recent substantial cut in the Rate Support Grant for 1977-8. This withdrawal of funds does not mean that central government is reducing its involvement with, or control over, the local authorities, rather the opposite. It represents a strong central move to force all local authorities to restrict their spending in line with central policy. It is also an astute move, for any council wanting to maintain current levels of services will have to face its local constituency with an even greater rate rise than the 15% average now being predicted for 1977-8. With wages held down and prices rising it would be a brave local authority which would dare.

The decision, profoundly political, and devastating in its implications both for local authority workers and those most in need, is, however, presented as a technical one, an adjustment to the economic machine, a righting of balances. Within the local state, corporate management and similar techniques have done the same for countless other, smaller issues. Today's worsening situation finds large areas of decision making transferred out of the realm of politics and into the hands of experts, reinforcing the notion of technical solutions and removing them from public debate. This in itself has been a major achievement in shoring up the power of the state, an achievement which has re-equipped the state to meet new pressures more efficiently.

Not only has the state reorganised as capital reorganised, but it has taken a lesson in management techniques from industry which makes it better prepared to meet the consequences of capital's activities.

CONCLUSION

The state's fight against urban deprivation has been exposed, like the 'emperor's new clothes', as empty rhetoric. But just as no one was foolhardy enough to laugh at the emperor, we too would be rash to disregard the reality behind the packaging of the Poverty Programme.

The basic dilemma for the state remains the same—how best to respond to the needs of capitalism on the one hand and maintain the consent of the working class on the other. Now in the mid-seventies the problems we have described over the last decade have become more acute. The economy is in crisis and desperate measures are being called for. The profitability of British industry can ony be restored by a reduction in wages and living standards. As the state responds to the needs of capital, the scope of the problem experienced by the working class can no longer be explained as a marginal problem of the inner city and the blame put upon the inadequacies of the people living there. The working class as a whole is being affected by reductions in real wages, by the threat of unemployment and by the fall in the value of the social wage, as public sector cuts affect services of all kinds from transport to health to social services.

This is the wider reality which puts the Poverty Programme in its proper perspective. For what kind of a 'Welfare' State is it which, at a time when economic recession is causing additional hardship, particularly among the people living in 'areas of special social need', cuts back the services on which people depend. Planned in the first place in order partly to protect working class people from the harsher consequences of unfettered capitalism, its very structure is now being dismantled to help shore up an economic system that has patently failed to provide decent living standards for all. It it not surprising, then, that in the final analysis the 'deprivation initiatives' where not about eradicating poverty at all, but about managing poor people.

Cracks in the State

The story of the Poverty Programme reveals the nature of the state's interest and activities quite clearly. The Programme has evolved as a testbed for new ideas and strategies for dealing with the working class. As such, it also provides a framework both for understanding better the variety of ways in which the state operates and for locating the weaknesses and contradictions within the state's structures and activities. In this report we have concentrated on drawing out the broader strands of the state's interests and objectives. In doing so we have run the risk of presenting the state as a monolithic force.

As workers for the state ourselves, we are aware of the extent to which this is an oversimplification. Our experience in CDP makes us acutely conscious of the range of opinions represented within the state structures. The state has now embraced the liberal conscience of the nineteenth-century philanthropists as well as the social-democratic values of people like Beveridge. As a result we have found clear political differences, for instance, between council employees and councillors, between central and local government, civil servants and MPs, council committee chairmen and 'backbenchers' in their own parties. It is also clear, with increasing public expenditure cuts, that of the workers employed by it are in opposition. Many of these workers, those at the bottom end of the state hierarchy, are also the ones at the receiving end of the Welfare State—who live in the declining area, who need the services most and find them least often provided. It has used them for years as cheap labour to perform manual jobs in the hospitals and local services. At the professional level, too, there is an increasing gap between the level of resources with teachers, nurses, social workers, public health inspectors and others need in order for them to do their job to their own and their clients' satisfaction and what the state is now prepared to fund. The resistance of state workers to low wages and, more recently, to the threat of redundancy and increased workloads yet lower standards, has been one of the most important recent developments in working class organisation.

But the struggle of state workers is not simply about wages and conditions of work, or restoring the level of services of a few years ago. The issues raised in this report show that it has to be about the content of the work to do, too. We have already shown how the state, in order to maintain control over a situation, defines the everyday problems experienced by people in terms which reflect *its* needs and interests. Thus the Poverty Programme, although arising from the problems of poverty and exploitation experienced by those living in the older declining areas, was not developed in order to solve or alleviate *their* problems, but to help the state meet its problems in dealing with these people. In the same way the successful working class demands for better living conditions, whether housing, health services or education, have in the past been translated into the language and needs of the state. They may be 'our' hospitals, schools and council houses, but they have been shaped by the state according to *its* interests, the interest of maintaining the necessary conditions for capital to flourish, not the interests of those who use the services. Questions about the kind of services and whom they are for, are central to furthering the interests of both the workers, who provide the services, and the consumers on the receiving end, for they are often the same people.

For CDP workers, the contradictions involved in being state employees paid to analyse the causes of poverty, meant that effective organisation of all the twelve projects, across the institutional barriers drawn up by the Home Office, was essential both to protect our jobs and to extend our understanding of the problems we were employed to deal with. This has enabled us to develop our analysis of the reality which faces people in the areas of industrial decline and reject the definitions of the problem handed to us by the state. We have only been able to do this because at the same time we fought for the right to control our work—what we do, for whom we are doing it and why. Breaking the geographical boundaries—through inter-project meetings and the CDP Workers' Organisation—not only helped us to reject the small area focus we had been given, but also to resist Home Office attempts at control, when our employers reacted to this analysis.

For other state workers, working in the health service, public transport, education, housing and other services, there are possibilities for similar activity once the contradictory nature of state services is recognised and the decision is made to work towards providing a service in the interests of the working class, not capitalism and the state. This means not just fighting against the diversion of resources away from the public services but also acting collectively to change the structures through which these services are provided so that both workers and consumers have a service which is geared towards their needs and over which they have control.

PART FIVE

The Future

Introduction by the Editor

Can town planning be part of a radical reconstruction of society? That question begs two others—What *sort* of town planning? What process of reconstruction? Both, however, cannot form the basis of firm prediction as they will only come about as the continuing product of class struggle. The current world crisis of capitalism or, specifically, the current *restructuring* of world capitalism and its crisis *effects* within advanced capitalist societies, necessarily makes prediction difficult. It is possible, however, to examine some dimensions of these questions and to attempt to indicate the major forces and relations which affect the future of planning.

In one sense town (and regional) planning has become increasingly irrelevant in its present forms and with its past assumptions. Urban planning under capitalism was predicated upon *growth*—economic growth, urban expansion and competitive capital investment. That assumption, it hardly needs to be stressed, no longer exists. Throughout the countries of the advanced capitalist world quite different processes are are work—deindustrialisation, deskilling, major jobs-loss in manufacturing, switches of capital both sectorally (the age of the microchip) and spatially (watch Southeast Asia over the next ten years). We must be prepared to consider real economic decline in the advanced capitalist world; not slower growth, but actual decline. Associated with these changes is the growth of the 'New Right' and systematic attacks on the assumptions and institutions of social welfare. This may be a transitory stage; in Britain at least there are signs of political realignment which has produced a 'centre party' capable of changing the structure of party allegiance and moving government policies in a 'social democratic' direction. I suspect, though, that the days of social democracy are numbered, and that the alternatives remain authoritarian capitalism or socialism of one form or another. Whatever the future, in Britain, the US and subsequently other Western countries, it is not likely to be one of growth—but if anything the need for planning has never been greater. Just as growth under capitalism never brought equity so it is even more likely that the effects of decline will be unjust.

If there is to be a viable alternative economic strategy, as Tony Benn and other Labour progressives argue, then investment in, and management of, the physical environment must be one component element of the reorientation of economic activity. This would involve a different *content* for planning but also, necessarily, a different form—based not on authoritarian law but on socially responsible and democratic principles of decision making.

Bob Kraushaar and Nathan Gardels put forward a provocative and stimulating analysis of current developments which tries to bring together socio-economic change and developments in the state and their implications for planning. Their position is much influenced by the theoretical perspective of Claus Offe and thus is a distinctive and, I should note, contentious radical stance. Their notion of the significance of the 'middle class' and their implicit assumption that planning will remain a middle-class profession may be questioned, but there can be few reasons for doubting their basic analysis: times are changing and planning will change accordingly.

Towards an Understanding of Crisis and Transition: Planning in an Era of Limits

ROBERT KRAUSHAAR and NATHAN GARDELS

A clear theme for the 1980s has emerged from the disarray of the previous decade: the post-World War II era has ended and the remainder of the century will mark the transition from growing affluence to an era of limits. It has become increasingly clear that the 'major capitalist countries will not exhibit the fairly continuous and often vigorous growth accompanied and assisted by an expanding public social sector which characterized post-war reconstruction and expansion and led to notions of a post-industrial society' (Miller, 1980,p. 1). In its place seems to be evolving, not the post-scarcity society as envisioned in the 1960s, but an era of limits. Numerous recent works, from a variety of perspectives, have reflected this theme (Barnet, 1980; Clavel et al., 1980; Harrington, 1980; Rifkin and Howard, 1979; Stobaugh and Yergin, 1979; Thurow, 1980).

. On one level it is an era of economic limits. There is the continuing economic turmoil in Western industrial countries, exacerbated by the depletion—and politicization—of the world's natural resources (Barnet, 1980). Traditional government policies of economic regulation, based on Keynesian concepts such as the tradeoff between unemployment and inflation, have proved ineffective. To maintain profitability, private corporations continue to rationalize production within the industrial countries or shift their productive bases to countries with lower living standards. The former tends to increase regional imbalances while the latter creates considerable absolute unemployment. The result has been a serious decline in the rate of economic growth as the constraints on an expanding economic system increase (Gold, 1977).

On another level, however, it is an era of profound political and ideological limitations. Simply put, not only is the state less effective in regulating economies, but it is less able to compensate for the resultant social and economic hardships by increasing welfare and public employment. A decline in economic growth also means a decline in the surplus that can be redistributed for these purposes. This has led to a general disillusionment with state institutions and towards the notion that state intervention in everyday social and economic life only makes the situation more acute. The political ideology which justified state actions, liberalism (or social democracy), has lost a great deal of credence in this process and with it the legitimation that the state needs in order to actively confront the demands placed upon it. In other words, the scope and degree of political intervention has also become constrained (see Mandel, 1978; O'Connor, 1973; Habermas, 1976).

The implications of an era of limits are immense, for both capitalism and liberalism are by their very nature expansionary and cannot survive long, at least in their present forms, without sustained economic growth (see Crozier, 1975; Lowi, 1969, for example). While capitalist collapse does not seem likely, it is probable that some sort of transformation of economic and political structures will occur. In fact, several possibilities have already been put forth (Birnbaum, 1977; Goodman, 1979; Henderson, 1978; Rifkin and Howard, 1980).

This paper neither thoroughly analyzes the overall societal implications of an era of limits nor the dynamics and contradictions within the capitalist economic system that have led to an era of limits, as both topics are beyond the scope of a single paper. Instead, this paper is an examination of the role of the state and its institutions, in particular planning, within a capitalist economy and an exploration of possible changes in that role to compensate for the changing economic environment. The importance of this is significant if one accepts the supposition that of necessity it will be the task of the state to re-create economic order and ideological consensus, as it did in the 1930s.

The paper is divided into four sections. The first examines the relationship of the state to the economic system, its evolution over time as a result of changes in that economic system, and the reasons for the state's present inability to cope with the current economic transformations. The second section explores the possible directions open to the state as it attempts to overcome its present 'crisis of legitimation'. The third section deals with the implications of an era of limits and the transformation of the role of the state for the main social and economic groups in society. The fourth section examines possible future roles for planners.

1. The Political Contradictions of Decline

A. *The role of the state*

The starting point for an understanding of the role of the state in capitalist society is the relationship between accumulation and legitimation, or as some choose to define it, between capitalism and democracy. Simply put, in a system of production dependent on private accumulation, a state legitimated by a democratic ideology must continually mediate or obfuscate the conflict between societal interests and the interests of private capital so as to maintain its authority. This relationship has been the basis for the 'political capitalism' which has predominated since the Second World War (Burnham, 1980). In this context, accumulation, as Offe (1975a, p. 126) noted, 'acts as the most powerful constraint criterion, but not necessarily as the determinant of content, of the policy-making process'.

Because of this, any capitalist state has two conflicting needs: efficiency and legitimacy (Offe, 1975b). Efficiency is not determined by the state's ability to be efficient in terms of its own internal operations, but on how efficient those operations are in maintaining and maximizing the accumulation process. Its legitimacy is based 'on the postulate of a universal participation in consensus formation and on the unbiased opportunity for all classes to utilize the state's services and to benefit from its regulatory acts of intervention' (Offe, 1976, p. 396). A direct contradiction to its role in the accumulation process, which leads to a very uneven distribution of societal resources, this means that 'the state can only *function* as a capitalist state by appealing to symbols and sources of support that *conceal* its nature as a capitalist state' (Offe, 1975a, p. 127, emphasis original), a process which is the source of the state's 'inauthenticity' (see Habermas, 1976, part III).

B. *The changing nature of state activities*

Since the role of the state is constrained by its relationship to the economic system, the evolution of that economic system has the effect of modifying the role of the state. The uneven nature of capitalist development is constantly imposing new functions on the state, both changing and extending its intervention in society. Increasingly, this intervention has been 'productive' as opposed to 'allocative' in nature (see Offe, 1975a).

State allocative activities involve the administrative allocation of resources controlled by the state (such as public monies or legal power) or the regulation of the material conditions that allow the continuation of accumulation (such as Keynesian economic policies). In modern capitalism the state has been forced to respond to situations where its actual involvement in production is required because allocative actions alone prove insufficient to maintain the accumulation process. Over time this has meant the increased direct intervention in such areas as education, manpower training, health, transportation, housing and energy. This increased activity is qualitatively as well as quantitatively different. State allocative measures are *inputs* into the accumulation process; state productive measures influence the *output* of that process.

The expansion of state activity has meant that many previously economic struggles have been transferred to the political arena. The resultant increase in political action directed against state institutions is one reason for their decline in credibility.

> By expanding social services and infrastructure investment, the state does not only exacerbate the systems of the fiscal crisis, but it makes itself the focus of conflict over the mode in which societal resources should be utilized. The state does not so much, as liberal reformers believe, become a force of social change and social progress, but rather it becomes increasingly the arena of struggle. (Offe, 1975b, p. 256.)

There are ways that the state has evolved to defuse this potential conflict, one of the most efficient being its ability to depoliticize and individualize collective protest through its everyday activities (see Kraushaar, 1980; Piven and Cloward, 1979b). The overall effect, however, has been that a new 'technocratic concept of politics' has become relevant in which the principle function is 'cautious crisis management and long-term avoidance strategy' (Offe, 1976, p. 415).

This approach to policy-making has not been sufficient to reconcile the state's efficiency and legitimation demands. In fact, because of the 'noncoincidence of its notions and objective function', the state's expansion under modern capitalism has magnified this inherent contradiction. Its present mode of functioning 'has absorbed the "anarchy" that it partially eliminated from the economy. In spite of all attempts towards urgently needed rationalization, "muddling through" with plan or praxis has become the official program' (Offe, 1975c, p. 104).

C. *External demands versus internal structure*

The root cause of this is a functional discrepancy between the external demands placed upon the modern capitalist state and its internal structure. Previously, when state activities were primarily allocative in nature, a bureaucratic mode of governance sufficed. As the state's activities have become, of necessity, more productive in nature, its mode of governance has declined in competence.

> The problem is that the application of predetermined rules through a hierarchical structure of 'neutral' officials is simply insufficient to absorb the decision load that is implied by productive state activities. In other words, the administration of productive state activities requires more than the routinized allocation of state resources like money and justice. (Offe, 1975a, p. 136.)

What Offe refers to here is the need for planning decisions, the setting of priorities for final products and outcomes of state activities within the efficiency of production. Productive state activities cannot be 'standardized, routinized and channeled through rigid hierarchies' and for that reason, bureaucratic structures become increasingly inadequate.

In the case of housing, for example, allocative measures consist of laws mandating certain behavior (such as zoning and building codes) or regulating the property market, and the allocation of state resources (for such things as loan guarantees and subsidies). Examples of productive measures, on the other hand, include urban redevelopment and public housing. While the first set of activities are perfectly suited to bureaucratic routines, the scope of data and events that productive measures necessitate is much broader, involving an increased interaction with external environmental conditions, and previous administrative structures are insufficient.

This discrepancy means that every problem the state must deal with has a dual nature: the problem itself and the problem of the state's internal mode of operation (see Offe, 1975a). As a result, the institutions that make up the state apparatus can never fully adapt to the changing nature of capital and, therefore, find it increasingly difficult to adequately respond to the demands made upon them by their environment.

There have, of course, been several attempts to overcome these constraints. One has been an effort by state institutions to incorporate bits of their environment into their policy-making process 'by increasing the information flows and other practical links between the two. . . . It is by integrating the local population into predictable "families" and "community groups" and by setting up "joint committees" between itself and them that the state can develop the level of information flow that amounts to "governance" ' (Cockburn, 1977, p. 100). The recent expansion of community development and citizen participation schemes can be partially seen as attempts to do exactly that (see Miller and Kraushaar, 1979; National CDP, 1977a).

Another has been an effort in many countries to make state policy-making a more rational, business-like process. These changes, from PPBS in the United States to Corporate Management in the United Kingdom, have proved marginal to the problems confronting state decision-making (see Lee, 1973; Benington, 1975; Cockburn, 1977).

A third direction has been the initiation of experimental programs, such as action-research projects, justified partly on the basis of later expansion if successful. This model, explicitly based on private industry's conception of research and development, proved unsuccessful because of the radically different context within which the state operates (see Marris, 1974).

Finally, there has been a move to make the state more responsive to its environment via the conception of its transformation to a 'learning system' (Schon, 1971). The rationale is that, in the past, the emphasis had been misplaced. Instead of concentrating on experimental models in the expectation of their successful duplication elsewhere, what was needed was 'a climate and organizational arrangements which make innovation easy and frequent' (Trow, 1971, p. 93).

A major emphasis of all these policy adaptions has been the evolution of a 'purposive-rational' model of governance, an attempt to make the internal policy-making structure of the state similar to that of private industry. The main contradiction in these efforts is that, unlike the private firm which is guided in its production decisions by the sole criterion of profit maximization, the state—as the guarantor of social well-being—must internalize all externalities in productive decisions and must consider all classes and constituencies in its decisions if it is to remain consistent with the traditional conceptions of democracy. As Offe has pointed out, this is something that the policy-making process of the capitalist state finds difficult:

> The variety of needs, interests, demands, crises, etc., that appear in the environment of state activity are of a contradictory nature . . . to allow the derivation of operational goals. Conversely, the state in its specific capitalist form is unable to impose on its environment its *own* definition of a set of goals that it then would pursue according to instrumental rationality. (Offe, 1975a, p. 138, emphasis original.)

At present, the evolving era of limits means that the state, in its present form, has increasing trouble in legitimating its own policies. Its inherent internal policy-making limitations exacerbate attempts to alleviate the conflicting demands on its institutions, demands magnified and multiplied by the collapse of 'political capitalism' and the generalized capital accumulation problem in Western industrialized countries (McCracken *et al.,* 1977; Thurow, 1980). On one level this has manifested itself in 'a systematic overloading of the public budget' as the state has attempted to deal with the increasing demands using a decreasing fiscal surplus (O'Connor, 1973). On a broader level, however, this has meant a decrease in the credibility of state intitutions overall, with potentially serious consequences. As Habermas put it:

> If government crisis management fails, it lags behind programmatic demands *that it has placed on itself.* The penalty for this is the withdrawal of legitimation. Thus, the scope of action contracts precisely at those moments in which it needs to be drastically expanded (1976, p. 69, emphasis original).

While the current dilemmas faced by the state do not necessarily mean its complete disintegration, they are certainly indicators of a growing 'legitimation crisis' (Habermas, 1976). Such a crisis necessitates a new mode of state intervention to regain, or transform, the basis of political authority. To overcome these present manifestations of its inherent contradictions, it is likely that the state will be forced to transform its policy-making structure—a transformation similar in scope to the earlier change in most Western industrial countries from *laissez-faire* to welfare state capitalism.

II. The Resolution of Crisis

A. *The reduction of legitimation demands*

There are two directions open to the state at this time. The first is an effort to reduce its legitimation needs, thereby reducing the demands placed upon its policy-making apparatus and allowing more scope in its support of the accumulation process. This is in accord with Miller's (1978) 'recapitalization of capital' thesis and would be a logical outcome of the present conservative backlash in many modern capitalist countries.

In order to reduce its legitimation needs, the state would first have to contract its extensive involvement in social intervention, thus reducing the conflict it has absorbed from the economy. This would also tend to reduce its fiscal pressures and help mute the present taxpayers revolt. Second, the state would have to reduce expectations. It would need to convince the various classes in society that, while it recognizes hardships and injustices, its powers are limited. Little state involvement to rectify matters should be expected or even desired.

Miller sees this intertwined with an attempt by the state to restore the manufacturing infrastructure and productivity to its preeminence in the world economy. In one sense, it would 'decouple Keynes from Beveridge'. This would be done through such devices as deregulation, lower taxes on businesses, and lower wages.

> 'Recapitalization' means, then, a social-political change away from a large social sector and an active government influencing the macro processes of enterprises; less government, then, means more capitalism. (*Ibid.*, p. 30.)

Increasingly, this has meant replacing discredited Keynesian economic policies with 'supply-side economics', a new conservative approach which has rapidly gained credence in the current economic debates. This shift has obvious ideological implications.

Keynesian theory encourages stimulating aggregate demand through tax cuts or national budget increases, a policy aimed at poorer people who are more likely to spend the money in the right way. The new conservative theory encourages tax cuts that can stimulate the supply of goods and services. This policy is aimed towards reducing the tax burden of the wealthy, who are more likely to invest rather than spend their money.

As the concern in the period of stagnation increasingly focuses on the reinvestment of capital, the Western industrial countries are implementing elements of this economic policy. In 1978, for example, the United States Congress cut the tax on capital gains from 49% to 28%. Four-fifths of the benefit from this reduction went to the richest 2% of the taxpayers (*The New Republic,* 1980). New proposals, such as one to change the depreciation allowance schedule, would cut corporate income taxes by almost half. Combined with the investment tax credit, this would amount to a virtual negative tax on investments profits: the government could end up paying business to make money.

What this argument obscures is the limited resources the state has at its disposal. In order to increase its resource allocation to recapitalize capital, the state must reduce its intervention in social welfare and other public services. Thatcher's economic policies and Carter's attempt at a balanced budget are cases in point. In this context, whether Miller's scenario will fully unfold is impossible to determine. What is clear, however, is its relationship to the present conservative trend within Western industrial countries, the cutback of government intervention and the increasing credence given to such slogans as 'lowered expectations' which can be 'a substitute for social expenditures and employment policies' (Miller, 1978, p. 30).

B. *The expansion of state intervention*

The second possible transformation is for the state to increase the legitimation it is able to achieve. In many ways this is a logical extension of its past attempts to modify its present bureaucratic mode of governance. The goal would be a 'purposive-rational' policy-making process which would utilize such management and planning techniques as program budgeting, cost-benefit analysis and social indicators to control objectives, outputs and outcomes. The present critique of this mode of operation stresses the limits placed upon the state by its lack of control over its economic environment (see Offe, 1975a). *The key transformation, therefore, would of necessity be an expansion of state intervention in the production end of the economy.*

In the present context, the mere regulation of the economy would seem insufficient. The purpose of supply-side economic policies, as already stated, is to increase productive investment. But with little control over where to invest the resultant increased tax revenues there is no guarantee that investment will be in areas likely to increase productivity. The beneficial effects of the 1978 capital tax cuts were minimal, for instance. Even the United States' President's Council of Economic Advisors judged it to be inefficient as a means of promoting productive investment.

No doubt these policies stimulate some kind of investment. The problem is relying on tax policies to stimulate uncontrolled investment, with no guarantee of its efficiency in meeting societal needs. Clearly here are the seeds for future state intervention in the production end of the economy. The emphasis on the efficient organization of the subsidy from society to capital logically extends to include the subsidy's investment back into society. Within this context, no longer would investment and disinvestment decisions be the prerogative of private capital, but subject to state controls. The growing dependence of capitalist economies on public monies and semi-public monies such as pension funds for investment capital makes this intervention even easier by assuring it a place on this decade's public agenda (Gardels and Williams, 1977; Rifkin and Barber, 1978).

C. *The expansion of democratic policy-making*

In the present state of turbulence, there is the possibility of a third alternative—a 'democratic consensus' model of policy-making.

> By this method production would not be made dependent upon a set of rules generated at the top of a hierarchical structure, or by a preconceived goal that is achieved by rules of technical effectiveness and economic efficiency, but by a *simultaneous determination of inputs and outputs* by clients of state administration or the recipients of its benefits. (Offe, 1975a, p. 139, emphasis original.)

This alternative seems less likely because 'it remains highly questionable whether a policy process that is directly dependent upon democratic pressures could . . . converge on a policy that is consistent with the functions that are required in a capitalist society' (*Ibid.,* p. 140). In other words, a democratic consensus model is not compatible with capitalist state activities. To achieve this change would ultimately mean a restructuring of the economic and social system. This is not to say that it is not desirable, just extremely difficult. Nervetheless, in a time of ideological disarray its partisans are gaining credibility (see Carnoy and Shearer, 1980; Hayden, 1979; Goodman, 1979; Harrington, 1980).

In part this is because the arguments for state intervention in production also contain the rationale for democratic planning. If investment is to be publicly subsidized, then it is logical to argue that it must be publicly steered to meet social needs. Economic rationalization then becomes combined with the democratization of decision-making.

D. *The restoration or transformation of legitimation*

Both the purposive-rational and the democratic-consensus policy-making models define intervention in the production process as a primary way of restoring or transforming legitimation respectively. Both alternative models require greater state intervention to control accumulation, investment and supply rather than manage effective consumer demand at the consumption end of the economy. A major difference between the two models, however, is in the criteria used as input and overall goals.

In the purposive-rational model, the decisions are primarily technical, aimed at maintaining the present industrial mode of social organization and the dominance of private accumulation as the 'most powerful constraint criterion' in the formation of public policy. The logical development of this mode of intervention, state-corporate planning, involves rationalizing the corporate system of production (i.e. eliminating parasitic and unproductive capital) while, at the same time, strengthening the systemic prerogatives of private accumulation. The major thrust is to restore the previous context of legitimation. Thus, while the social subsidy of capital is more effectively organized, there is no decisive control over production decisions in the private sector.

The democratic-consensus model, on the other hand, seeks to transform the entire basis of legitimation, democratizing the control of capital, thereby replacing private accumulation with democracy as the decisive constraint of policy. The public steering of investment would enable the state to engage in discretionary investment in vital areas of consumptions, such as housing, and in productive investment to assure guided and bounded growth to meet social needs. For, as the collapse of 'political capitalism' has demonstrated, by singularly employing policies which are limited to the regulation of the inequalities of consumption, the state is not in the position to control those factors which generate inequalities and which stimulate demands on the public budget for welfare services and expenditures. This theme is recognizable today in the 'Investitionskenkung' of the German labor movement, the Meidner 'economic democracy' plan of the Swedish blue-collar unions, and the emerging pension fund control struggles of the American labor movement.

Finally, it must be noted that state capitalist social formations—which both of these production intervention strategies imply—can be either the ante-chamber to socialism or fascism, particularly the subtle, technocratic forms of 'friendly fascism' (Gross, 1980). Since it is the supporters of the democratic-consensus model who are presently articulating 'production politics' (Gardels and Williams, 1978; Holland, 1975, for example), it suggests the possibility of their ideas being used to save the very economic system they wish to transform—a classic leftist dilemma. It can only be stressed that the 'active democratic' as opposed to the 'technocratic' context of policy-making makes the significant differences.

III. The Main Social Actors in the Transition from Affluence to Limits

The transformation of the state's mode of governance, coupled with an era of economic limits, will be greatly affected by the amount of political struggle it generates. As Piven and Cloward (1979a) have noted, political struggles occur predominately during periods of economic and political turbulence.

(It) is even more likely to take place, or to take place more rapidly, when the dislocations suffered by particular groups occur in a context of wider changes and instability, at times when the dominant institutional arranagements of the society, as people understand them, are self-evidently not functioning (p. 12)

An understanding of who will be the main social actors in an era of limits must begin with an analysis of which socio-economic groups will be most adversely affected.

During economic growth, the inherent contradictions between capital and labor have been controlled through the 'consumerization' of the economy. The promise of continued affluence in the post-war era was sufficiently realized through the growing ability to consume with rising personal income. Liberalism monopolized the political space and welfare planning, or redistributive public policy, dominated state intervention. Enough surplus was generated through taxation to subsidize the needs and pay the social costs of corporate capitalism.

During the peak of this period, from 1950 to 1970, the main social actors were the poor of the civil rights movement and the ghetto riots who sought greater political and economic enfranchisement; and the youth who rebelled against a generalized disenchantment of suburban affluence, the military draft and the Vietnam War. Piven and Cloward's (1979a) criticism of those who dismissed these social actors as not being the 'correct' ones is certainly valid, for within the particular circumstances of the post-World War II period, these were the groups who were either denied the benefits of or disillusioned with the growing affluence. As for the traditional working class, the institutional arrangements of the modern capitalist state and the economic surplus generated by continuous growth gave rise to particular forms of struggles, in conjunction with other class forces, which were fragmented and consumption oriented. Castells (1977; 1978) has made much of this in his discussions about 'popular' urban contradictions which arouse constituencies against the logic of capitalism in everyday life. This is the basis for such contemporary movements as the environmentalists, anti-nuclear/pro-solar groups, and rent control and housing struggles.

Today, economic stagnation, inflation and energy crisis are rupturing the 'praxis of consumption' (Lefebvre, 1967; Marcuse, 1964) which reproduces the social system at the level of daily life, and have opened up the space for transformation rather than reproduction. The present crises broaden the 'popular' constituencies set into motion by collective consumption conflicts and tend to activate that vast, nebulous stratum which bourgeois American sociology has labeled the 'middle classes'.

Whatever their location in the socio-economic continuum of class definition (i.e. 'blue-collar' organized working class, 'white-collar' professionals, small business petit-bourgeoise), these groups are unified in their common ideological perspective and consumption orientation. Unlike the poor, minorities and disenchanted youth, they above all believed in the 'promise of affluence' which the post-World War II economic boom sustained. However inequitable its actual material realization, this 'semantic field' ordered their consciousness.

Although the complexities of the simultaneous dimensions of class have generally eluded clear analysis by Marxist political economy, it seems evident that the self-consciousness of these classes, no matter how false, has tended to be defined (aided and abetted by corporate advertising and bourgeois sociology) with respect to the consumption of goods and status, not with respect to production or socio-economic class position. Well over a decade ago, Marcuse (1964) assessed the condition of a welfare state which bought off opposition through the ideology of the commodity as the 'rational and material ground for the unification of opposites' in a class society.

While there has been a good deal already written concerning class definitions in contemporary Western society (Mann, 1973; Walker, 1979; Gouldner, 1979 for example), the important point here is that, in their own self-consciousness as *labour and consumer,* more ideological weight has been given to the latter role—in part because of the degradation of labor (Braverman, 1974), the profound influence of the ideology of the 'American Dream', and the virtual identification of the 'pursuit of happiness' with greater per capita income with which to consume.

The ramifications of this reality are many. The deficit of consumption becomes, ultimately, not only a deficit of production, but also of ideology. As traditional social bonds have weakened, the only 'principle of social organization' of the present social structure is the steady rise of per capita income (see Habermas, 1976 on the destruction of tradition in modern capitalism and its effect on social life). The decline or levelling-off of economic growth, then, is enough to eventuate a 'legitimation crisis' in the sense Habermas (1976) defines it. The system of government intervention, which was supposed to guarantee the rise of income, has only succeeded in alienating its source of legitimacy—witness the tax revolt, spending limitations movement, and anti-bussing protest emanating from a disillusioned middle class. The potential struggles can only increase as this disillusionment increases. *Therefore, the transitions from affluence to an era of limits will spawn the rise of a demoted middle class as the agent of basic issues, as the central social actor on the stage in the 1980s.* Langston Hughes' 'dream deferred' for the poor and racial minorities will become a 'dream denied' for the middle class.

This transition may fracture or unify, that is, ally or oppose, the component socio-economic classes of this middle strata which the era of affluence had consolidated ideologically. In large part, this fracturing or unification will depend upon who must bear the costs of maintaining accumulation. If the political struggles of consumers and labor can combine to redirect the costs of economic growth, then a new ideological consolidation is possible. If corporate capital is able to make the middle class bear the costs of private accumulation, then fragmentation will likely divide its various component fractions. Therefore, a major question is which way this massive social force will move in response (or in reaction) to the present conditions in society. If the middle class follows *Business Weeks'* (1974) postulation that the American people will have to do with less so that business—which produces jobs and is responsible for accumulation—does with more, than a recapitalization trend is possible.

> It is inevitable that the U.S. economy will grow more slowly than it is has . . . some people will obviously have to do with less. . . . Indeed cities and states, the home mortgage market, small businesses and the consumer will all get less than they want. Yet it will be a hard pill for many Americans to swallow, the idea of doing with less so that big business can have more. . . . Nothing that this nation, or any nation, has done in modern history compares in difficulty with the selling job that must now be done to make people really accept the new reality (p. 14).

In the long run, such a trend seems unlikely to be sustained because of the basic need for a capitalist state to intervene in a capitalist society to stabilize accumulation and legitimation. So a more interventionist mode of state activity is necessitated and it will be the ideological and political battle for the support of a disillusioned middle class that may decide the type of transformation that occurs. The key factor is the alignment of class forces behind the technocratic and democratic tendencies of a state apparatus in transition.

IV. The Role of Planners

It is only now possible, within this framework of analysis, to examine possible future roles for planners. For Planning, as it has previously been conceptualized, evolved within the assumptions and boundaries of an era of affluence. Its purpose was to order growth so that its social value was maximized, or at the very least, its social disruption minimized. All of the traditional planning functions contained these underlying assumptions. So when the concept of an affluent society comes into question, so does planning. When the overall worth of state intervention is questioned, so is planning. The present task is to restructure our conceptions of planning to fit the economic realities of the 1980s (see Harvey, 1978; Sarbib, 1978).

> And so we find at each of the major turning points in our history, a *crisis of ideology*. Past commitments must obviously be abandoned because they hinder our power to understand and most certainly lose their power to legitimate and justify. . . . And as the pillars to the planners world slowly crumble, so the search begins for a new scaffolding for the future. At such a juncture, it becomes necessary to plan the ideology of planning. (Harvey, 1978, p. 229, emphasis original.)

In the present context, then, there seem to be three possible ideological directions for planners, which logicaly correlate to the possible future directions of the state policy-making process. But while these ideological directions are in the process of formation, it is difficult to forecast exact roles for planners, or even at which levels of society they would most likely work. Therefore, the types and levels of planning discussed are, of necessity, broadly defined.

A. *The planners as the manager of decline*

One of the consequences of making do with less, a central tenet of an ideological direction stressing the reduction of legitimation needs, is an acceptance of decline both in a physical and economical sense.

In most Western industrial countries there are specific geographic regions, economic sectors or social classes that will be severely affected by the transition to an era of limits. Usually these are the most economically marginal sectors of society, including central cities and industrial regions with outdated physical infrastructures and specific less flexible populations, such as the elderly. This, of course, is in addition to the general fall in the standard of living of the middle class.

The role of the state within this perspective, however, is not to rectify these conditions. Neither the resources nor the technical expertise are available to accomplish such a task which, in any event, is the 'natural' outcome of economic activity. The only options open to the state are to minimize the negative affects by maximizing the impact of dwindling resources.

For planners, then, the issue would become, as David Harvey stated, for the 'gospel of efficiency . . . to reign supreme' (1978, p. 231). Their role would be that of technicians and urban accountants overseeing the decline of state intervention. They would be required both to help supply the rationale for this withdrawal and to cushion its effects. Elements of this ideological perspective of planning exist today in both theory and practice. On a theoretical level, Edward Banfields's book, *The Unheavenly City,* was a fairly early (1960s) statement of this concept. Also the economic thinking of Milton Friedman (1977a; 1977b) reflects the perspective of economic decline as not only inevitable but beneficial in the long run. Friedman has acted as an economic consultant to several governments, including the United Kingdom, Chile and Israel. Thus many of his theoretical ideas have already influenced state policies.

On a practical level, an early example of this approach was Daniel Moynihan's 'benign neglect' racial policy. This theme has been revived as of late in relation to declining neighborhoods. The technical term for this rationalization of the economic abandonment of several cities and regions is 'planned shrinkage'. It can include anything from the systematic reduction of schools, fire stations and hospitals in poor neighhoods to the 'mothballing' of these areas until basic economic policies change. This frequently entails the restructuring of government policies, as in Britain during the 1970s when this process was facilitated by a shift from comprehensive redevelopment to housing improving programmes (Paris and Blackaby, 1979).

So far the various elements have not coalesced into a consistent national planning policy, except perhaps in the United Kingdom under the present Thatcher government and the Fraser government in Australia. As for the outcome of such policies, Hill (1978, p. 228) has defined one possible 'embryonic tendency,' 'the Pariah City . . . a 'reservation' for the economically disenfranchised labor force in a monopoly capitalist society'.

> A program of deliberately cutting back on public services in the most deteriorated (i.e., the poorest) sections of the cities is called for during the abandonment period to explicitly encourage the remaining population to leave, by moving either to low-income areas in other parts of the country, or to those parts of the cities where they can be more inexpensively taken care of by governments. (Goodman, 1979, pp. 69-70.)

B. *The planner as the technician of development*

The second ideological direction, related to a purposive-rational policy-making process, would likely stress economic development, both at the national and regional levels. The control and rationalization of economic development, directly relating it to the control and investment of capital, would be dominant planning concerns.

Up until now territorial governments have not exercised effective influence over the capital-flow decisions of the major multinational corporations. The use of business incentives (i.e. tax credits and forgivenesses, loan guarantees, industrial development bonds, low-interest loans), conventional public works projects and manpower training to create a 'pro-business climate' have proven ineffectual (see Harrison and Kanter, 1978; National CDP, 1977b). Indicative planning, which attempted to incorporate big business, labor and government into a bargaining process, occasionally resulting in 'planning agreements', was also unable to rationalize major investment and disinvestment decisions, decisions which generated inequalities and structural demands on the state for welfare and service expenditures. A recent example of this is the operations of the Chrysler Corporation in both the United States and the United Kingdom.

Therefore, the concept of economic development planning at the national level is rapidly becoming an 'idea in good currency'. In the

United States, which has a sporadic tradition of regional and national planning, there has been growing pressure on state governments in the declining industrial Northeast to regulate and plan present and future investment decision. At the national level, the Ford-Hawkins bill now in Congress would regulate, albeit only marginally, the investment decisions of major corporations (see Rifkin and Barber, 1978). Many intellectuals, politicians and even businessmen, however, seek a national planning system of wider scope similar to Roosevelt's National Resources Board. As Professor Wassily Leontief, an American Nobel laureate in economics, stated in response to the troubled Chrysler Corporation, 'We need a national planning board that would single out the problem areas, systematically evaluate shifts in the nation's industrial base, and anticipate the next endangered industries' (quoted in Miller, 1979). Corporate leaders such as Henry Ford and the President of the Atlantic-Richfield Oil Corporation favor more direct federal involvement in business as a way of insuring 'a more predictable supply of investment money, a market and price for (their) products, a steady source of materials as favorable prices, and less necessity to compete . . .' (Goodman, 1979, p. 149). On a local level, the Business Roundtable, a group of major US corporate executives, has issued a position statement calling for permanent 'Economic Growth Commissions' in every city in the country (*Ibid.,* p. 92).

Several European countries (i.e. France, Italy and the United Kingdom), of course, have a longer history of national and regional economic planning, but again this has been largely ineffective in resolving problems such as structural redundancies and geographical income disparities. Currently each of these countries have conservative governments, but if the present economic turmoil continues, more comprehensive forms of control, such as those suggested by Holland (1978) and Benn (1979), might predominate.

These policies, from a purposive-rational perspective, however, would be implemented only to stabilize national economies and severe regional imbalances. The control over the economic environment would allow greater efficiency in the use of social and physical infrastructure, but only from a technical perspective. The overall goal would be to rationalize private accumulation. A likely byproduct of the planning techniques needed to implement these policies, centralized administrative control and budgetary planning, might be the evolution of the 'social-industrial complex' envisioned by O'Connor (1973) in which the state institutions themselves are more directly involved in raising the productivity of the corporate sector at the expense of social needs.

C. *The planner as the facilitator of change*

The third ideological direction involves the development of a democratic-consensus mode of governance. Of necessity this will include the linkage of the *production* issues of the 1980s with the more popular based issues of *consumption*. Conflicts in the era of affluence, as well as the alliances built upon them, were centered around the plight of vulnerable neighborhoods and marginal workers. While these collective consumption concerns are merging with more privatized consumption issues (i.e. rising food and gasoline prices, higher property taxes) in the initial transition to an era of limits, their genesis, and thus solution, is found at the production or control end of the economy. But, as previously stated, the imposition of limits means a wider basis upon which to organize. Indeed, as economic rationalization proceeds in response to the accumulation problem, production issues, such as plant closures, and economic control issues, such as steering pension fund investments, will undoubtedly become more prominent. *It is this recognition which identifies the linkage of a 'production politics' with 'consumption issues' as the key to organizing political power in the transition to an era of limits.*

It is the effort to expand 'consumer deficit' struggles of the middle class to include production politics, something made easier by the shift of ideological and political space in the present context, which will detemine the success of supporters of 'economic democracy'. While the organized working class may be strong enough to defend its income against erosion, it will not be able to capture economic control without the other socio-economic classes which comprise the middle-class strata. And without democratic control of investment and production decisions, the distribution of unequal consumption in a period of decline by corporate economic rationalization will eventually break up any class alliance which could resist being burdened with the costs of economic growth.

A key component of this evolving strategy is the alliance between community and union organization. On a limited level, this is already in progress in Britain (Kraushaar, 1979). In the United States the issue of the spatial effects of union pension fund investments and the community effects of plant closures have necessitated union-community collective action (Rifkin and Barber, 1978; Gardels and Williams, 1978; Goodman, 1979). The Ohio Public Interest Campaign, a statewide coalition of union, church, minority and community organizations formed in 1975, has been lobbying for a state law which would require larger corporations to give advance notice of closures, grant severance pay for retraining and resettlement, and reimburse the affected community for the dislocation caused. One significant side effect of the near-bankruptcy of the Chrysler Corporation was its agreement with the United Automobile Workers to set up a joint advisory board to invest 10% of each year's next income in pension monies in socially desirable areas, such as low-to-moderate-income housing, child-care centers, or similar projects in communities where Chrysler employees work and live. Finally, the Campaign for Economic Democracy has been successful in getting the State of California to set up a public pension fund task force to explore alternative beneficial state-specific investment policies for its $40 billion in pension funds.

V. Conclusions

To planners who seek to transform the system of social relations rather than reproduce it within a slightly different context, a concern must be the location of a critical spaces within which to operate. At present, the contradictions inherent in an era of limits open up ideological and political space for intervention. Although the resolution of the present crisis requires a transformation, its direction is at the moment unclear and dependent upon the balance of social forces and their political power. Elements of all three ideological directions and planning roles exist at present; they are not mutually exclusive. The question is which one will eventually predominate?

This paper has shown that as situations continue to arise that cannot be managed by existing state institutions because of the imposition of an era of limits, structural pressures will increase for the evolution of alternative state institutions and forms of governance. This presents an opportunity to propose new theoretical frameworks which explain and new organizational forms of governance which attempt to overcome the apparent incoherence of everyday life. The difficulty is the linkage of these theories of social change and visions of a new society to immediately 'struggleable' policy proposals, viable in the momentary constellation of social and political forces and around which the forces and agencies of change can be mobilized. The only hope for effectiveness is for planners to be linked or to link their technical expertise to the political power of a middle class organized to democratize the economy as a response to crisis and transition. The potential of these linkages is not the issue, rather it is the role of the planner in facilitating these linkages.

References

Benn, Tony (1979) *Arguments for Socialism,* London: Jonathan Cape.

Banfield, Edward (1974) *The Unheavenly City Revisted,* Boston: Little, Brown

Barnet, Richard J. (1980) *The Lean Years: Politics in the Age of Scarcity,* New York: Simon and Shuster.

Benington, John (1975) Local government becomes big business' in Coventry CDP, *Final Report: Part 2 - Background Working Papers,* London: Home Office, May pp. 105-22.

Birnbaum, Norman (ed) (1977) *Beyond the Crisis,* New York: Oxford University Press.

Braverman, Harry (1974) *Labor and Monopoly Capital: The Degredation of Work in the Twentieth Century,* New York: Monthly Review Press.

Burnham, Walter Dean (1980) 'American politics in the 1980's, *Dissent.* May, pp. 149-160.

Business Week, October 12, 1974.

Carnoy, Martin and Shearer, Derek, (1980) *Economic Democracy: The Challenge of the 1980s,* New York: M. E. Sharpe.

Castells, Manual (1977) *The Urban Question: A Marxist Approach,* London: Edward Arnold.

Castells, Manual (1978) *City, Class and Power,* New York: St. Martins Press.

Clavel, Pierre *et al.,* eds. (1980) *Urban and Regional Planning in an Age of Austerity,* New York: Pergamon Press.

Cockburn, Cynthia (1977) *The Local State: Management of Cities and People,* London: Pluto Press.

Crozier, Michael *et al.* (1975) *The Crisis of Democracy: Report on the Governability of Democracies to the Trilateral Commission,* New York: N.Y. University Press.

Friedman, Milton (1977a) 'From Galbraith to Economic Freedom', Occasional Paper 49, London: The Institute of Economic Affairs, January.

Friedman, Milton (1977b) 'Inflation and Unemployment: The New Dimension of Politics', Occasional Paper 51, London: The Institute of Economic Affairs, May.

Gardels, Nathan and Williams, George (1978) 'A response to fiscal crisis and the tax revolt: toward public control of capital and credit.' Unpublished paper, School of Architecture and Urban Planning, University of California, Los Angeles. November 21.

Gold, David (1977) 'The rise and decline of the Keynesian coalition', *Kapitalistate* **6**, 129-161.

Goodman, Robert (1979) *The Last Entrepreneurs: America's Regional Wars for Jobs and Dollars*, New York: Simon and Schuster.

Gouldner, Alvin (1979) *The Future of Intellectuals and the Rise of the New Class*, New York: The Seabury Press.

Gross, Bertram M. (1980) *Friendly Fascism*, New York: Avon.

Habermas, Jurgen (1976) *Legitimation Crisis*, London: Heinemann Educational Books.

Harrington, Michael (1980) *Decade of Decision*, New York: Simon and Schuster.

Harrison, Bennett and Kanter, Sandra (1978) 'The political economy of States' job-creation business incentives', *Journal of the American Institute of Planners*, **44**, (4), October, pp. 424-35.

Harvey, David (1978) 'On planning the ideology of planning', *Planning Theory in the 1980's: a search for future directions*, edited by Rober W. Burchell and George Sternlieb, New Brunswick, New Jersey: Center for Urban Policy Research, pp. 213-34.

Hayden, Tom (1979) *Economic Democracy in an Age of Scarcity*, Los Angeles: Campaign for Economic Democracy.

Henderson, Hazel (1978) *Creating Alternative Futures: The End of Economics*, Berkeley: Windhour Books.

Hill, Richard Child (1978) 'Fiscal collapse and political struggle in decaying central cities in the United States', *Marxism and the Metropolis: New Perspectives in Urban Political Economy*, edited by William K. Tabb and Larry Sawers, New York: Oxford Unviersity Press, pp. 213-40.

Holland, Stuart (1975) *The Socialist Challenge*, London: Quartet Books.

Holland, Stuart, ed. (1980) *Beyond Capitalist Planning*, New York: St. Martin's Press.

Kraushaar, Robert (1979) 'Pragmatic radicalism', *International Journal of Urban and Regional Research*, **3** (1), 61-80.

Kraushaar, Robert (1980) 'Policy without protest: the dilemma of organizing for change in Britain', *Urban Change and Conflict*, edited by Michael Harloe, London: Heinemann Educational Books.

Lee, Douglas (1973) 'Requiem for large scale models', *Journal of the American Institute of Planners* **39** (3), May, pp. 163-78.

Lefebvre, Henri (1967) *Everyday Life in the Modern World*, New York.

Lowi, Theodore, (1969) *The End of Liberalism: Ideology, policy and the crisis of public authority*, New York: Norton Press.

McCracken, Paul *et al* (1977) *Towards Full Employment and Price Stability*, Paris: Organization for Economic Co-operation and Development.

Mandel, Ernest (1978) *Late Capitalism*, London: Verso Editions.

Mann, Michael (1973) *Consciousness and Action Among the Western Working Class,* London: McMillan Press.

Marcuse, Herbert (1964) *One Dimensional Man,* Boston: Beacon Press.

Marris, Peter (1974) 'Experimenting in social reform', *Community Work One,* edited by David Jones and Marjorie Mayo, London: Routledge and Kegan Paul, pp. 245-59.

Marris, Peter (1975) *Loss and Change,* Garden City, New York: Anchor Books.

Miller, Judith (1979) 'How can Congress help prevent other Chryslers?', *New York Times,* December 23, p. E4.

Miller, S. M. (1978) 'The recapitalization of capital'. Unpublished manuscript August, 1978; abridged in *International Journal of Urban and Regional Research* 2 (2) pp. 202-12.

Miller, Tom and Kraushaar, Robert (1979) 'The emergence of participatory policies for community development: Anglo-American experience and their influence on Sweden', *Acta Sociologica,* 22 (2), June, pp. 111-33.

National Community Develoment Project (1977a) *Gilding the Ghetto: The State and the Poverty Experiments,* London: Home Office.

National Community Development Project (1977b) *The Costs of Industrial Change,* London: Home Office.

O'Connor, James (1973) *The Fiscal Crisis of the State,* New York: St. Martin's Press.

Offe, Claus (1974) 'Structural problems of the capitalist state', *German Political Studies,* Vol. 1, edited by K. V. Beyme, Los Angeles: Sage Publications, pp. 31-57.

Offe, Claus (1975a) 'The theory of the capitalist state and the problems of policy formation', *Stress and Contradiction in Modern Capitalism,* edited by L. Lindberg *et al.,* Lexington, Massachusetts: Lexington Books, pp. 125-44.

Offe, Claus (1975b) 'Introduction to Part II: Legitimacy versus efficiency', *Stress and Contradiction in Modern Capitalism,* pp. 245-59.

Offe, Claus (1975c) 'Further comments on Muller and Neusus', *Telos,* No. 25, pp. 99-111.

Offe, Claus (1976) 'Political authority and class structures'. *Critical Sociology,* edited Paul Connerton, Harmondsworth: Penguin Books, pp. 388-421.

Paris, Chris and Blackaby, Bob (1978) Not Much Improvement— urban renewal policy in Birmingham, London: Heinemann Educational Books.

Piven, Francis Fox and Cloward, Richard (1979a) *Poor Peoples Movement: Why They Succeed, How They Fail,* New York: Vintage Books.

Piven, Francis Fox and Cloward, Richard (1979b) 'State Structures and Political Protest: notes toward a theory.' paper presented at Centre for Environmental Studies Conference on Urban Change and Conflict, January.

Rifkin, Jeremy and Barber, Randy (1978) *The North Will Rise Again: Pensions, Politics and Power in the 1980's,* Boston: Beacon Press.

Rifkin, Jeremy and Howard, Ted (1979) *The Emerging Order: God in the Age of Scarcity,* New York: G.P. Putnam's Sons.

Sarbib, Jean-Louis (1978) 'Notes on the legitimation of liberal reform', *The Structural Crisis of the 1970's and Beyond: The Need for a New Planning Theory.* The Proceedings of the Conference on Planning Theory. Division of Environmental and Urban Systems, College of Architecture and Urban Studies, Virginia Polytechnic Institute and State University. May.

Schon, Donald (1971) *Beyond the Stable State,* New York: Random House.

Stobaugh, Robert and Yergin, Daniel eds. (1979) *Energy Future: Report of the Energy Project at the Harvard Business School,* New York: Random House.

The New Republic, April 26, 1980.

The New York Times, January 6, 1980.

Thurow, Lester C. (1980) *The Zero-Sum Society: Distribution and the Possibilities for Economic Change,* New York: Basic Books.

Trow, Martin (1971) 'Methodological problems in the evaluation of innovation', *Readings in Evaluation Research,* edited by Francis Caro, New York: Russell Sage Foundation, pp. 81-94.

Walker, Pat, ed. (1979) *Between Labor and Capital,* Boston: South End Press.

The Future of Planning (Theory?)

THE EDITOR

Given the general perspective of this book, it may seem ironic that planning is unpopular with the political right. The current swingeing cuts in public expenditure have hit planning already—growing unemployment amongst planners, reductions in the scale of planning education—and are likely to continue to do so. Does this suggest that planning, after all, has been a radical force?

I believe not, for two main reasons. First, I have discussed my view of the ideology of planning and it is wholly consistent with the view that town planning can be both objectively useful for the capitalist state *and* valuable ideologically as a repository of blame for the social effects of capitalist urbanization. The second reason, and this may be distinctively new, is that we are entering a period when town planning is becoming *less useful* to the capitalist state, as the necessary costs of attempting environmental management outweigh their ideological merits: thus institutional planning, like other welfare state activities, is affected by the fiscal crisis of the capitalist state (O'Connor, 1973) and parallel legitimation crises (Habermas, 1976). What is happening today is that new forms of legitimation are being sought and during a period of limited investment or even overall disinvestment in the built environment town planning can be jettisoned. Clearly, the aspirations and assumptions of comprehensive planning embodied in the Planning Advisory Group (PAG, 1965) and the Town and Country Planning Act, 1968 have long been consigned to the trashbin of planning history.

I think that Gwyneth Kirk (1980) is absolutely correct in the concluding section of her recent book:

> One of the dilemmas for the state is that while facilitating the capital accumulation process, public intervention in a market-based economy, including land use-planning, is limited by the need not to encroach upon the profitability of the private sector (p. 196).

Thus in acting upon particular contradictions of capitalist urbanisation *new* contradictions have necessarily emerged. The central problem for planning theory as an abstract 'theory of planning' is that it cannot reconcile technical dimensions of decision making with the forces which shape and reshape the social world.

The heavily-blinkered horse stands comfortably in the eye of the storm. *At least* one worker in every ten in the UK is now unemployed, there is a civil war in Northern Ireland, major metropolitan authorities are increasingly unable to cope with providing the services necessary merely to maintain present inadequate standards. Town planning simply is not relevant to these major and critically significant events which will influence every part of Britain over the next ten years.

There cannot be a *technical* way out for planning, planners, or planning theory. The future of planning will depend on the outcomes of struggles currently going on between social classes, within and between political parties, both located historically in the most critical phase of post-war capitalist reorganization.

References

Kirk, G. (1980) *Urban Planning in a Capitalist Society,* London, Croom Helm.
Habermas, J. (1976) *Legitimation Crisis,* London, Heinemann.
O'Connor, J. (1973) *The Fiscal Crisis of the State,* New York, St Martin's Press.
Planning Advisory Group (1965) *The Future of Development Plans,* London, HMSO.

Notes on Further Reading

There is now a wealth of radical literature specifically on planning and more generally on urban and regional development. The best journal is the *International Journal of Urban and Regional Research*. An excellent outline of the field is contained in a working paper of Birmingham University's Centre for Urban and Regional Studies (CURS). This comprises a short introduction on the nature of urban and regional studies, the outline of a postgraduate course and an extensive bibliography: *Social Theory, The City and the Region,* CURS Working paper 68 by Ray Forrest, Jeff Henderson and Peter Williams, is available from CURS, University of Birmingham, PO Box 363, Birmingham B15 2TT.

Gwynneth Kirk's *Urban Planning in a Capitalist Society* is the only full-length book dealing with British planning from a Marxist perspective, though other authors have made major contributions in the debate on urban politics and, *inter alia,* discussed planning. In particular see Dunleavy, P. (1980) *Urban Political Analysis,* London, Macmillan, and Saunders, P. (1979) *Urban Politics,* London, Penguin.

The two most influential theorists during the early 1970s were David Harvey (1973) *Social Justice and the City* and Manuel Castells (1977 English edition) *The Urban Question,* London, Arnold; (1978) *City, Class and Power,* London, Arnold. David Harvey is currently completing a major work on the urban process under capitalism, and a taste of what is probably to come is his essay (1978) 'The urban process under capitalism: a framework for analysis', *International Journal of Urban and Regional Research,* Vol. 11, No. 1. See also Harloe, M. (ed.) *Captive Cities* (1977) London, Arnold, and Pickvance, C. (ed.) (1976) *Urban Sociology: critical essays,* London, Tavistock; these two collections of essays bring together much of the best essays in the 'new urban sociology' up to their date of publication. Harlow and Pickvance both provide incisive and critical reviews of the field.

Much work has been done on critical urban analysis in the USA since the mid-1960s, and a series of useful collections of readings published. In particular there are three readers which tend to focus on American issues, from broad 'left' and Marxist perspectives: Cox, K. (ed.) (1978) *Urbanisation and Conflict in Market Societies* and Tabb, W. and Sawers, L. (eds.) (1978) *Marxism and the Metropolis,* Oxford, Oxford University Press, and Scott, A. J. and Dear, M. (1980) *Urbanisation and Urban Planning in Capitalist Society,* London, Arnold. The growth of concern about 'urban fiscal crisis', particularly in New York but also as a more general problem of state intervention in cities has led to a spate of publications, notably Alcaly, R. E. and Mermelstein, D. (eds.) (1977) *The Fiscal Crisis of American Cities,* New York, Vintage; for a less radical treatment of these issues see Blair, J. P. and Nachmias, D. (eds.) (1979) *Fiscal Retrenchment and Urban Policy,* Beverley Hills, Sage. An interesting political analysis of the relationships between capital investment/disinvestment processes, and their social effects is in Bluestone, B. and Harrison, P. (1980) *Capital and Communities,* Washington, The Progressive Alliance. Based in North America, Scott (1980) seeks to develop earlier work with Roweis into a theory of the relationship between capitalist forms of land use and state intervention: *The Urban Land Nexus and the State,* London, Pion.

The issues of state/capital relations and planning, central to much recent and current radical analysis, are now being explored worldwide. Stilwell, F. (1980) *Economic Crisis, Cities and Regions,* Sydney, Pergamon, is a political economy approach to Australian city and regional development. Kilmartin, L. and Thorns, D. (1978) *Cities Unlimited,* Sydney, Allen & Unwin, seek to apply 'the new urban sociology' to Australian and New Zealand society and include an interesting chapter on urban planning. From a liberal interventionist stance Sandercock (1976) *Cities for Sale,* London, Heinemann, also looks, though more specifically, at town planning in Australia.

Much research and theoretical development has also been undertaken in continental Europe, though unfortunately there is a considerable time-lag before any of this is available in English translation. Elizabeth Lebas (London) is finishing a major survey of recent international developments in critical urban analysis and her forthcoming work will be of invaluable assistance in charting the field. One notable book, not necessarily specifically on planning, is Mingione's (1981) *Social Conflict and the City,* Oxford, Blackwell; Mingione uses the concept of hegemony to examine the nature of state intervention in processes of territorial uneven development and, amongst other questions, he studies the role of planning in relation to politics and state intervention.

Much radical work has focused on housing, in particular numerous Community Development Project Reports: (1976) *Whatever Happened to Council Housing?,* (1977) *The Poverty of the Improvement Programme* and (1976) *Profits against Houses: an Alternative Guide to Housing Finance.* See also Lambert, J., Paris, C. and Blackaby, B. (1978) *Housing Policy and the State,* London, Macmillan; Paris, C. and Blackaby, B. (1979) *Not much Improvement: Urban Renewal Policy in Birmingham,* London, Heinemann; Conference of Socialist Economists (1975) *Political economy and the Housing Question,* (1976) *Housing and Class in Britain.*

The Community Development Project Workers have also written more generally on the state poverty programme (1977) *Gilding the Ghetto.* A good introduction to Marxist writing on the state is Miliband, R. (1969) *The State in Capitalist Society,* London, Weidenfeld & Nicolson. See also Cockburn, C. (1977) *The Local State,* London, Pluto; Wright, E. O. (1978) *Class, Crisis and the State,* London, New Left Books; Holloway, J. and Picciotto, S. (1978) *State and Capital,* London, Arnold; Gough, I. (1979) *The Political Economy of the Welfare State,* London, Macmillan.

A note of caution

Readers unfamiliar with current debates within Marxist and neo-Marxist studies should be careful not to treat 'radical' or 'critical' literature as a homogeneous whole. Different authors start from and develop distinctively different stances, which are not always made explicit. So do not assume that all the works mentioned above, or included in this book, represent 'The Marxist Approach' to planning and planning theory. This cautionary note is *not* intended to put you off exploring this literature; quite the opposite! It is my sincere contention that Marxist and 'neo-Marxist' approaches to the study of everyday life offer us the only way to penetrate beneath the banalities of 'common sense' understanding of the world. Hence we can move on to better arguments, better analyses, and more adequate political practice.

Name Index

313

Subject Index

317

Other Titles in the Series

NEEDHAM, B. B.
How Cities Work: An Introduction (Volume 17)

LEE, C.
Models in Planning: An Introduction to the Use of Quantitative Models
    in Planning (Volume 4)

LICHFIELD, N. *et al.*
Evaluation in the Planning Process (Volume 10)

MASSAM, B. H.
Spatial Search: Applications to Planning Problems in the Public Sector
    (Volume 23)

MOSELEY, M. J.
Growth Centres in Spatial Planning (Volume 9)

McAUSLAN, J. P. W. B.
The Ideologies of Planning Law (Volume 22)

RAPOPORT, A.
Human Aspects of Urban Form (Volume 15)

SANT, M. E. C.
Industrial Movement and Regional Development: The British Case
    (Volume 11)

SOLESBURY, W.
Policy in Urban Planning Structure Plans, Programmes and Local Plans
    (Volume 8)

STARKIE, D. N. M.
Transportation Planning, Policy and Analysis (Volume 13)

The terms of our inspection copy service apply to all the above books. A complete
catalogue of all books in the Pergamon International Library is available on request.
The Publisher will be pleased to consider suggestions for revised editions and new titles.